Eli Whitney

History Maker Bios

Catherine A. Welch

LERNER PUBLICATIONS COMPANY • MINNEAPOLIS

The author thanks Judith Stark, Jackie Hoffman, Raymond Bouley, and the staff of the Southbury Public Library in Connecticut for help in gathering material for this book.

Illustrations by Tad Butler

Text copyright © 2007 by Catherine A. Welch
Illustrations copyright © 2007 by Lerner Publishing Group, Inc.

Lerner Publications Company
A division of Lerner Publishing Group, Inc.
241 First Avenue North
Minneapolis, MN 55401 U.S.A.

Website address: www.lernerbooks.com

Library of Congress Cataloging-in-Publication Data

Welch, Catherine A.
    Eli Whitney / by Catherine A. Welch ; illustrations by Tad Butler.
        p.   cm. — (History maker bios)
    Includes bibliographical references and index.
    ISBN: 978–0–8225–7607–5 (lib. bdg. : alk. paper)
    1. Whitney, Eli, 1765–1825. 2. Inventors—United States—Biography.
    I. Butler, Tad. II. Title.
    TS1570.W4W45 2007
    609.2—dc22 [B]   2006036728

Manufactured in the United States of America
1 2 3 4 5 6 – JR – 12 11 10 09 08 07

TABLE OF CONTENTS

INTRODUCTION

Eli Whitney grew up in Westborough, Massachusetts. The United States was not a free country when he was young. It was under Great Britain's control. Americans were fighting for independence in the American Revolution (1775–1783).

The United States won its freedom. But Great Britain still supplied Americans with goods. Eli knew the United States wanted to end its need for British goods. But the country didn't have skilled workers or machines.

Eli had a mind for invention. He created a machine called the wire-toothed cotton gin. It got Americans excited about using machines. Eli looked forward to his country's future. He encouraged others to look forward to the future too.

This is his story.

1 A SPIRIT FOR INVENTION

Eli Whitney was born on December 8, 1765. His parents were farmers. Their families had moved to the United States from Great Britain.

Eli and his father shared the same name. Eli's father was a kind man. He loved Eli and the other children, Elizabeth, Benjamin, and Josiah.

Eli's mother, Elizabeth Fay, became ill when Eli was five. She was so sick that she couldn't look after the children. Eli's brothers and sister were even younger than Eli. He worried about them.

Eli, his parents, and his brothers and sister lived in this farmhouse in Westborough, Massachusetts.

In 1777, Eli's mother died. A housekeeper helped Eli's family. She took care of Eli and his sister and brothers. Eli helped his father with farm chores. But Eli missed his mother. And he never liked farmwork. He would rather be in his father's workshop, using tools to make things.

When Eli was twelve, he took apart his father's watch. Then he put it back together in working order. He loved seeing how things worked.

Eli learned about the many gears of a watch like this one.

CHORES AND SCHOOL

Eli worked hard when he was growing up. In summer, he helped harvest hay. In winter, he watered and fed the cattle. Then he walked across snow-covered fields to go to school. Eli was a slow reader, but he learned math quickly. He practiced his penmanship until it was perfect. He liked using his hands.

Eli also had a mind for business. Nails were expensive during the American Revolution. They were hard to find too. All goods were needed for the war. When Eli was fourteen, he decided to make nails. In his spare time, he made tools for nail making.

By then, Eli's father had remarried. His wife's name was Judith Hazeldon. She was a widow with children. Eli's new stepmother helped care for his younger sister and brothers. Eli had more time for himself.

In Eli's time, blacksmiths crafted tools and other items by hand.

Soon, Eli thought about hiring a helper to make nails. He didn't tell his father about his plan. He left the farm for three days. He began searching for a man who could help him. Eli went from town to town. He talked to carpenters and blacksmiths. He learned new ways to make tools.

Eli's father was not happy that Eli left the farm. But Eli found someone who could make nails. The man made nails with Eli for three months. Eli made money by selling the nails.

After the American Revolution, nails were easy to find. People didn't want to pay as much money for them anymore. Eli stopped making nails. He began making other things, such as walking sticks and hatpins. Women used hatpins to hold their hats to their hair. Eli earned more money by making these items.

Eli was always thinking. When he was nineteen, he thought about going to college. Back then few people went to college. But Eli wanted to learn new things and meet new people.

Hatpins and walking sticks were expensive. Owning a walking stick or showing off a pin on a fashionable hat displayed wealth.

Eli's stepmother didn't want Eli to go to college. College cost a lot of money. Eli's father worried about the costs too. He also knew that Eli needed to study more to get into college. To get in, he would have to pass a test.

Eli didn't let these things stop him. He got a job teaching school. He taught in nearby towns for the next three winters. He made enough money to study at Leicester Academy in the summers. Leicester was a very good school.

Leicester Academy opened in 1784. It had only two teachers.

Harvesting hay was hard work. The hay had to be cut and gathered quickly before it could be ruined by rain.

At the academy, Eli studied English grammar. He also studied Latin and Greek. He struggled with these subjects. But he did not give up.

Eli was tired from working so hard. In the summer of 1788, he went home for a visit. While he was there, he helped harvest hay. This work wore him out even more. Eli caught a bad cold. He also suffered from a leg infection.

Eli's stepmother did not take good care of him. When his father found out, he became angry. He loved his son. And he knew how hard he worked. He thought he deserved better treatment.

Eli's father decided to let his son go to college. In March 1789, he gave Eli money for his college education. Eli set out for Yale, a college in New Haven, Connecticut.

2 ELI GOES SOUTH

When Eli got to Yale, he still needed to take the entrance exam. He took the test on April 30, 1789. Eli's hard work paid off. He passed the exam. He began his college work right away.

Yale College was founded in 1701.

New Haven was an exciting city. Eli met people from all over the United States. Many students at Yale were wealthy. They were also bright. Eli had to study hard. He planned to become a lawyer.

Eli learned how to debate. He learned how to be like the Yale men. He studied how the wealthy students spoke and dressed. Eli wanted them to accept him.

Eli enjoyed college. He learned a great deal. But when he graduated in September 1792, he had very little money. Eli heard of a teaching job in South Carolina. The job would give him enough money for his daily needs.

Eli thought South Carolina's hot weather was unhealthy. But he traveled south to get work. He sailed on a ship with a man named Phineas Miller. Phineas was a little older than Eli. He had studied at Yale. He managed a plantation, or large farm.

Eli also sailed with Catherine Greene and her five children. Catherine owned the plantation where Phineas worked. Catherine was the widow of Nathanael Greene, a war hero. Catherine invited Eli to spend time at her plantation. It was in Georgia. The plantation was called Mulberry Grove.

Nathanael Greene (RIGHT) received Mulberry Grove as a gift of appreciation for his service in the Revolutionary War.

In the 1700s, many wealthy women passed their time with complicated needlework. They used round frames to hold fabric tight while they worked.

Catherine saw that Eli was skilled at fixing things. He made her a frame for holding her needlework.

Then one day, planters visited the plantation. Eli heard them talking. Tobacco crops had worn out their soil. Tobacco was hard on the land. The planters needed a new crop. They wanted to grow cotton.

But cotton wasn't worth growing, the planters grumbled. The kind of cotton that grew best in Georgia had sticky green seeds. The seeds had to be removed before the cotton could be made into cloth. Removing the seeds took time.

Some planters used machines to remove the seeds. These machines were called roller cotton gins. But the machines left bits of seed in the cotton. Planters needed a new type of gin.

Catherine said Eli could help. She showed the planters the needlework frame. She explained that Eli was good at making things.

Eli didn't know anything about cotton. But he was curious. He studied a cotton plant's seed pod, or boll. He felt the velvet coating on the cotton's seeds. He tugged at the cotton and tried to separate it from the seeds.

These cotton bolls are ready to be picked.

Then Eli got an idea. It was hard to separate the seeds from the cotton. But it might be easier to separate the cotton from the seeds. Eli decided to build a machine that would do just that.

Phineas and Catherine thought Eli's idea was brilliant. Eli chose not to take a job teaching after all. He went straight to work on his cotton gin.

It didn't take Eli long to build a model of his gin. The gin had a place to put the cotton in. Wire teeth on a rolling drum caught the cotton. The teeth tore the cotton from the seeds. Eli's gin cleaned cotton ten times faster than other methods.

COTTON AND TEXTILE MILLS

Cotton is a good fabric for clothing. It is soft but strong. In the 1700s, Great Britain needed large amounts of cotton for its textile (cloth) mills. But the country couldn't grow its own cotton. By the 1800s, the United States was selling millions of pounds of cotton to Great Britain.

Eli's model of the cotton gin was small. If it worked, he planned to make large gins for big cotton farms.

Catherine was excited to show the model to her friends. But Eli and Phineas were afraid others would steal Eli's ideas. Eli wanted to patent his gin. That meant Eli would be the only person allowed to make gins like the one he had designed.

On May 27, 1793, Eli and Phineas agreed to work together. Phineas would give Eli money to build cotton gins. The men would share the money they made from selling the machines.

On June 1, 1793, Eli headed east. Georgia did not have the supplies or workers he needed to build gins. Eli wanted to go to New Haven. But first, Eli stopped in Philadelphia. At that time, Philadelphia was the country's capital. In Philadelphia, Eli applied for a patent for his gin. On March 14, 1794, Eli got his patent. He was very happy. He wrote his father a letter. He wrote that men were calling his gin "the most perfect and most valuable invention that has ever appeared in this country."

3 COTTON GIN TROUBLES

In June 1794, Eli and Phineas became business partners. Phineas began urging planters to grow cotton. He believed that if more people grew cotton, there would be more customers for Eli's cotton gin.

But most planters could not afford cotton gins. The machines were expensive. So Eli and Phineas offered to use the gin on planters' cotton. They offered to separate the seeds from the cotton for a fee.

But the men soon faced a problem. Georgia's planters didn't think Eli's patent was fair. They thought that everyone should be allowed to sell Eli's cotton gin—not just Eli and Phineas. And Eli's patent wouldn't end for years.

Eli's cotton gin had many different parts. Each piece was made by hand.

Planters hoped large cotton crops would help the South make money. This painting by William Aiken Walker shows a huge cotton field in North Carolina.

Eli didn't understand how angry the planters were. He wanted to make more cotton gins. He still thought planters would hire him to run the machines.

Eli hurried to his workshop in New Haven. He began making cotton gins. He worked until the spring of 1795. Then a fire broke out in the workshop. The building burned to the ground. Eli's work came to a stop.

Small cotton gins could be turned with a hand crank. Large gins used horses or waterpower.

Everything was lost. The fire destroyed all the tools and machines. In Georgia, blacksmiths and carpenters began making gins of their own. Planters still needed machines to help remove seeds from their cotton.

Eli worked on rebuilding his shop. Then he worked on building gins. In seven months, he built twenty-six of the machines.

Before long, cotton prices rose. That meant planters could make more money than ever by growing cotton. Planters had an even greater need for gins. And they didn't want to pay Eli and Phineas to gin their cotton.

Blacksmiths and carpenters claimed that their gins were better than Eli's. They spread rumors that Eli's gin damaged cotton. The rumors weren't true. They were just a way to try to stop planters from buying Eli's gin.

The rumors spread throughout the South. Eli and Phineas had trouble selling gins. They began to run out of money.

COTTON AND SLAVERY

Cotton gins were a big help to southern farmers. The machines made it easier to harvest cotton. But planters needed workers to run the gins. Many farmers relied on slaves to do this task.

Farmers thought of their slaves as property. The slaves worked hard running gins. As cotton crops grew, farmers used more slaves.

People worked in special sheds made for ginning. The sheds provided shade and kept the cotton from blowing away.

Eli and Phineas managed to keep their business running. And they got some help from Catherine Greene. Catherine and Phineas had married. Catherine believed in the men's work. She gave them money to continue their business.

The money helped a great deal. But other men had begun making cotton gins. Edward Lyon and Hodgen Holmes were two such men. Hodgen's gin was a little different from Eli's machine. But it worked the same way.

It seemed others were stealing Eli's idea. Eli and Phineas thought this was wrong. They took Edward Lyon to court. But they lost their court case. And they kept on having money problems.

Finally, the men decided to let others build gins like Eli's. They charged a fee to anyone who wanted to build the gin. They also rented gins to planters. They made some money this way. But they were still struggling. Phineas and Catherine had to sell Mulberry Grove. They could no longer afford the plantation.

Eli approached Congress twice to renew his patent (LEFT).

4 MAKING MUSKETS

Eli and Phineas were upset about their cotton gin troubles. The men didn't know what to do. Eli thought about starting a new business. But he didn't have enough money.

By 1798, it looked as if the country would soon be at war with France. The United States would need muskets. Eli decided to make guns. The U.S. government could lend him the money.

At that time, there were no factories to make weapons. Workers made guns one at a time. Eli had never made a gun. But he was good at planning and inventing. He began planning a system that would allow workers to make guns quickly.

Eli planned to use machines to make large numbers of gun parts. No worker would make an entire musket. Each worker would be trained for one job. That way, Eli could make thousands of muskets quickly.

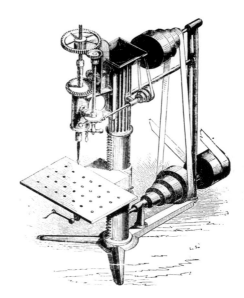

Eli wanted to use machines such as this drill press to make gun parts.

Eli's idea to make many guns at once was not new. A musket maker in France had had a similar idea. He had made many identical musket locks at once. Thomas Jefferson had met the man and sent samples of his locks to the United States. Eli may have seen the locks.

Eli thought his musket-making idea was a good one. He was eager to try it. He hoped his new business would be a success.

The U.S. government sent Thomas Jefferson to France. He was to strengthen business ties with the country. He inspected French muskets during his visit.

Gunsmiths in the 1700s made muskets one at a time. The parts of one gun did not work on any other gun.

Eli had many powerful friends. Many were Yale men. One was named Oliver Wolcott Jr. Oliver was secretary of the treasury. That meant he managed money for the U.S. government.

Eli wrote Oliver a letter about his musket-making plans. Oliver liked Eli's ideas. In 1798, the government gave Eli and twenty-five other men contracts to build muskets. Eli got the largest contract. He was to build ten thousand muskets in two years. Eli had no factory or workers. But a New Haven businessperson helped Eli find land where he could build a factory.

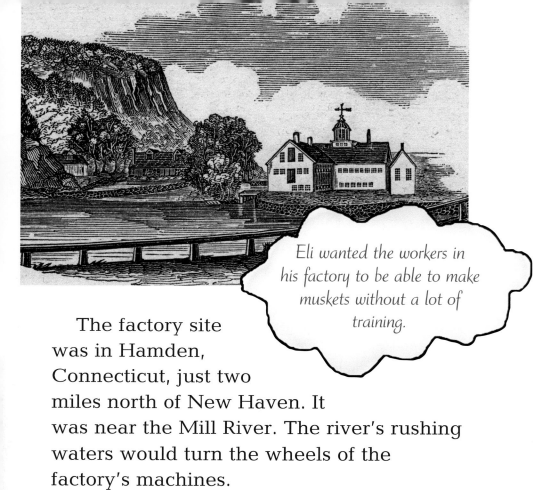

Eli wanted the workers in his factory to be able to make muskets without a lot of training.

The factory site was in Hamden, Connecticut, just two miles north of New Haven. It was near the Mill River. The river's rushing waters would turn the wheels of the factory's machines.

The factory's location was perfect. But construction moved slowly. Heavy snowstorms stalled the project. When the building was finally ready, Eli wasted no time getting to work. He bought finished wooden gun handles and barrels. He had his workers make locks for the weapons. This was the most difficult part of the gun to make.

A good part of the work was hand filing. Workers were trained to use tools called filing jigs. These steel patterns helped guide workers' hands as they filed gun parts. Eli planned how workers could put the parts together quickly by hand.

Eli's men worked hard. But by September 30, 1800, Eli had delivered only one thousand firearms to the government. He was nine thousand muskets short of his goal. Eli needed more time and money.

ELI'S VILLAGE

Eli wanted to take care of the workers at his musket factory. He wanted to keep them happy and working for him. Eli built a special village where his workers could live. It was known as Whitneyville.

Whitneyville had stone houses where workers and their families could stay. It had a house for unmarried workers. Eli created rules for those living in Whitneyville. They could not swear or drink alcohol. Workers did not always like Eli's rules.

In January 1801, Eli met with important leaders in Washington, D.C. President John Adams was there. So was Thomas Jefferson. He'd been chosen to be the country's next president.

Eli spread out musket parts in piles on a table. He began putting together locks and muskets. He showed that ten locks fit the same musket.

The leaders were amazed. They had never seen so many locks made to fit the same musket. At the time, no one had heard of machines that could make many identical parts.

This is one of Eli's early lock designs. Each lock had an eagle stamped on its side. The eagle was Eli's factory mark.

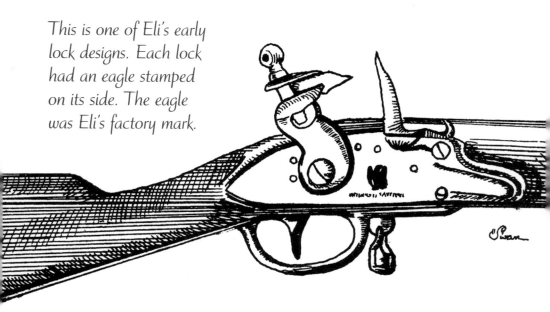

Eli put on a good show that day. But he may have fooled the men. They thought Eli had invented machines that could make many identical locks quickly. His lock parts may have been specially made to show off at the meeting. But the country's leaders were excited about Eli's muskets. They gave Eli more time and money to make his weapons.

Eli's new business was doing well. But he was still fighting those who tried to steal his cotton gin idea. He went to court many times and never made much money with the gin. Then, in 1803, Phineas suddenly died. Eli was alone in the fight to protect his cotton gin. Just a few years later, Eli's father died. It was a very hard time for Eli.

5 LIFE'S END

In January 1809, Eli delivered the ten thousand muskets he'd promised to the government. The government paid Eli. He had just enough money to settle his debts.

At this time, Eli lived on a farmhouse near his factory. He was surrounded by workers, housekeepers, and his three nephews. But Eli was lonely. He didn't see his family in Westborough very often. And he wanted to be married. In a letter, he told a friend he was "an Old Bachelor, overwhelmed in business."

Then, on June 18, 1812, the United States declared war on Great Britain. Eli got more work. He signed a contract to make fifteen thousand muskets. The first set of muskets was due on May 1, 1813.

The War of 1812 (1812–1815) hurt the cotton business. The British navy stopped U.S. merchant ships from sailing.

In June 1813, a man named Captain Callender Irvine inspected Eli's weapons. He complained about them to John Armstrong. John was the secretary of war. He was in charge of the U.S. Army. "The bayonet is two inches too short," Callender said. "The barrel is very crooked."

Eli argued with Callender for months. He worried about Callender's complaints. Eli's health grew worse. And in September, he got more bad news. Catherine Greene had died.

Before the War of 1812, John Armstrong (LEFT) served as an ambassador to France.

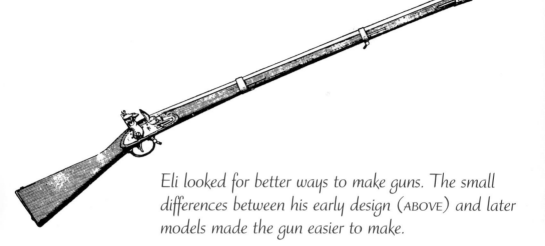

Eli looked for better ways to make guns. The small differences between his early design (ABOVE) and later models made the gun easier to make.

By May 1815, the problems with Callender had ended. The government had sent another inspector to look at Eli's weapons. This inspector thought most of Eli's guns were of good quality.

And soon, something even more wonderful happened. Eli fell in love with Henrietta Edwards. She was the daughter of his friend Pierpont Edwards. Henrietta was thirty-one years old—twenty years younger than Eli. But the age difference didn't matter to Eli. He and Henrietta married on January 6, 1817.

WHITNEY'S NEPHEWS

Eli loved his nephews Eli, Philos, and Elihu. He often gave them advice. He urged them to improve their handwriting. He told them to speak clearly so others could hear them. He scolded them when they didn't sit up straight. Eli gave his nephews tips about dress and manners. He prepared them to meet the children of his important friends.

Eli was happy to have a wife. He and Henrietta had children right away. In just a few years, Eli had three daughters and a son. Sadly, one of Eli's daughters died in 1823.

Eli and Henrietta rented a house on Orange Street in New Haven. But Eli's health got worse. He asked his nephew Eli Blake to help run his factory.

Eli worried about his factory as he grew older. He wanted someone to manage it after he died. On January 7, 1825, Eli decided to leave the factory to Eli and Philos Blake. The next day, Eli Whitney died.

Eli was loved by his family and friends. Many people attended his funeral. The minister who spoke at Eli's funeral praised Eli's spirit for invention. He also said that Eli had a special "energy . . . which carried him through difficult times."

TIMELINE

In the year . . .

1777 Eli's mother died.

1780 he started making nails during the American Revolution. `Age 14`

1785 he began teaching in nearby towns.
he began studying at Leicester Academy.

1789 he entered Yale. `Age 23`

1792 he graduated from Yale.
he traveled to Georgia and learned about cotton gins.

1793 he invented the wire-toothed cotton gin.

1794 the U.S. government granted him a patent for his wire-toothed cotton gin.
he became partners with Phineas Miller.

1795 Eli's New Haven, Connecticut, workshop burned to the ground. `Age 29`

1798 he got his first contract from the U.S. government to make ten thousand muskets.
he started to build a firearms factory in Hamden, Connecticut.

1807 his cotton gin patent expired.

1809 he finished making ten thousand firearms for his first government contract.

1812 he got another contract with the government to make fifteen thousand muskets. `Age 46`

1817 he married Henrietta Edwards.

1824 he signed his will, leaving his wife and children money for living expenses. He also left money to his sister, Elizabeth, and his nephews.

1825 he died. `Age 59`

DIGGING FOR THE TRUTH

The Eli Whitney Museum in Hamden, Connecticut, honors Eli Whitney. Many of Eli's personal papers are kept at Yale University. Eli's grave is in Grove Street Cemetery in New Haven. His tombstone reads: "Eli Whitney, the Inventor of the Cotton Gin."

Eli was the first person to create a wire-toothed cotton gin. But historians know that he was not the first person to build a machine for removing cotton seeds. They also believe he never invented machines for mass-producing musket locks.

Archaeologists—scientists who study the past—have been digging at the Hamden Whitney factory site since the 1970s. They are trying to discover the truth about Eli and his inventions.

The Eli Whitney Museum is located on the site of Eli's musket factory.

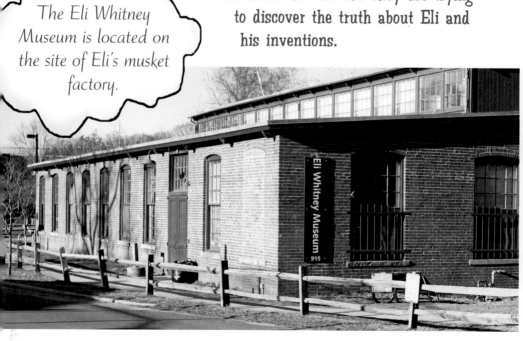

FURTHER READING

Elrbach, Arlene. *The Kids' Invention Book.* **Minneapolis: Lerner Publications Company, 1997.** Learn all about fun and useful inventions created by kids.

Gibson, Karen Bush. *The Life and Times of Eli Whitney.* **Hockessin, DE: Mitchell Lane Publishers, 2007.** In this book, you can read more about Eli Whitney's life.

Gleason, Carrie. *The Biography of Cotton.* **New York: Crabtree Publishing Company, 2006.** Find out more about cotton in this fun book.

Zuehlke, Jeffrey. *Henry Ford.* **Minneapolis: Lerner Publications Company, 2007.** Read the life story of Henry Ford, a pioneer of mass production.

WEBSITES

Eli Whitney Museum
http://www.eliwhitney.org This website from the Eli Whitney Museum in Connecticut includes detailed information on Eli's life.

The Story of Cotton: How Cotton Is Grown
http://www.cotton.org/pubs/cottoncounts/story/how.cfm
This website shows how farmers grow cotton.

SELECT BIBLIOGRAPHY

Green, Constance McL. *Eli Whitney and the Birth of American Technology.* New York: Longman, 1956.

Lakwete, Angela. *Inventing the Cotton Gin: Machine and Myth in Antebellum America.* Baltimore: Johns Hopkins University Press, 2003.

Mirsky, Jeannette, and Allan Nevins. *The World of Eli Whitney.* New York: Macmillan Company, 1952.

Starbuck, David R. "Re-Inventing Eli Whitney." *Archaeology* 50, no. 5 (September–October 1997): 100.

Woodbury, Robert S. "The Legend of Eli Whitney and Interchangeable Parts." *Technology and Culture* 1. (1960): 235–253.

INDEX

Acknowledgments

For photographs and artwork: © SuperStock, Inc. / SuperStock, pp. 4, 28; Courtesy of the Eli Whitney Museum, pp. 7, 36, 41, 45; © David Jay Zimmerman/ Corbis, p. 8; © Getty Images, pp. 10, 39; © North Wind / North Wind Picture Archives, pp. 11, 16; Courtesy of Leicester Historical Commission, p. 12; © Bettmann/ CORBIS, pp. 13, 21, 34; © CORBIS, p. 17; © Historical Picture Archive/CORBIS, p. 18; © Inga Spence / Visuals Unlimited, p. 19; © The Print Collector / Alamy, p. 24; © Christie's Images / SuperStock, p. 25; © Kevin Fleming/CORBIS, p. 26; National Archives, p. 29; The Granger Collection, New York, pp. 31, 40; © Stock Montage/Hulton Archive/Getty Images, p. 32; The Art Archive/Gunshots, p. 33;

Front cover, © Stock Montage/Hulton Archive/Getty Images
Back cover, © Time & Life Pictures/Getty Images

For quoted material: pp. 22, 39, 40, Constance McL. Green, *Eli Whitney and the Birth of American Technology* (New York: Longman, 1956); p. 43, Denison Olmsted, *Memoir of Eli Whitney, Esq.* (New York: Arno Press, 1972).

When We Talk about God . . .

Let's Be Honest

Dedicated
to the Family of Faith
and
to the Faith of Family

When We Talk about God . . .

Let's Be Honest

R. Kirby Godsey

SMYTH & HELWYS
PUBLISHING, INC.

Macon, Georgia

ISBN 1-57312-028-6

When We Talk about God
Let's Be Honest

R. Kirby Godsey

Copyright © 1996
Smyth & Helwys Publishing, Inc.®

6316 Peake Road
Macon, Georgia 31210-3960
1-800-568-1248

Library of Congress Cataloging-in-Publication Data

Godsey, R. Kirby (Raleigh Kirby), 1936–
    When we talk about God: let's be honest / R. Kirby Godsey.
    x + 214 pp.   6" x 9" (15 x 23 cm.)
    ISBN 1-57312-028-6 (alk. paper)
    1. Faith.
    2. Theology, Doctrinal.
    3. Christian life—Baptist authors.
    4. Godsey, R. Kirby (Raleigh Kirby), 1936—Religion.
    I. Title.
    BT771.2.G57   1996
    230`.61—dc20
                                                    96-11331
                                                        CIP

Contents

Preface

Plain talk about our faith is hard to come by. Theologians often talk above our heads, their language remote and obscure. Pulpit talk wanders into a different kind of obscurity. It is not remote or esoteric; it is specialized. There is often a disconnection between the language of preacherly admonition and the ordinary field of discourse of where we live each day. My writing here is driven by the conviction that we can talk and that we need to talk about our faith in ways that are straightforward and open.

In my own experience, religion was so much a part of the culture and the family tradition that "unreligion" would have been unthinkable. We were Baptist back when Baptists were the ruling class in the South. People who belonged to other religious orders were regarded with some condescension, if not outright disdain. In our town, St. Paul's was a magnificent Catholic cathedral standing near the center of the busiest part of downtown. It was a stately, eerily quiet, Gothic-looking building anchored by awesome towering steeples. The low-hanging clouds of morning would hide the large stone crosses that marked the height of the steeple's reach into the clouds. A certain mystery seemed to shroud this place.

We Baptists grew up being suspicious of Catholics. They ran a close second to Jews as being the religious outclass. We were never taught explicitly to be anti-Semitic or anti-Catholic. Indirect teaching of religion is always far more powerful than direct religious instruction. We got the message more by a downward glance and a tone of voice. We walked on the other side of the street. We were taught that Baptists were right, Catholics were wrong, and Jews were not even in the game.

It is wonder that any of us young fledgling Baptists stayed with the faith at all when we got old enough to see for ourselves that a lot of bad religion was being passed off as devout Christianity. The fact is that a lot of Baptist neophytes did not stay around. The sham and shame of religion eclipsed the wonder of belief. Some of my friends signed up with other Christian troops such as Methodists and Presbyterians—even a few high-brow Episcopalians. At least in these religious environs, it seemed that religion was a little less hostile, less defensive, and a little more tolerant of our differences.

If straight talk teaches us anything about our faith, it should cause us to face up to a mountain of bad religion. Digging out of the debris of bad faith requires patience and courage. This book is about whether faith makes sense and whether we can lay claim to a life of devotion without the nonsense of a good deal of our popular religious rhetoric. I believe that we can find our way toward a faith that enlightens and sustains, a faith that lifts us up instead of putting us down.

In this book, I am not into high language. I do not wish to become mired in words that only the theologically educated can understand. I want to talk about what the Christian faith means in a way that is honest, frank, and approachable. My aim is to encourage us to face together some of the basic issues of faith about which we all can and should become more conversant. I offer no final authority on what we ought to believe. Instead, I invite you to join me on a journey of confessing our faith. I am confident that the church will be strengthened by talking openly and forthrightly about what we believe and even what, in good faith, we cannot believe. We have walked on the other side of the street long enough.

The problem with the Christian religion is that it often turns out to be more religion than Christian. Let me explain. When we look closely at the Judaism of the first century, we begin to see a world where religion had become complex and weighted down with doctrine. Jesus' intent was to bring the meaning of faith back out into daylight.

The faith of the children of Israel was born in relating to God as their deliverer. God had sustained them through the wilderness. As the years went by, Judaism had become a formal religion—institutionalized and written down in heavy tomes. The simple trust of a delivered people had been structured into a rigorous web of doctrines. It is not surprising that Jesus wanted to break through the accumulation of religious tradition. The tradition had grown sterile. Well-schooled and proper, the religious establishment became nervous about this renegade named Jesus. He spoke against the rites of the temple and the complicated laws that enslaved rather than set people free.

Christianity has suffered much the same fate. What was born as a new way of seeing and relating to God has come to consist of a carefully crafted set of religious doctrines. To be Christian is to be a member of the Christian religion and to adhere to an intricate set of religious traditions. Our challenge is whether the passion and promise of the light that broke through in Jesus can find its way back down where we live. Christianity is not a set of doctrines. We miss the point when we convert Christianity into an elaborate system of religious theories. We make Jesus into an object of worship. The message of the Christian faith is not to worship Jesus. It is to follow him.

Jesus points us to God. In the light of Jesus, we are able to see ourselves and where we are going more clearly. Jesus enables us to break out of the catacombs of doctrine and trust God's presence in our lives. We are able to meet God, not as a remote, extraterrestrial figure, but as a reality that is present with us and within us. Religion comes off the shelf and down to earth when we take seriously the reality that we are in God and God is in us.

This book is first and foremost an acknowledgment of my own journey of belief. I intend to speak plainly about where I stand. Naturally, I speak with a bit of uneasiness. That uneasiness stems, first, from wishing to avoid the arrogant presumption that your beliefs should fall in step with mine. My journey is not and should not be a measure for yours. Surely, we have come along different roads. Nevertheless, I want to say what I have come to believe in order to encourage you to explore and to confess your own beliefs more fully and more openly.

A hint of uneasiness also arises for me because, in confessing my faith, I am placing my own personal sense of religious meaning on display, as it were. My path has certainly been a mixture of joy and pain, of defeat and fulfillment. Candor always brings a sense of vulnerability.

A final word for beginning: All our work and all our speaking of faith suffers from the frailty of language and the limits of our own experience. I am acutely aware that I cannot say all that I mean and our experiences diverge. The richness and diversity of what you and I believe cannot ever be adequately conveyed by the language we use. Whenever we speak or write, we have to be prepared to speak again. We will need to speak again, in part, because we come to see our world and our faith more clearly. Your experience will enrich my experience. But even more, we will need to speak again because new truth will break through the boundaries of the frail words we used before. The light of faith remains more than any words can ever contain and more than any one person's experience can ever grasp.

Chapter 1
Marketplace Religion

When we meet at church, the mantle of believing can be worn without putting us in a bind. Sitting in our hallowed sanctuaries, bowing our heads and bending our knees seem the natural things to do. We have been trained to worship. No sweat. Believing comes easy. In the marketplace, earnest believing is another matter. There our resolve to believe runs headlong into our efforts to succeed and make a living. The tension between believing and behaving brings on headaches and causes knots to cramp our stomachs. Honest faith up against dishonest religion becomes a tangled web of uncertainty and guilt. Living and believing collide in the marketplace.

I learned my first lessons about honest religion behind a soda fountain where work after school provided far more than a little spending money. This fountain was my window onto a world of theatre and commerce, a world of discord and celebration, a world of trading and profits. It was a world of very different people—black and white, high dressers and street people, well-positioned and unpositioned.

My brother, Jack, had worked there as a college student, and I could think of nothing grander than to follow his steps into the calling of being a "soda jerk." That's what we were called because that's what we did. In that day and time a person "jerked" sodas, spewing high pressured carbonated water into tall glasses of ice cream, foaming our way toward a soda to be topped with a mountain of whipped cream and a syrupy red cherry. To sip an ice cream soda before low fat milk and doses of aspartame made mockery of such festive indulgences was a treat that would draw a person again and again to straddle the bar stools at the "Alabama Cigar and Soda."

The soda fountain was located three doors down from the Alabama Theatre, an ornate, chandeliered place built when big-time downtown theatres and playhouses were in their heyday. This theatre was the center of virtually every gala that came to town. Long lines would snake their way around the corner, waiting for a seat to watch the crowning of the next Miss Alabama. Stan Malotte, when he was sober (actually he played better when he wasn't completely sober), would mount this large gilded pipe organ, rising from beneath the stage with sounds and color that brought the audience to its feet and sometimes to its knees.

The Alabama Theatre was a movie house but a great deal more. It was the people's gathering place for premiers and live performances. The crowds would stand for hours on end waiting to see the latest debut. And on their long, waiting way, I would fix them sodas and sundaes to restore their stamina and to add enough festivity to their wait so that they could hold out a little longer to see the main attraction.

Nighttime was party time. It was unspoiled by the insulation and loneliness of a television bounded by four walls. Television has made our world both larger and smaller. Daytime was work time. During the day, this soda fountain stood at the center of commerce where deals were made and shopping was done. We had not yet learned to retreat to the corridors to do our shopping in hundreds of little hamlet malls where the faces and races of the customers are more predictable. The action was downtown. We were all in it together.

Mink and sable fur coats were sold in the store adjacent to the Fountain, and on the corner sat a blind man with his shepherd dog, patiently sitting alongside him. The blind beggar played the guitar with his hat upside down, collecting coins from passersby who were either lifted by his music or injured by his misfortune. Fur merchants, beggars, soda jerks—we were all in it together. The contours of our world were shaped by the lame and the strong, the middle class and the upper class, the in crowd and the out crowd all intermingled downtown, unable to keep our distance from each other.

The black members of our community were still expected to take a back seat, to come to the rear of the soda fountain, to sit in the third balcony of the theatre—if to sit there at all. Even so, we were all in it together. Society just made sure that black folk were at the end of the line—or in a different line where the water fountain would be marked "colored only."

We were the ordinary people, and I learned more about faith and dysfunctional faith fixing sodas than I did on Sunday mornings when we all went our separate ways into our cocoons of worship, pretending we didn't belong together. We could work together, shop together, and drink sodas together, but not worship together.

The churches were segregated by races and classes. The ruling religion was silent when it came to racism and class divides. We could get our dander up about alcohol. Our church would sponsor Bible conferences decrying the evils of whiskey to an all-white audience. The Bible conferences about alcohol weren't much about the Bible since the Bible seems to waffle a little on alcohol. The conferences were more about whipping up an urgent commitment to abstinence.

My lessons of belief and unbelief began in a soda fountain where the well-to-do came to theatre galas and the down-and-out gathered spare coins from the crowds, where blacks were definitely restrained into being an underclass and where religion had yet to see the sin of its exclusive ways. Real faith has to be born in this kind of setting. It has to be born where we live. We were ordinary people separated by race and money and status. We were faithfully pursuing our religious lives with little or no thought given to the fact that if we believed what we were singing and praying, our comfortable and separated worlds would surely one day collapse.

The talk of God belongs to the marketplace. We should not be paralyzed because we do not see everything aright. The faith of the church has to be born among people who are caught up in the web of racism and sexism and other sins we yet have the wisdom to name. Faith does not belong mostly to scholars or to people who have all the right answers. Faith belongs to us who stake our lives on the claims of faith and who sometimes get our beliefs and morals wrong.

There is real mystery in religion, but the mysteries of faith need not be confused with vague talk and esoteric language. If we who call ourselves the church are to sustain our faith with any measure of passion or promise, we must become a part of the conversations about what is reasonable to believe. Too long we have left the responsibility to think about faith to the clergy or, even more remotely, to academics. As a result, those of us in the church wind up becoming the audience. We are trained to listen passively to exposition, affirmation, and admonition. It is not surprising that we lose interest. The whole point of the Christian revelation is to engage people in the life of faith. Enough of passive religion. Faith, if it matters at all, should have a bearing on living. All else is dead religion.

As we range over the lofty fields of theological subjects, we begin to discover that the real issues of faith are very close to where we live. Whereas the discourse of professional theologians may seem distant, the daily fray of our lives raises all of the really important issues. Our beliefs about God come to life in the everyday struggles with life and death. If our talking of God does not help us make sense of the struggles, our talk will be largely unimportant.

The life of faith and doubt is intertwined with the ups and downs, the triumphs and tragedies of living on Main Street with merchants and beggars and soda jerks. If plain talk about God constitutes a serious reflection on what we believe, that talk must take into account the rough and tumble of ordinary experience. The terraces of our own journeys of belief that take place downtown and in the suburbs, in the city and in the country, become the best context for beginning our conversation.

The future of the church as a relevant voice in our world requires that we find a way to move beyond being passive believers. We should not be content to serve as pawns in other people's belief systems. The conversations of faith should enable us to exchange ideas and to test what we say against the reality of one another's experience.

When it comes to honest talk about God, there are no right answers. Life is not lived by finding the right answers. When we think about it, we realize that life does not center chiefly around questions and answers. Being here is about living and dying, feeling joy and fighting with depression. It is about believing devoutly and being clouded with doubt.

That is where you and I as ordinary people who make up the church actually live. We do not live in a context where glib answers to deep questions are very satisfying. The neat categories of religious doctrine often seem unrelated to the world where we reside. We live where life is difficult. We live where people cheat on their income taxes and where a few coins in the hat are the difference between a meal and falling asleep hungry. Folks get hurt. Life gets broken. The faith of ordinary people takes place in this kind of setting. Thinking and talking about what we believe helps us make sense of the chaos and stave off the uncertainty and the dread.

While this book unfolds along the lines of the major issues of faith, doctrines themselves are often rather "off-putting." They intimidate. They seem so high-sounding and abstract. Our challenge is to find a way to link our thoughts about God to the concrete and particular avenues of our life. How do we get theology out of the clouds and onto our terrain?

Throughout these reflections, my goal is to say "let's talk about God," or "let's talk about Jesus," or "let's talk about the church." In other words, our task here is not primarily to instruct, but to foster a believing community that takes faith seriously enough to talk about it. The power of thought and dialogue can become a rich resource for strengthening our faith and undergirding the church. Clearly, this kind of give-and-take among the people of faith can become a source for authentic renewal with the church. Reaching for more honest religion changes the life of the church. We have a chance to move from being objects of preaching to active bearers of faith and witness. Conversation about our beliefs and even our disbeliefs brings a new sense of integrity to our religious commitments.

Beginning with Confession

Taking the first bold step to talk about our faith—to put what we believe into words—may be the most difficult. At first, we only know to repeat what we have heard. We are reminded of the great affirmations of faith. Listen, for example, to the Apostles Creed:

> I believe in God the Father Almighty, maker of heaven and earth. And in Jesus Christ, his only Son, our Lord; who was conceived by the Holy Ghost, born of the Virgin Mary; Suffered under Pontius Pilate, was crucified, dead, and buried. He descended into Hell; The third day he arose from the dead; He ascendeth into Heaven; and sitteth on the right hand of God the Father Almighty; From thence he shall come to judge the quick and the dead. I believe in the Holy Ghost; the Holy Catholic Church; the communion of Saints; the forgiveness of sins; the resurrection of the Body, and the life everlasting.

The Apostles Creed is repeated Sunday after Sunday in thousands of churches. There are many others: the Philadelphia

Confession adopted by the Baptist Association in 1742 and the New Hampshire Confession of 1833 on which the Baptist Faith and Message was based and adopted in 1925. Baptists, like the Congregationalists, tended always to lower the importance of creedal statements. Creeds were regarded more as declarations of faith than entrenched and flawless statements to which faithful members were required to give assent.

I believe that creeds should never be used as tests of orthodoxy. But I believe as well that confession is deeply important because it provides an affirmation of who we are and where we stand. No person's confession should ever have a binding force on another believer. We do not know enough to do that. A confession is a gift, not a test.

Have you ever wondered where these confessions came from? At one time, they came from the ranks of devout Christian believers, earnestly thinking and probing what they believed. They were not, at first, creeds to be set in concrete and recited. They were confessions of faith to be heard and repeated with sanctity and gratitude.

All our statements of faith begin as such simple affirmations. In a manner of speaking, they describe how far we have come in our life of faith. Confessions become markers along the way. Stating what we believe should not be done as a way of taking a hard and fast position from which we never move as if our understanding of faith becomes frozen in place. Affirmations of faith serve, rather, as a point of reference.

Today's confessions may be tomorrow's uncertainty. Tomorrow's confession may be today's heresy. Our affirmations of faith are rarely a place to stand forever, unchanging. Today's confession is a place from which to move and to grow. It is a place to be open to the study of Scripture. It is a place to be open to the light of the church and to be open to hear the continuing voice of God. We leave the creeds at church to repeat when we return there. The confessions we take with us downtown. They stay with us while we work, while we buy and sell, while we celebrate and while we weep. They grow and change there because that is where faith meets life.

The Life of Devotion

The most compelling conversations about God spring from devout people earnestly seeking to know what the presence of God means for their lives downtown and in the kitchen. The life of devotion is the engine of theological discourse. For that reason I have called what I am writing here "devotional theology." This description seemed fitting to me for several reasons.

First, I want to convey that my writing is far more a confessional interpretation of what I believe than a rigorous, systematic treatise that is based upon reason alone. This book is not about proposing a hypothesis or making a series of logical inferences from abstract theological propositions. I am writing about what I believe because I do believe. I am a person of faith, and my reflections flow, first of all, from the reservoir of my own faith.

Being devout does not mean that we have it right. We never do completely have it right. Devout people embrace foolish beliefs and commit terrible wrongs. Devotion is not about having religion just right. It is about pursuing our commitments of faith with honesty and integrity. Most of us will shudder when we look back and see some of the things we believed and did in the name of being upright and religious people.

Devotional theology, then, means that I am writing as a person "devoted" to the Christian faith. Even so, I am not a person whose faith is concluded or whose devotion is closed to new light. Blind obedience to abstract doctrines or to human preachments is never the point of religious belief. The Christian faith does not call upon us to become servants of anyone's system of beliefs. To the contrary, our faith will be strengthened by being a part of a community that raises vital questions that issue from an open commitment of faith. We have only begun to see the light.

Second, our common devotion is the best foundation for exploring our faith. There is a place for skeptics' conversations, but there is also a place where earnest believers can face up to and talk about their uncertainty. Together, we all participate in the inexorable difficulties of life. We do not do "good" religion by pretending that life is always smooth and undisturbed. The Middle East where Israelis and Palestinians face off against one another teeters on the brink of being an inferno. Every community of devotion faces into the turmoil of everyday life.

From the territory of the unexpected, the community of devotion breaks bread together, embraces one another, and explores the meaning of faith in the kind of world where we are awakened each morning by the news that fighting has erupted again in Bosnia and the threat of AIDS is gaining on us. We seek an understanding of our faith that will help sustain us even through each new season of turbulence. Devotional theology is not an understanding of our faith that is handed down in a tidy package. It rises up from the twisting turns and sharp curves that mark the common traffic of the community of devotion.

Third, my use of the term devotional theology means to suggest, perhaps above all else, my conviction that piety and thought belong together. I have found that the life of faith can stand up under the light of reason. The light of reason is never the enemy of faith, and intelligence does not require faith to take a back seat. Thinking about our faith does not diminish our commitments or undermine our belief. We should let theological conversation go on alongside worship and instruction. Otherwise, our religion withers. Earnest and honest reflection on what we believe is the best pathway to a healthy and stable church.

The ability of the church to make a difference in a difficult world requires that you and I not become passive recipients of religious doctrine. While our commitment to the church is an act of devotion, that act of devotion includes taking responsibility for practicing our faith. We make choices. Sooner or later, serious religious convictions have a bearing on some of those choices. Unthinking devotion is more emotion than substance. Thought is not a denial of devotion. The contrary is true. The search for understanding is the fulfillment of devotion. Piety and thought belong together. Devotional theology reminds us that every serious act of theological discourse is rooted in the wellspring of devout commitments of faith.

The life of devotion teaches me never to become disheartened by the failures of reason. I am astonished by the gap between what we actually know and what we hold to be true. Knowledge and belief—we balance them. We are foolish when we treat what we believe as a substitute for what we know. Belief does not call upon us to ignore or to deny the lessons of reason. Equally so, we should not permit our claims of knowledge to become pretentious or arrogant. Knowledge is woefully limited. We do see through a glass darkly. Our understanding runs toward mystery. We live on the edge of understanding.

By calling this endeavor devotional theology, I am reminding us that we should never lose sight of the significance of faith to human experience. We are believing creatures. Tear away our will to believe, and we will be something less than human. All the people I know are shaped as much by what they believe as by what they know. It was true for the beggar, and it was true for the merchant. It is not wise to treat our beliefs as a settled core of truth to which we pay homage. Beliefs are changing affirmations to be probed and tested and lived by. They are a dynamic force, guiding our living and molding our character.

Talking about God is a task that should be taken up by people like you and me. We are men and women of faith, seeking to know what it means to love God with all our hearts and to love our neighbors as ourselves. Life is not lived on a pedestal, above the noise and conflict. Life is not lived in some abstract forum. We live in a world where it sometimes seems that God is nowhere to be found. If we are to live our faith in the real world, we must work toward building a faith that brings our hearts and heads together.

Theology is about the extraordinary, but speaking of God does not belong to a special or extraordinary class of people. Speaking of God is up to you and me. Speaking of God is a child of the church. It is devout people thinking about what they believe. Theology arises from ordinary people who, as a community of devotion, reflect upon and come to grips with the power of the extraordinary within their lives.

Chapter 2
Confessions of the Heart

Confessions are born of the heart, and they reach toward the mind. We want to say what we sense. Confessional theology challenges us to believe passionately and to think clearly. Growing in faith means listening to the counsels of both the mind and heart. People cannot live well by attending only to the whispers of the heart. Neither can we live by thought alone.

Confessions are like hymns, more poetry than science. They should not be read or recited as admonitions where we must get every word just right. Confessions are vulnerable statements. They convey the power of belief—full of anxiety and devotion. They are not rational expositions that will withstand the rigors of logic. They are more like exclamations, affirmations that precede understanding.

Confessions honor the mystery of belief. We see more than we can say. We believe more than we can put into words. Confessions are poetic remnants of our meeting the Holy. The precision of language is rarely the strength and value of a confession. Confessions are the linguistic residue of meeting God. Instead of being silent, we speak. Even so, the confession can rarely convey the power of our experience of the Holy. The mystery of confession is born amidst the labyrinth of real life. I learned a lot about the labyrinth and the meaning of confession from my mother.

My mother, Chloe, worked for a living before working moms were the social norm. My most unyielding impressions of her, even at a young age, were of fortitude and resolve. I didn't know what to call it. Perhaps I called it determination. Chloe had three sons: Jack, the brightest; Max, the kindest; and me. I was conceived in joy but was born in the shadows of her sorrow. Her husband and my father, Spearman, was killed in an accident at work, leaving her pregnant and scared.

She found work and raised three sons. She did it the hard way. She labored long hours in the school lunchroom and on World War II assembly lines. Not well-educated herself, she wanted to assure that we were well-fed, well-churched, and well-educated. At the time, it never occurred to me that we were poor. We were nurtured with good food, strict discipline, and lots of up close lessons about self-reliance.

I learned from her about confessions of the heart. She was devout but always seemed to struggle with a thinly veiled sense of guilt. I learned that guilt didn't have much to do with what you do. It has more to do with self-blame. By any theological definition, my mother was a fundamentalist long before the politics of fundamentalism came into vogue. We used to talk about religion, especially after I started to college. By then, I could say a lot more than I knew. Talking beyond our understanding is a malady to which young people are especially susceptible.

Those conversations, which I enjoyed and my mother endured, were an avenue of growing for me. Our disagreements and all my ideas didn't seem to matter much to her. She showed no signs of backing away from this college boy with all his eruditions. She taught me by her tolerance that all our doctrines are passing chapters in the autobiography of our lives. Frederick Buechner said that all theology is autobiography. He was right.

Getting our minds and our hearts together is one of the challenges of faith. Thought can never displace sight, but we should never be content not to think about what we believe. Confessions are sustained by the evidences of the heart. They stay alive through the light of day and the dark of night through the power of thought and reason.

Experience and reason converge in the person who believes. We believe many things—some of them foolish, some fleeting. They fade away into the night. A few beliefs, very few, turn out to mold our character and influence our understanding. They create our values. Certain beliefs cause us to take on an identity. We begin to make formative commitments that give texture to the character of our lives.

The decision to believe, or even more descriptively the experience of being taken hold of by some fundamental commitments, is an experience that both binds us and also sets us free. We become bound to a certain and clearer sense of who we are. At the same time, we achieve greater freedom from the tyranny of every immediate circumstance. We are tossed about less by the prevailing currents of thought or action. We begin to see and to think and to believe on our own. Chloe took me to church, but she also sent me to school.

The Joy of Confession

In a world where we get confused and burdened down, the notion of joy can seem a little out of place. When chaos and quiet desperation intrude into our lives, we are tempted to judge life in terms of the difficulty and pain. Our lives do become terribly crumpled. Confessions always course down the jagged edges and sharp crevices of our crumpled lives. Otherwise, our confessions are make-believe.

The Christian faith is about finding a new center from which to see and understand our world, even when agony and ugliness are abundant. If we are simply in search of an easy fix for the pain, the Christian faith is not likely to be much help. The numbing need to feel good is the tragic side of our relentless pursuit of pleasure. Beyond the call to mere pleasure, the Christian faith offers as a pathway toward strength and wisdom and hope. Faith gives us the courage not to define life by its difficulties. When we really believe that God will never abandon us, regardless of the trouble, a quiet joy slips into the inner recesses of our souls. The Christian faith teaches us that failure and loss should never become the defining essence of our lives.

Prior to every doctrinal elaboration, faith is a celebration of this quiet joy. Joy is born of the grace of seeing through the confusion and frustrations that distract our lives. Where there is no underlying sense of joy, our theological discussions remain more an academic exercise than a reflection of inner light. The history of the church is the history of people bearing witness to their most compelling beliefs. The church's witness, however, can never be carried solely by those who lived and spoke before us. In our own time and place, we also have to speak. It is the only voice from God some people will ever hear.

The task of interpreting faith is never finished. Our faith continues to unfold. We speak and then we have to listen again. So, in the midst of our speaking, there is silence. These interludes of silence are as crucial to the conversations about faith as the rush of words. While we are often tempted to talk our way through life, we cannot. There can be no genuine speaking unless it is interrupted by the quiet times. The silence enables us to be in touch with the source of our joy. The joy of believing is grace. The joy of confessing springs from finding common ground for meeting each other.

The quiet joy from which confession springs is not trivial or pretentious. Quite to the contrary, it is often wrestled from the arena of suffering. The Christian confession of faith does not deny the reality of suffering. It does not call upon us to diminish the impact of pain upon our lives. The simple truth is that we hurt. Tragedy invades our quarters and chills our laughter.

Suffering is real. It imposes dreadful consequences upon us. It leaves us angry and frustrated. We tumble into the valley of despair. Yet, it is sometimes out of these very moments of anguish that a deeper sense of joy is born. Faith enables us to learn the difference between pleasure and joy. Joy arises from the transforming realization that God holds onto us even when we feel that we are not worth holding onto. The lesson of our faith is that God's grace stands against our suffering and pain. Suffering and pain will not be the last words. Grace does not displace or disguise the hurt. Grace embraces us even while we hurt, and in God's embrace lies the new light from which our confessions flow.

Moving beyond the "Once and for All"

Believing is never done once and for all. We have to keep returning to the altar. The notion that we achieve a posture of faith that resides within us pure and unquestioned assumes that we can discard our humanity. We are frail people who get confused. Life changes. The father is killed. We go to school. We experience new events. We ask new questions. The dynamic and changing nature of our experience means that the confession of our religious experience must be done over and over again. Our words are halting. Our speech is stumbling. Accurate and settled beliefs continually elude us.

As it turns out, I believe that openness will strengthen the life of the church more than accuracy. Your life and my life in the church is a changing and an open relationship. We have to be willing to revisit our affirmations of faith if those affirmations are to stay in touch with our actual experience. Unless we remain willing to return to the altars of belief, our statements of faith weaken into hollow rhetoric. Our affirmations become more recitations than confessions.

In this recurring exploration of what we believe, we must learn to listen without becoming uncritical disciples of those who teach us. Learning to repeat after someone is not the best evidence of gratitude. Gratitude is evident by exercising the courage to struggle with the meaning of our own faith. Each new or revisited confession of faith can, at best, provide a clearing from which to examine where we go from here. Our confessions remain tentative and open, giving us enough wisdom and light to proceed on a little while longer.

Keeping religion in touch with the actual life of faith remains a constant challenge for the church. Though the church cannot be sustained by theology alone, the church gains real energy from genuine religious dialogue. Whenever we rely upon the development of great church organizations or complex religious programs as the principal means for sustaining the family of faith, we will fall short. Faith is sustained and flourishes in a context that honors both genuine piety and intellectual integrity. Piety is rooted in taking seriously our commitments of belief. Intellectual integrity enables us to affirm our faith, while seeking rational exposition of belief. It applies reason to the leanings of the heart.

We are inclined to compensate for our limited understanding of faith by sermons and church programs that are stocked with certainty and clarity. The last thing we want from our faith is more uncertainty. As a consequence, we rush to build make-believe harbors of safe and sure statements where religious truth is absolutely clear and precise. We long for secure places where we can rest indifferent to the troubling storms that blow across the terrain of daily life. We substitute fervor for conviction.

A make-believe world of faith might seem to serve me well until the chaos of personal experience becomes intense, until I become weighted down with tragedy or guilt. Religious fantasy fades when life gets tough. Christianity is not a religion to make us feel good; it is a faith that gives us hope. An enduring and resilient faith is hammered out upon the anvil of real experience. Faith becomes significant when our convictions about God's presence become a factor in our voyage through the very center of life's storms. Pretense makes no sense. The harbor of hope lies in holding our bearings through the distractions of the bright days and the loneliness of the dark nights.

We should not think that the struggle with belief is one frightful and furious battle. If that were the case, we could engage the struggle and record our theological statements of victory. Confession is a recurring act precisely because our struggle with belief is not to be completed and laid aside. We lose our way and have to search all over again.

Theology has been described on the log books of those who have traveled the sea of Christian experience before us. That description simply means that faith is born of life, while theology is fostered by reason. Faith is a way of relating; theology is a rational exposition of the life of faith. Using the right words to speak of God becomes entirely secondary. We should not be afraid. There are no right theologies. The most significant ways of speaking of God emerge from the honest reflections and conversations among a community of believers about their commitments of faith. No one has a set of answers that settle life or religion "once and for all."

Shared Confessions

Creeds can be recited alone. Confessions have to be shared. They deserve to be discussed and weighed. Listening and speaking belong to the essence of confessing. Conversation has a winnowing effect, helping us to grow up spiritually along with our physical and social growth. The failure to discuss what we believe leaves us as toddlers of belief, never sure of our footing and always a little off balance. For this reason, my mother's tolerance of my questions and my tentative affirmations that were veiled with certainty encouraged me to crane my neck in search of better understanding. Shared confessions are the only route to shared convictions. Otherwise, we simply adopt others convictions as our own and recoil from any setting where we might need to explain what we mean. It is easy enough to say, "I believe in Jesus." It is more difficult to explain.

Sharing our confessions requires a measure of courage. Our courage can be strengthened by the realization that every effort to formulate a final and absolute set of religious answers is in vain. Life is larger than words. Faith stretches beyond our talk and endures beyond our speaking. Our confessions form a rhythmic pattern of listening and speaking. Speaking without listening is empty; listening without speaking is immoral. The problems of our world are complex and confusing, and people long to hear a word that will bear some light from God. You and I can only confess the light we see. We cannot see for someone else. We cannot believe for another. But we do have an obligation to say what we see with clarity and good sense. We bear witness intelligibly so that the light by which we walk has a chance to light the path for someone else.

Deep within us, we know that people need more than what we can say to them. Words turn out not to be enough. People need to experience grace in person. They need to feel a fresh sense of hope. When the preachments of the church become coldly unrelated to people's desperate cries for help, all our confessions lose their power. In order to be instruments of hope, our affirmations must remain unconditionally open to new light. Remaining open to the transcendent claims of God shatters our inclination to believe in belief itself.

All our doctrines and creeds will not bring hope. We should not be tempted to depend upon the stability of our own fragile statements. We should not rely unconditionally upon our limited theological truths. Whenever we try to build doctrinal empires that admit or reject people on the basis of agreement and consent, we are simply wrong. Believing should never be equated with doctrinal soundness. Doctrinal soundness is arrogant theological nonsense. We are substituting our doctrinal constructions for God's reality. God's truth gives hope. Our propositions of belief inevitably fade. All our theologies and statements of faith are crafted by frail people. They should never be trusted for their finality. Theology itself is not the source of human hope. Our hope rests only in God.

The Centrality of Love

I should not leave this early discussion of the power of confession without confessing the core of my own belief. Throughout this book, I will return again and again to the centrality of love. It will recur in my writing like the chorus of a hymn. Its repetition is meant to connect everything else that is said. It is like a thread that weaves through the fabric, holding together all the rest. Whether we know it or claim it, I believe that we are all sustained by the reality of love.

The confessions of my heart begin here: All real living is about relating. Relating, at its highest, means loving. The central reality of the world is that God is love. Every expression of God and every manifestation of God is the articulation of love. Love never fails. Love abides. Love endures. Love is the beginning and the end. Jesus brought God's love down to earth, living out God's love up close. Every person is born to be a person of love. The call to follow Jesus is the call to live in the light of love.

Love as the embodiment of God's grace is the pervasive theme for my speaking about my faith. It is the touchstone for conveying my vision of God. For me, the reality and hope embodied in God's love defines God's character as clearly as language can come to that definition. Love, as lived out in the life of Jesus, represents the Christian faith's most important gift to the world. Love's light remains our best hope for dispelling humankind's darkness.

I lay claim to the centrality and significance of love while being fully aware of the word's woeful ambiguity. Both language and culture have distorted the meaning of love. In ordinary parlance, love is often confused with sentimentality and the notion of love has eroded into relationships of lust and envy. These counterfeit expressions of love are so commonplace that they blind us to the powerful reality of God's presence in the world.

Even so, I urge us not to abandon our confession of the centrality of God's love or abandon our language. Love remains the best language to describe the reality of God's nature and the substance of our highest calling as persons of faith. We are called to love. Without love's reality transforming the ways we are together, we will either wither in greed and despair, or we will destroy ourselves with the carnage of fear and hatred. Love's power is the world's best hope.

Even with its limitations, love provides the highest and best category for interpreting faith for two reasons. First, we are our relationships. Separate any of us from our relationships, and nothing is left. We are born of relating. We live all our days relating. The pain of death's loss is the loss of relating. We are children of our relationships. The Christian faith defines for us the highest form of relating: loving.

Second, love most clearly and powerfully describes the character of God. Look at the eloquent witness of the Gospel of John and

1 John. The issue is to take with utter seriousness the affirmation that God is love. It is to say that the ultimate enduring reality of the world is love. We should not be hindered because our vision and understanding of love is limited and clouded. Both the lessons of the church and the canons of Holy Scripture teach us that God's love never abandons us. Love makes sense of our lives. Love makes sense of the world. And love, above all else, makes sense of God. Love was Jesus' calling, and it is ours. The confessions of my heart begin and end with the affirmation that God is love.

Chapter 3
The Courage to Doubt

Honest confession will sometimes lead us to genuine doubt. Doubt is the growing edge of faith. We do not live with perfect sight, and our understanding is always limited. The call to faith is a call to follow. It is not a call to pretend that we do not get frightened along the way. Making significant commitments always leaves a residue of uneasiness and a whisper of uncertainty. We cannot see exactly where our large choices will lead. We do not know every twist and turn that our journeys will take.

A seminary professor named Billy McMinn made me question everything. He introduced me to thoughts and ways of looking at the world I had never heard, much less seriously considered. He taught me one of those high-sounding courses called Systematic Theology. Before he was finished, he had stretched some new creases into my religious skin. One of his tools was the first volume of Paul Tillich's *Systematic Theology*. The other two volumes of this giant book hadn't even been published yet.

I read and heard of new metaphors for speaking of God such as describing God as the "Ground of Being." Perhaps for the first time, I realized that all of our speaking of God is metaphor. Since we cannot get our mental arms around God, we turn to image and symbol. Turning to myth and symbol is never wrong unless we stop there. Golden calves and crosses become troublesome when we cannot see beyond them to the God beyond our gods. All our symbols testify that we cannot get our arms around God. The beginning of faith is learning that God's arms are around us.

I learned in that seminary course that doubting is a crucial part of believing. Without the courage to doubt, it is very difficult to sustain the will to believe. As I watched Billy, I also learned that in a seminary confessing your doubts will get you fired. Billy was more than an orthodox seminary could stand for long. They nudged him out of the door even though, maybe even because, his teaching drew crowds of students and his probings made all of us think more precisely and speak more clearly. He was drawing too many crowds and threatening too much decaying religion. We could not have preachers doubting what they were doing, or professors shaking the foundations of established belief. As for me, I found a principle. It is this: Never trust a preacher that doesn't doubt what he or she is doing. Doubting is the human side of ministry.

But there I was in this crevice of history before the heresy hunters could get their work done and get some of these dangerous disciples out of the faculty ranks. The work of purification began while I was there before my very eyes. I watched as they exorcized Professor Ted Clark because he dared to suggest that we might be saved by Jesus' life as well as his death. Heresy hunting is swift and intolerant. Any hurt can be justified in the name of protecting God's turf. In the heat of battle in which I was mostly a bystander, I learned that God's turf doesn't need protecting. God's truth is secure. Honest doubt will be a greater ally of God's truth than all the fires that burn books and char the lives of devout teachers who teach the truth by exposing untruth.

Doubting is an integral part of making important commitments. The process of developing commitments is a process of redefining ourselves—whether it be a career commitment or a marriage commitment or a faith commitment. Commitments are nurtured. They come about in stages. Their beginning may be quiet, or they may be dramatic and stunning. But their growth is always marked by the interaction of clarity and confusion. We are settled and certain, and then we wonder. Something doesn't fit. We run into doubt.

The admonition merely to stand firm, deny the doubt, gives rise to religious dishonesty. It undermines the very security and certainty for which we are reaching. The winds of doubt inevitably blow through the fields of belief. We can go along, chanting such clichés as "The Bible says it. I believe it. That settles it." In the deep night, however, when no one is listening and watching, the doubt usually catches up with us. We find ourselves wondering and feeling guilty for wondering. We feel guilty for doubting.

The guilt is misplaced. The plain truth is that doubts do occur and some of them are helpful. Strong faith is not born of denying wonder and doubt. A strong faith is born of the tensions of devout struggle with believing. Becoming faithful means facing squarely into genuine questions and difficult circumstances. Faith should not pretend the questions do not exist. Faith cannot deny the trouble that makes us wonder if God is really there.

The church is foolish to shield people from the pain of facing difficult issues and raising tough questions. Quite to the contrary, the church should be the one place we can bring our difficulties, where we can probe our questions and doubts. It is intellectually dishonest and morally wrong to say "Don't worry. Have faith. Everything will be alright." We are worried, and everything is not alright. Faith is not an armor to protect. It is more like a sword with which to do battle. Faith that is thoughtful will be far more power-ful in confronting life's most difficult moments than faith that is defensive, naive, and doctrinaire.

Ironically, we seem especially inclined to shield the young from their questions and uncertainties. Youth is filled with uncertainty and consumed by questions. Doubts arise on every corner. The young are prone to challenge every assumption. It is bad faith and poor discipleship that discourages the young from asking their questions. Furthermore, it is dangerous and unwise. Refusing to face questions leads either to a deadly religion of guilt or eventually to discarding religion as irrelevant and out of touch with where they live.

Day after day, it occurs. Religion loses its power because it will not stand beside people in facing the most difficult questions of life. The Christian's response to life should not be "Just believe." The failure to speak a question does not mean that the question has not been raised; it means only that the question has not been faced.

The church can become the kind of setting where the search for truth and struggle to gain a more mature faith can be carried on. After all, the church is not an organization for which agreement is the central issue. The heart of the church is not agreeing with each other; it is believing in each other. The church is made up of people who are learning as they go. Disciples are learners. The church is a community of believers who accept each other regardless of differ-ent ideas and different life histories. Walking together through the shadows of doubt and the valleys of grief is the church's best hope for developing a faith that has the power to sustain.

We need not fear that questioning our faith threatens or disap-points God. God is quite secure. God not only accepts our inquiring search, but stands alongside us in that search. Even when the very foundations seem to be shaking around us, God's loving confidence in us is unshaken and unyielding. We need not be afraid. Both doubt and faith enable us to grow. Facing up to our questions can transform them into vehicles for gaining insight and understanding.

Believing in the Face of Doubt

The highway to a strong, resilient faith runs through the valley of doubt. There is not another road to the other side. We can try to go over or around or under. We can try to deny doubt, or ignore it. The more honest way of dealing with uncertainty and doubt is to face it. If we have the courage to face up to these shadows of doubt, we will find the wisdom to walk through those shadows into the light.

Life is not random. When our life is done, it will have meant something. Some pattern of meaning and devotion will be evident, if only in hindsight. One of the gifts of religious dialogue is that our give-and-take clarifies what we do believe. Conversation provides a platform as it were, to stand above and to look at the range of our affirmations. We get to hear what others heard us say. We often discover that what they heard was not what we really meant at all. We are able to see how one affirmation of faith relates to another. We are able to discover our own contradictions.

The interplay of belief and doubt arises from the complex lives we live. When you and I add up what we have done—the decisions we have reached, the sermons we have preached, the meals we have cooked, the nails we have driven, the books we have written, the letters we have signed, the lectures we have given, the families we have reared, the miles we have walked—we become painfully aware that none of these endeavors usher in the good life. Much of our real living lies between the pages and the meals, between changing diapers and visiting Kroger. Amongst our chores, we experience moments of real anguish, and we experience times of breathtaking grandeur.

Though these moments remain mostly unnamed and even unacknowledged, they leave their mark upon us. The fleeting glance away that breaks the stream of thought, the breath between appointments, the quiet between a child's insistent calls nurture the nuances of our character. The character of our lives is not colored chiefly by the major events that happen to us. We are shaped by a broad constellation of simple relationships and quiet events that shape the contours of our life of belief.

In the face of diverse and sometimes conflicting relationships, we long for our life to have some purpose. We long to be whole. Our journey of belief is about helping us get a sense of what all of life means. It is about helping us lay claim to some pattern of meaning by which we can make sense of our private and public lives. We are pulled in many directions. We need some center that can help us stay intact, instead of being torn asunder by every competing claim for our time and attention.

Unless we can find a center, life remains scattered. While we are doubting, we need to doubt the wisdom of living continually scattered lives. Thinking and talking about what we believe becomes a force establishing some stack poles of belief around which to make our choices. Finding this integrating center requires real engagement. It is not enough to be spectators of the conversation. Being a spectator of faith can be very attractive. We can relax in cool isolation from any personal investment with the problems and issues that are raised. We stand above the battle. The debate interests our heads but never touches our hearts. The alternative is to enter the search for the meaning of faith as an honest believer.

Religious life, at its deepest, is full of passion. The light breaks. The truth "dawns" upon us. The light of truth does not completely do away with the darkness; it pushes it back. We have seen dishonesty too long in the forums of religion. We cannot be content to feed off the residue of the past. The ability of the church to make a difference requires that we take people where they are and point to light that will help them on their human journey. Our point is not to win in a battle of religion, but to help people in their struggles with life.

Coping with Dead Language
Dead language is usually the first symptom of dead religion. We learn to chant religious words before we understand them, and we often recite them long after we stop believing them. Growing up invested many of us with a religious vocabulary. We were schooled in words that we hear at church, weddings and funerals, and public prayers. This language is reserved mostly for religious occasions.

We don't talk much about such things as salvation and sanctification in everyday discourse.

Only later do we discover that we don't have the vaguest notion what many of our words really mean. They are hollow—devoid of substance and emotion. We have learned to use the right words in the right setting. We have learned to say the right thing. Our language has grown stale. We find it more and more difficult to maintain a live faith with a dead language.

Language is not the only problem. The people who use the language are changing. When people change, their language must change along with them. Even when the essential truth of a matter does not change, the way we convey it to others does. The answer is not to talk louder. We have to wrestle with new ways of conveying old truths. If those old truths cannot be placed in new linguistic clothing—new wineskins—the old truths will lose their power to persuade. If we cannot put what we believe into new words, it may mean that we have remembered the words but forgotten what they mean.

A part of our problem with religion is that it is such an everyday occurrence. There are steeples on every block, and the sounds of church bells are never far away. Religion is so common that its basic irrelevance can go unnoticed. For most of us, the ordinary task of making a living, and living together with husbands and wives, children and parents, the young and the elderly consumes us. At times, we may really wonder if it is possible to affirm a religious faith that has any relation to these everyday responsibilities. I believe it is. Our challenge is to discover how it is possible. Finding an idiom of faith that is not foreign to our actual lives is critical to the credibility of religion. Unless we do so, our churches, like our language, will become increasingly barren. The bells will ring, but there will be no sound. Our religious affirmations will be recited without conviction. Passion will abandon the life of belief.

Beyond Doubt

The courage to doubt is the prelude to living beyond doubt. Doubt belongs to the avenue of faith. We should not try to drown out doubt with louder religious noise. The fear of doubt inhibits the courage of faith. Doubt is not our destination. If we are to make our way beyond its grip, we must wrestle honestly with its questions.

Wrestling with doubt will leave bruises and bumps, but the process of resolving doubt becomes a great reservoir for strengthening faith.

We can, of course, become enamored by doubt itself. We can become fascinated with the freedom to raise questions so that we enjoy our ability to serve as a gadfly of doubt within the community of belief. We become stalled on the shoals of unanswered questions. The danger lies in beginning to enjoy our role as a cynic. Constructive doubt prompts us to grow. Growing in faith that is open and honest will take us beyond the stages of doubt.

Doubt has to be resolved one day at a time. It is resolved not only by questioning our faith, but questioning our doubts as well. The courage to doubt includes the courage to doubt our doubts. Moving beyond doubt means facing into it and learning that the foundations that have been tested by doubt are generally more secure than those that have pretended that the ill winds would never blow. Moving beyond doubt means confronting life's most serious dilemmas and realizing that faith is built in the arena of risk. Faith is not blind. Faith sees the doubt but, instead of being paralyzed by its questions, embraces doubt's uncertainty as one of the conditions of faith.

Doubt can teach us that we should not believe some things. Doubt has a winnowing effect. We learn that a mature faith does not mean becoming an uncritical follower of every religious parade. It means realizing that those who proclaim the gospel are fallible men and women. Faith is nurtured in the crucible of reason and experience. Out of this cauldron of reason and experience, where life is not clear and precise, we find a place where we can stand with integrity and openness.

Our culture of belief generates an ocean of bad religion where people are manipulated and abused in God's name. Religion is marketed on television as a sure way of winning God's favor. The blessings of God are meted out like prizes on "The Price is Right." Open the right door. Say the right words, and God's blessing will be your prize. It is the same old urge to get something for nothing.

Honest doubt and critical skepticism can help to save us from the trivialization of religion that is so rampant in our culture. Religion has become big business. It produces lots of income, while sometime leading people down the pathway to emotional turmoil and unstable commitments. The volume and impact of bad religion that manipulates people's fear have injured our capacity to foster a mature and thinking faith. In all candor, the church needs to become more self-critical. The church should be a living protest against bad religion.

To live beyond doubt means to accept responsibility for our life of belief. It means to stand somewhere instead of trying to stand everywhere. Belief rarely means achieving objective certainty. Commitment, more than certainty, focuses our living. Open commitment, in contrast to a commitment that is closed and defensive, recognizes that our minds will change. Our beliefs will grow. We will see things more clearly. The anticipation that our minds will change should not silence us now, however. It should help us avoid dogmatism and exclusiveness. It should encourage us to listen to one another with more care.

Faith does not deliver perfect clarity. We do not speak of God because we know everything about God. We speak of God from the deep and persistent reservoir of faith that has been cleansed by the winds of doubt. The most enduring commitments of faith have been discovered while traveling down the avenues of doubt. Though it cost him his career as a seminary professor, Billy McMinn was right. The courage to doubt helps us find a better reason to believe.

Chapter 4
A Reason to Believe

The courage to doubt will wind its way home toward a reason to believe. Believing in God is both easy and difficult. It is easy because God-talk is so common. Most of us grow up with the sounds of religion all around us. God has become a television star. The channels are filled with preachers and somebody selling a new book on angels. It is easy to say that we believe in God because everybody seems to be doing it.

Believing is difficult because we don't know what to believe. There are so many gods to believe in. Everyone on the air and in the pulpits seems to have a different "take" on God. At times, we find ourselves put off and even offended by the unscrupulous and petty descriptions of God. The language of God is used to manipulate people who are weak and hurting. Some people send in their life's savings in the hope that it will win God's favor.

We also find it difficult to believe because of the real trouble and pain around us. How could God, if there is a God in charge, let such tragic things happen? We live in a world where there seems to be little relation between what people deserve and what they get. Believing in God in this kind of world where good people are senseless victims can make believing a difficult mountain to climb. CNN will not let us rest from the world's nightmares.

My reason for believing was bracketed between two people: Janie Scott and Mabry Lanceford. Janie was my father's mother. I did not know my father, though his genetic code must be intertwined with mine. But I knew Janie. She was a fortress—a strong, beautiful woman who could make any day a good day. Mabry was a teacher and a friend. He taught me in college, and years later we studied together in another academic program that caused our lives once again to converge. As it is with most teachers, he didn't really suspect that he was important to me, but the imprint of his words and his spirit lingered with me long after the ink on college diplomas had faded. Janie embodied unencumbered grace. Mabry embodied thoughtful believing.

Mabry Lunceford listened as much as he taught. It is hard to find listening teachers. Most of us who teach are so intent on telling what we know that we find it a high hurdle to listen. He would ask questions and actually listen and take our lesson down the alley ways to find unsuspecting lessons behind the formal lesson. I still recall his using a textbook by Edgar Brightman that opened up whole new rooms of ideas that I had never considered. Mabry combined intellectual understanding with a gentle and caring commitment to his students. He would accept nothing less than our most rigorous and disciplined thinking, but his hard expectations were matched by his gentleness. I learned from Mabry that my believing need not always fly in the face of reason and that reason can be an ally of faith.

Janie, on the other hand, didn't teach me. She led me. I spent every summer until I was fifteen years-old with her and my grandfather. She lived on a cotton farm. They raised most of what they ate. They didn't have much need for money, except to buy tools for the farm and a few staples from the "rolling store." Janie possessed an unusual combination of dignity and kindness. Dignity often comes across as being cool and aloof, but her dignity embraced and lifted people's spirit. She had plenty of difficulties. She was no Pollyanna. Yet she carried herself with more peace of mind than the circumstances could possibly have justified.

She was a strong woman—outlived three husbands. The only one I knew was Peter Scott, a stern man who worked hard in the field and had little to say. Janie told me that he was a "hardshell" Baptist. I didn't know what that meant, but I wondered at the time if that made us "softshell." Day by day and year by year, I learned of grace through her sensitive and liberal spirit. She didn't have any theology to teach me. I learned from her boundless openness, her enduring patience, and her unfettered compassion. From Janie, I learned that grace is the power of salvation.

My reasons for believing, and I believe most people's reason for believing, are grounded more in the people of faith than the doctrines of faith. Janie and Mabry, of course, stand in here for many others whose experience of believing has had a bearing on mine. The worst reason for believing is the fear that God is going to get you if you don't believe. "Gotcha" is a human game. It is not God's game. Belief is not a way of getting God on our side. The truth of the Christian faith, if there is any truth, is that God is on our side. Believing means tuning our heart to God's presence.

The Meaning of Belief

In gaining a reason to believe, it will be helpful to come to terms with the meaning of belief itself. Believing changes people's lives—sometimes in radical ways. Countless times we have witnessed people for whom their drama of belief has changed their values. It has changed their priorities and passions. We have seen drug addicts walk away from their addictions. We have seen alcoholics never take another drink and credit their religious conversion. We have seen people whose lives seemed to be a total wreck apparently transformed by their compelling and consuming beliefs. The history of belief is actually quite astonishing: the apostle Paul, Sister Teresa, Albert Schweitzer, Rosie Grier, Chuck Colson. More important than these are the people whose names are not in lights. Belief plays a leading role in human history. Take away the driving force of religious belief, and the human scene would reflect a radically different landscape.

What shapes the person of belief is not what happens to her, but how she sees what happens to her. If we wish to verify the prophet, we cannot simply look at what he says. We must look at what he sees. Belief has to do with seeing—seeing ourselves and seeing our world in a different way. Different beliefs provide different ways of seeing the world. The Palestinians and Jews look at the same land, but they see that land in a dramatically different light. Believing compels how they behave. Belief can be power for good, and belief can be power for destruction. People who believe commit atrocities in the name of God. People who believe build houses for humanity in the name of God. The substance of belief matters profoundly. Belief in belief is not belief enough.

Faith has become a terribly ambiguous term. We confuse faith with accepting something for which there is insufficient evidence. It is as if someone said, "Don't question; just believe." Faith becomes a substitute for knowledge. Belief is not meant to be a second-class kind of knowing. Belief is not a substitute for knowledge. Believing offers a new way of knowing, a new way of seeing and understanding ourselves and our world.

We are very good at acquiring manageable bits of knowledge. We customarily divide the world up into consumable parts. In a university, we divide the world up into subjects such as history and psychology, mathematics and chemistry. We create smaller and smaller versions of the world so that we can get our arms around them, trying to understand each part. The search for knowledge divides and redivides the world, aiming to know more and more about less and less.

Believing takes place in a different arena than the acquisition of knowledge. Knowledge focuses mostly on the parts and aims to know the whole by carefully studying the parts. Faith is focused on the whole and aims to understand the parts by focusing on the meaning of the whole. Knowledge aims to generate understanding on the way to finding meaning and wisdom. Faith grasps hold of meaning and wisdom on the way to acquiring understanding.

Believing focuses on our reason for being here. The Christian's faith or even the Muslim's faith has to do with life's center. What on earth am I doing here? To become a believer does not mean to adopt a certain intellectual viewpoint. It means to follow some reason for being here. The Christian faith is, in its simplest terms, one option for ordering our lives. To be sure, other choices are possible. We can be guided or driven by economic or political power. There are other religious alternatives: Islam, Hinduism, Zen. To believe means to bring our lives into some kind of order. Faith means making choices and staking our life and character on certain realities.

Belief, if it makes any difference at all, begins to reconcile our contradictory yearnings. We begin to live in more harmony, chasing less after each new experience that makes us feel good. Our talk about believing will always be frustrated by the limits of language. The light of faith cannot be completely described in language. Life is larger than language. Nevertheless, it is clear. Believing redefines who we are, what we value, and the intentions with which we live. Believing changes what we want out of life.

Believing is both an act and a relationship. When Jesus spoke to his disciples, he gave them no statements to accept. He gave them no tenets to adhere to. Instead, he asked that they follow him. There lies the heart of believing. It is the act of following new light and transforming our relationships in that light. To believe means to relate to all of life in a new and decisive way.

Each of us lives as though something is real and true. We all live out certain life commitments, whether we confess those commitments or not. For the Christian, the primary focus of meaning turns on the character and presence of Jesus. Regardless of our particular religious faith, believing refers to the ultimate act of choosing some center, some integrating force, for our lives.

In a sense, believing may be life's greatest risk. When we believe, we are choosing a life center. Christians claim to be followers of Jesus. This act of following provides light to their path and priority for their decisions. In becoming Christian, or for that matter, in becoming Muslim, we are choosing a place to stand. We are making a conscious commitment that something in the world is real and true. Our commitments of faith mean staking our lives on this certain center of being that gives us meaning and purpose. Believing provides a defining foundation to which we return even when we are weary and afraid.

Believing changes everything. Relationships form the reservoir of our character. Believing means relating in a new way. For Christians who believe, their relationships become transformed by the character of Jesus. For Jewish believers, their relationships are transformed and informed by their relation to God as the people of Israel. They are God's chosen people. This understanding of themselves changes everything. For fundamentalist Muslims in Iran, the power of their belief embodied in their leader, Khomeini, led to the overthrow of a king and the demolition of an embassy because they earnestly believed that the American embassy represented the evil empire.

In religious faith, the center of belief becomes the defining center for all other relationships. All our experience comes to be understood around the centrality of this one ultimate relationship. Nothing escapes the light of belief. Everything changes. The world is seen through different eyes. It is not that we see with certainty. It may be that we see with fear and trembling. Nevertheless, we see. And what we see, what we believe, changes the emerging character of our lives. We are never quite the same.

One reason to believe is that we cannot *not* believe. We can follow many pathways, all at once or one at a time. We can be many people. But the course of our lives will make us into somebody. At the end of our journey, we will have become some person. We will have believed. What makes us different from one another is how we order our lives and whether we take responsibility for ordering them. We can always follow the herd, join the parade, do whatever feels good. We can believe by default, simply repeat what we have heard. The alternative is this: We can face openly and honestly into our own destiny and choose to live out our special gifts. The challenge of faith is to live by the highest and best light we can see. For me, that has been the light of Jesus Christ. But you must follow your own light and believe. Following God's light is the most personal act of all.

Believing and Obeying

Obeying is the substance of believing. Belief without obedience is fanciful, largely rhetoric. Obedience is simply how belief acts itself out in the real world. The failure to "do the faith" springs from the failure to "believe the faith." Faith without obedience is empty and hollow. It means dressing up and having nowhere to go.

We need to think and act with great care when we interpret religious obedience in the Christian faith as adherence to a prescribed set of regulations. There is a place for rules. Rules are shortcuts. They keep us from having to think through every situation all over again. Obedience means being "faithful"—full of faith. It entails the responsible exercise of human freedom. Following Jesus or following any light of truth changes what we do. We cannot confess belief in Jesus without caring for the people for whom Jesus cares. The Christian is free to love and responsible to discern what love requires in every particular time and in each special circumstance. The rules help us discern, but they do not give us the answers. Love is alive, and the force and character of love can only come alive in the actual act of loving.

We cannot describe beforehand how love will behave in every situation. Only the life of believing can prescribe what the life of obeying requires. Life would be simpler if we could make absolute rules. We would like to spell out what specific behavior faith will require, every time. Nevertheless, we should resist the temptation to become the advance arbiter of love. The relationship of faith must remain the judge of obedience. The demands of believing are rigorous. Everything has changed. But the expectations of faithfulness cannot be laid out completely in advance. Believing implies obeying, but the act of obeying can only be determined finally in the actual context of being faithful. Life cannot be lived ahead of time. Love is not an abstract principle to be embraced. It is a concrete, specific way of life to be followed.

Faith and Reason

Reason is not the enemy of belief. The fact is that people think and believe. We have been mistaken when we have regarded believing and thinking to be mutually exclusive. Reason is on the side of believing, and believing should be an ally of thought. Some believers have actually avoided thinking and talking about their faith, fearing that their questions might incur the disfavor of God. We should not fear. God embraces us mind and heart, and we do well to keep our mind and heart together.

This interplay of faith and reason is deeply rooted in the history of the Christian church. Devout Christian leaders such as Thomas Aquinas, Anselm of Canterbury, and Saint Augustine have wrestled with how faith and reason are related. Thomas Aquinas, who lived from 1225 until 1274, was a devout Dominican monk who even by today's measures may be regarded arguably as the most important theologian in Christian history. His great *Summa Theologica* continues to instruct us as a chief reference for Christian thought. Before him, Anselm, born in 1033, shaped many of the issues of faith and crafted many of the church's doctrines, through his writing and preaching. He was the archbishop of Canterbury from 1093 until his death in 1109. Augustine, the bishop of Hippo, was born centuries earlier in 354 in northern Africa. His theology is known best through his treatise called the *City of God* and an earlier book about his own spiritual pilgrimage entitled *Confessions*. These three devout Christian interpreters framed the issues of faith and reason with such compelling persuasiveness that every serious religious thinker, medieval, modern, and contemporary, has been affected directly or indirectly by their reflections.

Aquinas was clear that reason is a gift of God. The gift of mind makes us distinct from the rest of creation. Aquinas was even convinced that through the power of reason alone we could demonstrate the existence of God. So for Aquinas, reason is where the life of faith begins. Faith, however, gives us a higher vision of God that reason alone can never provide. Anselm and Augustine were more focused on the centrality of believing. Faith sets the stage for reason. Reason strengthens faith, but our belief never rests on the effectiveness of our logic.

The challenge of keeping faith and reason together remains with us even today. Over and over again, we can and should affirm the legitimacy of both clear thinking and right believing. Thinking and believing belong together because that's where we live. We think and we believe. Life cannot be lived well without either faith or reason. Every act of believing is an act of a thinking person. Similarly, every act of thought is an act of a person who believes. Our beliefs color our thoughts and affect what we think about. We need believers who can be dispassionate and objective in their pursuit of truth wherever it leads. And we need scientists and mathematicians who acknowledge the joy of believing. Belief does not tell us much about how the world was made. Belief tells us that the world is rooted in God's being and God's purpose. The future of the church requires believers who think and thinkers who believe.

Faith, then, should not fear reason. A closed mind that refuses to hear the call of reason leads to a life of faith that will be shallow and afraid. It will be defensive and protective. Blind faith is more likely to yield to the call to do evil in God's name. As our faith grows, we learn that our inquiry leads us to clearer sight and deeper commitment. We are fallible believers. We do not have all the answers. There is much we do not know. Our understanding is limited, and our belief is clouded. Therefore, both faith and reason should remain open.

We have only begun. The aim of reason is to help us reach a more coherent and consistent system of thought. The goal of faith is to give us a sighting of reality by which we can live. Faith shows us more than reason can ever conclude. But faith never requires the denial of reason or the assertion of the irrational. We should be suspicious of any call to believe that asks us to defer thought. The mind, too, is a gift of God. Believing and thinking belong together.

The reason to believe is that belief provides the power for integrating life. If we are to be whole persons, persons for whom the world and our place within it makes sense, we must believe. The only alternative to belief is living from one passion to the next. But the need to believe does not mean that we should believe anything. Unthoughtful and uncritical believing leads to casting our faith aside as irrelevant or embracing a faith that justifies atrocities. A thoughtful, probing, growing faith can give us a reason to believe in ourselves, a reason to believe in others, and a reason to believe in God. A thoughtful faith will teach us, however, that the real foundation of our faith is not that we believe in God, but that God believes in us.

Chapter 5
The Dawning of Light

Light was the first evidence of the presence of God. Brooding over the darkness, God spoke and there was light. Still, you and I live between darkness and light. We live between chaos and order. We are often uncertain what step to take. We are continually confronted with decisions where the eventual outcome of our choices is not at all clear. We strain to see what is coming over the horizon. We are unsure what we should do or what we should believe. We want to believe, but we are not sure what to believe. Even worse, we want to leave the impression that everything is crystal clear and that we have life completely under control. We act as if there are no shadows. We are determined to be self-assured, even if it comes across as arrogance.

When we are honest, we all want light to live by. We want to know the reality behind the shadows. Coming out of the shadows can be blinding. Jesus was killed because he was more light than people could tolerate. When that is so, we pull down the shades to block the light. The light is too much. The astronomer, Galileo, brought too much light. He had to recant. Martin Luther brought too much light. He was excommunicated. Martin Luther King, Jr., brought too much light. He was assassinated. Yitzhak Rabin brought too much light. He was murdered. God's light is very often more than we can bear. We search for ways to make God's light more bearable.

Our religious systems become one means of managing the light. The Bible becomes a way of shading the light. The church becomes a way of shading the light. Theology becomes a way of shading the light. When God's light breaks upon us, we are inclined to build barriers between God and us to make God's light less blinding. Revelation is the dawning of God's truth. It is often very painful.

The Meaning of Revelation

We are intrigued by life's mysteries, enamored with magicians and fortunetellers. Education and research, and even gossip, are ways of pulling back the veils that shroud the unknown. Research in medicine, geology, psychology, and a host of other disciplines is trying to gain a better view of our world. We want to know what things are really like. We want to unravel the mysteries that continue to elude us. We want to discover what causes the cells of the human body to turn on themselves and begin to destroy other cells. We work frantically on a deadly disease such as AIDS in order to understand how and why this deadly virus operates and to find a means of stopping its relentless destruction. We search for facts and information and truth that will be revealing.

In our restless pursuit to push back the boundaries of the unknown, we usually stake out a little corner of life and work feverishly to uncover its mysteries. We dissect, inspect, and label a piece of the world. Our goal is to know it, master it, and control it. The persistent human desire to "name" new species, even to name the hurricanes, grows out of our effort to gain control. If we can name it, we have taken one step toward controlling it. The power to name symbolizes our desire to control. The Hebrews never spoke the name of their God, *YHWH*. To speak God's name would have been an act of trying to control God. So, God's name, *YHWH*, remained unspoken.

Even the philosopher Aristotle wrote about the impulse toward knowledge when he wrote that "all men by nature desire to know." Survival is not enough. We want to know how we fit into the larger scale of things. We want to belong. We want to know why we live and die. The unknown makes us restless. Columbus searched the mystery of the earth; Audubon, the mystery of plants; Admiral Byrd, the mystery of the Arctic; Jacques Cousteau, the mystery of the sea; Mozart, the mystery of music; Jonas Salk, the mystery of polio; John Glenn, the mystery of space. These are our kind of people, pushing back the horizons of the unknown.

We long for revelation. We yearn to bring the hidden to light. So, revelation is by no means simply the language of religion. The longing for revelation is indigenous to our character. Probing and searching lie deep within our souls. Where there is mystery, we work to uncover its inner secrets. We want to give all the world a name.

This longing for revelation also affects our personal lives. Our individual lives seem to be the greatest puzzle of all. We wonder about who we are and what on earth we are doing here. We consult astrologers and palm readers. The burning issue of "Who Am I" is rarely posed from outside us. It bubbles up from deep within. The question of personal meaning may not ever be raised as an explicit question to be answered. We are more apt to hear the question as an inner sense of discontent, wondering what we ought to do or wondering about life's problems that seem to have no "rhyme nor reason." Whether spoken or unspoken, the mystery of our own lives can be haunting. We are eager to see our way clear, to see our place in the world.

The religious impulse is born of this longing to see our place in the world. Our investigation of the world and even our probing of the human psyche does not reveal how we belong in the world. We learn more and more about the world, but all of our learning does not seem to tell us how to relate to the world. The life of faith springs from questions that are too large for the mind's eye. We want to see more than our intellectual inquiries will reveal. All world religions are about revelation. People are not religious because they engage in religious ceremonies. They engage in religious ceremonies because they are religious at the center of their souls. Even when viewed as human structures, all world religions are enduring monuments to the human longing for revelation.

The heart of religion, the primitive yearning for revelation, is born of wonder. In the quiet, reclusive moments, we wonder. In the noisy, busy world of making a living, we wonder. In times of good health and in times of dreadful disease, we wonder. Even when the wonder is submerged beneath the busyness of work or the pursuits of religion, it will not turn loose of us. We cannot keep it away from our door for long. In the soul's deep night, it creeps out from the recesses of our thought so the need for revelation springs from deep within the human spirit. The longing to dispel the mysteries of life is a part of our character that we share with every other member of the human family. Both separately and together, we long to know who we are.

Revelation is God's gift of light to us. The history of revelation
is the history of God showing us the ultimate meaning of our being
here. It is the history of God coming to us and walking beside us
even when we do not acknowledge God's presence. Sometimes we
hide our eyes. The truth hurts. Sometimes we do not see God
because we do not want to see God. We prefer to attend to the passing pleasures of the moment. Becoming open to God's presence
means beginning to see beyond the limits of our most recent
pleasure and to see beyond our hurried lives. Revelation is the
experience of seeing that our lives and our world are rooted in a
reality that is larger than our limited years. The story of our lives
begins to be written in the light of God's presence.

Seeing God through Nature and History

We ought to be careful about drawing the circles of revelation too
narrowly. When it comes to receiving light, we should let it shine in
from any window that opens onto our lives. It is easy to become
defensive, implying that our way of knowing God is the only way of
knowing God. Theologians have spoken of "natural" and "revealed"
religion, trying to draw the distinction between what we may know
of God from nature itself and what we learn of God from God's
special acts in history.

When people speak of "natural revelation," they are speaking of
what we can know of God through nature, human reason, and history. People often disagree about how clearly God can be known
through these means. They rarely disagree, however, that nature and
history shed light on the work of God. Even the biblical writers
were clear in their witness to the power and presence of God in
nature and history. In other words, God is not mostly present
through the "supernatural." God is present in the natural order of
things and in ordinary human history. Our Jewish forebears teach
us that the entire drama of history is taking place under the watch-
ful care of God. God is not a spectator. God joins us in the struggles
of our daily affairs. We can meet God in the ordinary events of
history.

If God can be known through nature and history without the
assistance of any special revelation, the question arises as to what
we can know. What do we know of God through nature and history?
Among the most immediate responses would surely be the oft-cited

"inalienable rights of man"—human rights. These values and truths are often presented as being "self-evidently" true and certain. "We hold these truths to be self-evident, that all persons are created equal." This notion that we all have a sense that certain things are true and right recurs throughout human history.

In addition, many persons, Christian and non-Christian alike, claim some knowledge of the goodness of God simply through nature itself. The beauty of the earth, the awesomeness and splendor of the world, convey the goodness and wonder of God. People are left speechless by the simple beauty of a sunset or the staggering beauty of a natural wonder such as the Grand Canyon or the aesthetic power of a Bach prelude. The beauty and awesomeness of the world inspires people to worship. The stars and heavens proclaim the grandeur of God.

Even as we are astonished by the wonders and awesome beauty of the world in which we live, an order and beauty that reveals God to us, we also face up to our larger experience of nature and history. Beside the beauty of the sunset is the destructive force of the tornado. The witness of nature and history is ambiguous. There is the beauty of birth. There are the inexplicable ravages of cancer. In nature, order is bounded by the inexplicable. Disorder also abounds. The orderly processes of nature are interrupted by catastrophes that leave people feeling helpless and alone. Order is punctuated with chaos.

History remains a mixture of good and evil, comfort and hurt, hope and despair. When we look at history and nature alone then, our reading of God's presence is apt to leave us uncertain, perhaps bewildered. Where has God gone? How could God let such tragic things happen? We retreat into stone-faced silence. In our silence we learn that history and nature alone are not enough to understand our lives.

The fact is that we not only live in history, we interpret history. Everybody's history is colored by their experience of that history. The history of racism is different for black and white people. History is a collection of what happens to us and our reaction to what happens to us. We are not defined simply by the whirlwind. We are defined by how we live through and beyond the whirlwind. The events of our lives are affected by what we bring to those events. An unpleasant and painful church experience of a child affects how we experience church as an adult.

I learned that my friend and colleague, Emily, was the youngest church organist her church had ever engaged. I was surprised. I learned that she grew up holding every office one could hold in the church—except those restricted to men, of course. Most of our churches have a patron saint. Her father was the patron saint of that congregation in Columbus, Georgia. On one of our day's travel, I asked about her experience of church in those younger years, and I heard one of the most moving stories of a church in conflict that I have ever heard.

In reflecting on her childhood, she spoke of seeing the church in all of its regal splendor and also its unsightly ugliness. She witnessed a church at war—a war that left her jarred at the prospects of the church being and behaving as church. Children set against children. Families divided. Friends parted. It taught her to keep her distance. She admits that she is Baptist to the core, but she also knows how bloody and brutal Baptists can be. For her and for scores of people who witness evil at the hands of the church, learning to trust the church again has been a long road.

When the church abandons the light of grace, and forgiveness, it casts a long shadow of failure. Mahatma Ghandi said, "I would have been a Christian had it not been for Christians." What happens to us is never a solitary, disconnected, isolated event. The baggage of previous events bears down upon our present experience. Who we become tomorrow can never fully escape who we have been yesterday and who we are today.

Our actual history, with all of its baggage, is the context for revelation. Our ability to see God's meaning for our lives cannot be wrestled from someone else's experience. Revelation occurs when the light breaks into our own history. Our ability to see the light depends largely upon our willingness to set the immediate events of our lives into the context of a larger reality to which we belong. If we live for the present moment only, we are likely to be overcome by the chaos and focused on the pain. The present moment rarely provides enough light to live by.

The Gift of Light

Revelation is always a "dawning." Through the life and the work and the words of Jesus, it "dawns" upon Christians what God is really like and what human life means. For others of the human family, Jesus is not the turning point of revelation. Every claim of revelation causes people to see the world differently. Revelation opens our eyes to see our world and to see God and to see ourselves in a new light.

The exodus from Egypt offers a wonderful example of the meaning of revelation. From the view of an Egyptian journalist, the exodus from Egypt would have been seen as the escape of a battered group of slaves from a hostile and foreign land. For the children of Israel, the exodus was deliverance. An Egyptian saw the event as escape. A Hebrew saw it as deliverance. The difference did not lie in the event. The difference lay in the meaning of the event. The difference lay in the light by which the event was seen. The difference between the perception of the Israelite and the Egyptian "Morning News" was the ability to see through the base event to the meaning of that event. The Exodus was experienced by the Hebrew people as the act of God. That vision was possible because they interpreted their history in the context of their ongoing relationship with God.

Similarly, Christians do not approach the coming of Jesus Christ in terms of historical data. The data of history about Jesus is interesting but not conclusive. We do not meet Jesus as historians might meet Jesus. We meet Jesus in terms of the meaning of his life for our own lives. Many events and people enrich the meaning of our lives. For Christians, Jesus makes a radical and formative impact on their lives. Jesus becomes the central focus for understanding what human life means. Other persons, indeed most other persons, may not be struck with the significance of Jesus. Most of them will even respect his words and be attracted by the character of his life. For Muslims, Jesus may be admired, but he is not the radical defining point for their lives. Jesus may be a source of light, but he is not the ultimate, defining revelation of God. Jesus is not the light by which they live.

Revelation, then, refers to an intelligible experience that makes all other experiences intelligible. It is the enlightening event that illuminates all the rest of life. For the Christian, Jesus is such an event in history. Jesus becomes the center of history and the event by which all of history, including our own personal histories, is understood. The Christian lives her life in the light of Jesus.

For all of us, whether we are Christian or not, revelation points to the principle or the person or the reality around which we order our lives. Revelation is a centering event in our experience. Revelation is not irrational. Revelation is more than rational. We see more than human reason alone will ever show us. Revelation uncovers the comprehensive, integrating reason of the universe that can never be understood by examining each part of the world with the mind's eye alone. Revelation discloses what the world is all about. It unveils the ultimate mystery that shrouds our being here.

The heart yearns to see ourselves and the world more clearly. Revelation ultimately fills that yearning. The pursuit of learning itself is prompted by that yearning. But no amount of human investigation ever completes the human picture. Around the edges of knowing lies the quandary of meaning. Revelation is the light that enables us to interpret the world and our place within it. When the light dawns, when some sense of purpose and order takes hold of us, we are never quite the same. We see life differently.

We are reminded of Jacob wrestling with the messenger of God. That experience changed who he was, and his name changed from Jacob to Israel. There could be no turning back. His name had changed. It changed how he met his brother, Esau. In our individual ways, we are all somewhat like Jacob. God visits us and we live by the light we have seen. What distinguishes us from one another is not the dark nights. Each of us experiences the dark nights. Indeed, the light often dawns in the deepest night. What distinguishes us is whether we have awakened to the dawning of light. Light was God's first word of bringing order from the chaos. God's light of revelation is the beginning of bringing order to our lives.

Chapter 6
Reliable Sources

The Christian religion has become very competitive. Good people quarrel about what they believe. Friendships are dashed, and families are fractured over conflicting religious views. On a global level, nations collide and wars erupt over issues that find their roots in competing religious beliefs. So, religion has been a source for soaring human hope and woeful human tragedy. Religious disagreement has led to anger, and anger has bred resentment and bitterness and warring. Much of our religious controversy springs from the fear of being on the wrong side with God. We defend our place as the right place—the only right place. The ugly face of religion has led many people to walk away from any serious religious involvement.

Even the most faithful and devout should work toward finding a place to stand that preserves respect and genuine communication with those who stand somewhere else. In the world of religious faith, we will have to learn that no one has final answers. When we set forth our belief as the only right belief, we are wrong. No finite person has absolute answers.

Rather than striving for finality, we should work toward finding a place to stand that we can affirm with integrity and honesty. The errors of the church have usually been generated by misplaced authority. We have wanted to lay hold of a solid and unimpeachable authority that will justify what we believe. Our search will be in vain. Instead of absolute authority, we need to search for reliable sources for our confessions of belief. We have placed on some resources of faith a greater burden than they can carry. Much of the splintering of Christianity into competing religious groups and denominations has grown out of disagreements over the issue of authority.

Truth and error about authority lie perilously very close together. When it comes to defining the foundations for belief, we need to be very careful about requiring infallible sources. The health of religion does not depend on infallible sources. The errors of religion spring over and over again from claiming too much for a single source of truth. The study of Christian history shows us claiming too much for the church or too much for the Bible or too much for our own experience with God. Genuine belief listens to all these sources. Each can be reliable. On the other hand, the elevation of any of them to the status of final authority inevitably leads to error and conflict.

The Church

For large segments of the Christian tradition, the church itself has been the primary source of authority for belief. The church, through its councils and bishops, historically determined for many persons what they should believe. One test of devotion was to submit yourself to the teachings of the church. In this tradition, the church serves as the major point of reference for determining both what should be believed and how people should behave.

The authority of the church contains an important element of truth. The church plays a high and significant role in our searching for what we should believe. The elevation of the church as the absolute source of belief is a mistake, however. The era of the Reformation served as one historical correction for an excessive reliance upon the church as our absolute authority in faith and order. The Reformation was a reaction to the excesses and abuses of church authority. Even so, the church as the community of faith remains a critical and indispensable resource to our life of faith.

Being in the church teaches us that we are never faithful alone. We believe in community, and the community of faith remains instructive for what we ought to believe as individual Christians. The notion that beliefs are solely individual and that believers should ignore the voice of the larger community of faith leads to religious arrogance and intolerance. We are a community of believers, and what we believe should be determined in community.

The church is a community of devotion, and the church stands alongside other reliable sources as an instrument of grace and revelation. Where love and fellowship abide, God is present. Where God is present, God's word can be heard. The church is the living presence of Jesus in our midst. Christians do not listen enough to each other in the community called "church." If we are to grow in our own spirituality, it will require us to take one another more seriously. People must meet, spirit to spirit. They must meet without barriers of position or standing, without the encumbrances of wealth or power. The church is where people meet heart to heart.

The church is something that happens when people meet and worship, transcending the barriers that separate them. In the church, the Word of God comes alive in a way that it can be seen and heard. That is what is meant by the "communion of saints." It is the church setting aside all of its frail and petty divisions. It means embracing one another as the children of God and the family of faith.

The Bible ought to be read in the context of the church, because the Bible is, in part, a gift of the church. Listening to the Bible in the church will sharpen and focus our ability to hear the Word of God. The isolated reader of the Bible, unconnected to the church, may be unable to see the implications of the Bible's teachings for his own life of faith. We are not faithful alone. We should learn to read and to listen to the Bible in the context of the church. There we can submit our interpretation, our hearing, to the judgment of fellow Christians. We must underscore that the community of grace also bears eloquent witness to God. Therefore, the word we hear from God through the Scriptures will not contradict the word we hear from God through the community of faith. God's presence is not divided. We are fallible. Our reading the Bible in the church enables our fallible ears to hear God's word more clearly.

The church should not be the sole authority. If revelation may be described as the dawning of light, coming to know God more fully rests, in part, with opening more widely the window of God's presence. We meet God through the church. We hear God's word through Holy Scripture. We know God through our own relationship with God. We should close off no avenues for hearing God. At the same time, we should resist every effort to make one way of knowing God the only way. The light of God comes through the church. The light of God comes through thought and study. The light of God comes through meeting and caring.

The Bible

In searching for a place to stand, many Christians, especially since the Reformation period, have placed an extraordinary focus on the Bible. Christians will often describe themselves as "people of the book." "Bible believing" becomes a code phrase for being a real

Christian. It is largely a foolish error, an effort to force upon the Bible a role that the Bible never claims for itself.

Our reason to believe reaches beyond the boundaries of the Bible. In all likelihood, the authority for our faith should not rest upon the Bible alone, or even primarily. For the Christian faith, the Bible is not the center of faith. The Bible is an instrument of the life of faith. The simple identification of the Word of God with the Bible is a grave mistake. Far from being the principal focus of our faith, the Bible is the record of God's revelation and how people responded and interacted with God's presence in their history.

God's revelation continues. And, indeed, the continuing presence of God in our lives and in our histories provides the context for our study of Holy Scripture. The Bible, then, should not be viewed as a boundary of belief. The value and critical importance of the Bible is tarnished by our unwarranted dependence upon the Bible as itself the object of belief. Believing the Bible is not the goal of faith, and it certainly should not be made a test of faith.

Revelation is personal and relational. Revelation is God's light breaking in upon us. The Bible is a window for God's light. Revelation, through whatever window, connects God's truth with our living. What is conveyed in Christian revelation is not information to be learned, or facts to be recited. Revelation is not information about God. Revelation is God's presence with us and for us. The goal of revelation is meaning, not data and propositions. Christian revelation does not offer us a statement of faith to be endorsed, but a way of life to be embraced.

The pages of Scripture reflect the interaction, the confession, the dialogue, the faithfulness, and the breakdown of faith among people of faith. We hear God speaking. We see people believing and refusing to believe. We see God's light break upon human history. God calls to us from its pages, and we find ourselves identifying with the struggles and conflicts of those people of faith. The Bible bears witness to the events that turn out to have extraordinary significance for Jews and Christians. The Bible is deeply important to the history of God's speaking and to our hearing God's voice.

Our confidence in the Bible as Holy Scripture should not rest upon believing the book to be a miraculous, divine dictation where its writers simply serve as God's recorders. The writers of the Bible were inspired persons of God, not secretaries empty of will and vision and insight. They wrote because they heard the truth and saw the light. The events, the relationships to which their writing bears witness, are the gifts that lie behind Holy Scripture.

The Bible is complete; revelation is not. To ascribe infallibility to the written words of the Bible is wrong. God's light has not gone out. God is alive and speaking, and God's word is not captive to history. To treat the Bible as infallible limits God's revelation to the past. Some events of history clearly take on crucial dimensions for our life of faith, but they take on those dimensions in our present experience. The Exodus is a larger event in the life of faith than the Torah can ever contain. The coming of Jesus bears a significance for our faith and living that cannot be limited to the pages of the New Testament.

Jesus often tried to bring his followers beyond the pages of Jewish Scriptures. No human words are sufficient to contain God. Jesus breaks the boundaries of any book. Through parable and deed, through speaking and touching, God's word took on living form and real substance. Jesus would demonstrate in his life and decisions, as well as his words, that the Sabbath was not a legal prescription. People were not created to serve the Sabbath. The Sabbath is a gift. The Sabbath is God's way of caring for us and our well-being.

We should also be reluctant to translate the Gospels and the Epistles into codified rhetoric for behavior. Turning the Bible into a rule book distorts the power of the gospel and misappropriates the teaching of Scripture. Let me illustrate in two ways. First, the sacraments of baptism and the Lord's Supper are important symbols of worship. In these events of worship, we act out our commitment and join together in a sacramental community of devotion. These sacraments are not biblical injunctions to be followed as formal religious requirements. They are powerful experiences for conveying our common life in Christ.

Second, the call to proclaim the gospel to all peoples is not carried out as a legal response to a biblical command. Our proclamation of the gospel burst forth from our own encounter with God. God is with us, and we proclaim the good news of God's presence. Wherever our proclamation is not rooted in a compelling sense of God's presence, our words fall as empty preachments. We proclaim the gospel because God has entered our sphere of experience.

The notion of the Bible's infallibility, instead of giving honor to the Bible, actually leads to a treacherous idolatry of the Bible. A person's understanding of the Bible becomes the acid test of faith. We should re-center our thinking. In the Christian faith, the Bible is not the focus of faith; Jesus is the focus of faith. If the Bible is beyond all criticism and analysis, it becomes absolute itself instead of pointing to God who is Absolute. Beyond the religious error of ascribing infallibility to anything but God, the notion of inerrancy also falters on the fallibility of people. An infallible book could be infallible only if it were infallibly read. So, in addition to writers whose inspiration was infallible, there must be infallible copyists, infallible translators, and even infallible readers.

Regarding the Bible as inerrant and holding fast to its inerrancy as the *sine qua non* test of faith exposes the human sin of trying to possess God. We really want God to belong to us, even if we can only manage that feat between the covers of Holy Scripture. We want to make sure that we have God possessed and secure in our understanding, either in a book or a doctrine or in a sermon. The truth is that God cannot be possessed. God remains beyond us. God gives us light by which to live, but we are wrong to worship the light. We can manage no final absolute knowledge of God.

Jesus Christ, not the Bible, lies at the heart of the Christian revelation. For the Christians' faith, Jesus embodies what God is like. In Jesus we see God's nature and character and purpose. Jesus is God's light, breaking in upon us. We are able to see God's kind of life and God's kind of spirit. We see in living color God's kind of love. In Jesus, the Word of God takes on historic personality. God comes and lives among us. We see how we would behave and respond to people if God's spirit were in us. We see God's way of behaving up close, and we begin to sense the unconditional character of God's love.

Jesus is present in our lives through the church, through the Scripture, and through our own living experience. Finding a place to stand means listening for God and seeking to know what it means to be a follower of Jesus in our time and place. There are no easy answers. Being Christian is a challenge that remains with us throughout our life of faith. We listen and speak, and then we have to listen again.

Our challenge is not to worship the Bible; it is to listen to the Bible. While not being an absolute authority, the Bible is indispensable to a full understanding of our life of faith. The Bible is crucial to our growing life in the Christian community. The Bible provides a unique and singular witness. The Old Testament places us before us the life and travails of the Jewish people in their journeys of faith. The people of Israel are the family of God through whom God speaks to us. The New Testament offers us the primary historic witness to the life of Jesus. The New Testament was born of the apostolic circle and gives us a firsthand view of the work and presence of Jesus within the early church. The Bible speaks from those who stood in closest historical proximity to the mission and ministry of Jesus and to the ministry of the earliest disciples. Therefore, while wanting to avoid a mindless and idolatrous worship of the Bible, we can hardly overestimate the significance of the Bible in our own searching for God's will.

Devout and open study of Scripture is a deep reservoir through which our life of faith is continually strengthened. The Bible informs and instructs. It inspires and lifts us beyond the preoccupations that consume us day to day. We learn from the intensity and anxiety of Abraham's faith. We learn from the self-reliance and brokenness of Jacob's struggles. We learn from the triumphs and tragedies of David's leadership. We learn from the lessons given by Jesus on the mountain. We learn from Paul who labored on behalf of an underground church trying to find its way in a hostile world. Through the Bible, God teaches us in our life of faith. God speaks to us again and again through the pages of Holy Scripture. We should let the Scriptures remain open to the Holy.

Spiritual Experience

Finding a place to stand requires listening to both the Bible and the church. We should not stop there. The third component of living faith is learning to trust our own experience with God. You and I can hear a personal word from God. Revelation continues because God continues to speak. We sometimes refer to this experience as "being led by the Holy Spirit." Still others may simply cite the overwhelming sense that a certain course is right. It seems inexplicable. We feel an ineffable, inescapable tug to take a certain step or to make a particular, specific decision.

I believe that God lives within us. When we will listen, God guides and directs our lives. We should learn to trust our life with God. Our lives can be tutored by disciplined devotion to hear and to follow God's calling. Listen to the sacred. God speaks to us in our everyday experience if we can but hear. Our own spiritual formation is a powerful source of revelation.

Our spiritual experience with God should be heard and lived in the context of the church and Scripture. God is not divided. The lessons that come from listening to the sacred, listening to the voice of God in our own experience, will not be alien to the lessons of grace that come through the church and Holy Scripture.

We have at least three reliable sources. We should listen for God within the church. We should learn from Holy Scripture, and we should listen to God in our own lives of disciplined devotion.

Finding a place to stand is dynamic. God's authority is alive. We must listen for God's voice again and again. Our authority for faith arises from the converging voices of God. If we are to discern God's word, we must listen to the common word that is heard through our living interaction in the church, our study of the Bible, and our own spiritual discipline. Together, they form our most trustworthy foundation for knowing God's will.

Most of the difficulties relating to knowing what to believe come about because one avenue of God's speaking becomes elevated above the rest. There lies the essence of idolatry. Neither the Bible nor the church nor lived experience should be allowed to become the single focus of faith. Our knowledge of God is a growing experience. God speaks to us in many ways. We have reliable sources for our faith. To claim any forum of God's speaking to be absolute exposes our lust to possess God completely. The truth on which we must live is that we do not possess God absolutely in a book, or in the church, or in our own experience. God's nature and presence are communicated to us most clearly and intimately in Jesus, and God continues to come to us throughout our life of faith. God comes to us through our own spiritual discipline, through Holy Scripture, and through the church.

We are often frustrated by uncertainty. We want a church or a preacher or a Bible to tell us what to do. Uncertainty may cause us to refuse to believe anything at all. But skepticism turns out to be not only hopelessly futile, it is also inhuman. The fact is that we do believe. Our lives actually do reflect certain values. We do not know everything. But God does not ask us to be gods. Our calling is to be human. Human life is a venture of faith. No authority can liquidate the ultimate risk of faith. To become Christian means to choose to stand somewhere. We make that choice amidst all the competing claims for our devotion. As Christians, our choice grows from the ultimate conviction that God has come to stand with us. We should keep the windows of God's light open. God continues to speak.

Chapter 7
Speaking of God

Life is precarious. People are born, and they die. Some live for only a few years. Others live for a hundred years. Even for the long-lived, life is precarious. In the stretch of history, the difference between 20 or 30 years and 90 or 100 years almost becomes trivial. Life, by any measure, doesn't last long in years. The edges of birth and death are precariously close together.

The question of God is raised by people living between the boundaries of birth and death. We want to know if those boundaries define who we are and what we are up to. The question of God does not begin as a distant philosophical abstraction. We feel the question of meaning before we ask the question of God. The day's burdens cause us to sense that we are fragile creatures living in a world that leaves us diminished and insecure. The issues of God's existence and God's nature can be framed as interesting intellectual puzzles, but the truth is that God is an issue of life and death long before God ever becomes an issue for thought and debate. There is little urgency in the intellectual discussion of the existence of God. There is not even much urgency in the abstract question of the nature of God.

Urgency arises when we earnestly wonder what we are doing here. There can be urgency in finding food to eat and water to drink. In 1995, a pilot shot down in a Bosnian war zone survived by wringing drops of water from sweat-soaked socks and eating bugs and ants crawling around him. The urgency of survival takes on flesh and blood. Walking closely to borders of survival raises within us the question of why we survive. The "so what" of surviving erupts within us, triggered by the border experiences of life.

The "so what" of surviving is the embryo of the question of God. The truth is that we are seldom sure how to ask the question of God. When the noise fades and the light dims, we simply wonder what it all means. So, whether spoken or unspoken, the question of God lies deep within the human spirit. We don't know how to say it, but it is there. We want to belong here. We want the world to be a different place because we are here. We want to be missed when we are gone. Our being here bears an unalterable connection with what has been and what is to come. The question of God is the question of what connects us to anything and everything else.

I first came to a conscious struggle with the question of God during my college years. I had been brought up to believe in God, but I had never wondered much about what it means to believe in God. As an even younger person, I had felt the inner pain of the tragic and senseless death of my three-year-old nephew, Jack, Jr., who drowned in a small stream swelled by a thunderstorm. I could make no sense out of God's connection to that event. The death of that beautiful young boy brought death up close to me for the first time and left me terribly bewildered. I had no answers.

Some years later, my reflections about the conflict between God's presumed omnipotence and the irrational presence of evil caused all of those memories and uncertainties to flood back in upon me. Life pushes us to wonder, "Who's in charge here?" In the face of trauma that is frightening and real, we find ourselves asking if God lives in these parts. We seem to be on our own. And we seem to be losing. Irrational, inexplicable tragedy mounts up. We try to keep faith while facing into bitter winds. We wonder if God really is in control. We wonder if God cares. We even wonder if God exists.

In this setting of uncertainty, the personal question of God has priority over the academic question about God's nature. The academic question tumbles out of the passion of the personal question. So when we speak of God, we are trying to get at the issues that roll out of our living experience. The most compelling questions about God arise from being here trying to make sense of it all. We learn that we cannot predict life by even the most clever and agile mental gymnastics. In the seriousness of life, we want to know if there is a God, and if there is, to understand God's ways in the world.

To believe in any god at all means to believe that our being here is connected to what has been and what is to come. It is to believe that we are not an isolated happening. We belong to a world that is whole and connected. The belief in God is a belief that we are not ultimately alone. The world and its history have some meaning and purpose. History is more than a collection of loose ends. The god that we create from our own understanding will always be too small. The question of whether God exists springs from the anxiety of whether we exist as an isolated event that has no reference or significance beyond the limited scope of our years. Are you and I anything more than a blip on the screen of time?

Belief in God can be wrecked on our misconceptions of God. For example, our belief in God is not much help when we think of God as one more object in the world. This idea of God goes something like this: The world is composed of many things—plants and trees, animals, skyscrapers, clouds, stars, planets, and God. God is the ruling thing. God is the most powerful thing in the world, but when all is said and done, God is one more thing in a world full of things. The question, "Does God exist?" often seems to be predicated upon this kind of conception of God. We want to know if, among everything else in the world, there is also a god. In this case, God is one more fragment of the world.

The idea of God as a fragmentary element in the world seems only to make our lives more scattered. We are already divided. We already serve diverse allegiances. One more fragment to claim our loyalty simply accentuates the exhaustion we feel. We are torn and tired from being pulled by competing forces. We do not need to believe in a god that stands alongside all the other gods we serve. We do not need one more god to worship. What we want to know is whether some enduring reality underlies all of the competing claims upon us.

For those of us who are already pulled in different directions by work and family and friends, by desires to succeed and passions to acquire, it is easy to discard or ignore one more call for devotion. A god that is nothing more than one more fragment of devotion only intensifies our dense jungle of commitments. The God that sustains cannot be one more object in the world, not even an object that is omnipotent. We are so accustomed to seeing the world as a collection of things that it is easy for us to describe God to be one more thing in the world. I believe this kind of God does not exist.

Our complex rhetoric about God obscures our ability to speak plainly of God. We learn to recite lots of language about God. In fact, we often recite more than we believe. So, a good place to begin our speaking of God may not be with believing more but with believing less. We busily chase after many gods, hoping to find some object of devotion that will make us feel good. Our frantic grasping leaves us feeling helpless. It is when all our gods are gone, when all our religious exercises seem in vain, that the God above language has a chance with us. Organized religion is mostly built around our trying to take hold of God. The heart of Christian belief is centered around God taking hold of us.

In ordinary affairs, it is when we seem utterly alone and at the end of our rope that we begin thinking seriously of God. In the face of being alone and feeling at risk, we at first work feverishly to pull everything together. When things fly out of control, we redouble our efforts to regain control. Along the way, we discover that we cannot get it all together. God is the only ultimate "together." The truth of God's ultimate grace is that you and I belong to God. It is only when the gods of our own making seem to have abandoned us that God above the gods can take hold of us. God is not a pot of gold at the end of our search for truth and wholeness. God holds us before the search, sustains us in the search, and, most importantly, becomes our ultimate hope when we abandon the search.

Generally, we prefer a more domestic god. We like the idea of claiming a crystal clear understanding of God. If we can wrap our minds around God, we can gain a measure of control over God. We want to name God along with all the world's creatures so that we can make God our very own, tame and domestic. We create a place for God—in God's heaven. It is our way of managing God, of being sure we have our arms around God. We want to be sure that we know God's expectations and can keep God's will clearly in view. We prefer a God with no surprises. All our talk about God becomes a way of disguising our ignorance of God. Ultimately, our words turn to stone, and our talk gives way to silence. When the silence comes, God is able to speak to us.

Philosophers Speak of God

Speaking of God is not limited to those who believe. The life of belief rarely arises from a logical inference. No one is likely to believe in God because they conclude that God exists. The God of belief transcends the god of logic. Nevertheless, the power of logic should not be discounted. There is a logic to the world that the mind seeks to fathom. Indeed, the mind is continually probing the insights that logic uncovers. We are creatures of logic, and logic reflects the rigorous exercise of the power of the mind. Logic sheds light on the evidence of God's presence.

There is a certain beauty, an aesthetic appeal, to the precision and economy of logic's delineation of the world. Logic illuminates. It pushes back the shadows of ignorance and enables us to understand our world more fully and to live in our world more competently. Logic is a gift of the mind, and the mind is a gift of God. Therefore, while we should not claim too much for the power of logic, we should pursue its insights vigorously and gratefully. Critical thinking about the world and our place within it is not only a possibility; it is a responsibility.

With the mind's eye, philosophers and theologians speak of God, using the tools of reason and logic. They wager arguments for the existence of God, and the idea of God plays a critical part in their interpretation of the world.

Two Christian thinkers who were devout persons of faith stand out for the power and influence of their historic discussions of God. I allude to them here because anyone who speaks of God should be aware of these high reference points for the philosophical defenses of God's reality. No major interpreters of faith have escaped their influence. While these historically important arguments rarely become the focus of faith, they do contribute to the intellectual debate about the reality of God. Therefore, our efforts to speak of God and to translate the heart of belief into intelligible language should be informed by these giants of thought and faith.

Anselm, the archbishop of Canterbury to whom we referred in chapter four, believed that the existence of God could be demonstrated by the power of reason alone. In doing so, Anselm was confident that reason was simply establishing what the heart already knows. Anselm's argument seems so simple as to be disarming. It is called the "ontological" argument, meaning it is an argument that hinges on the fact that anything exists at all. The argument centers around the nature of being. Anselm began with the assertion that "God is that being than which none greater can be conceived." In other words, a being none greater than which can be conceived is what we mean by God. He then added, "A being that exists is greater than one that does not exist." He concluded, therefore, "God exists."

Throughout modern history, there are hundreds of variations on Anselm's theme. Yet, the substance of these arguments remains very much the same. Anselm was saying that the very idea of God carries within it the implication that God actually exists. The very fact that you and I can think of God and speak of God means that God exists. Our ability to conceive of God implies God's existence. Anselm's argument stands as a simple and profound statement regarding the existence of God. The conclusion tells us no more than we knew in the premises, but the conclusion does draw out the inference that our ability to conceive of God is primary evidence of God's presence in the world.

The theologian Thomas Aquinas took a different direction. Aquinas certainly stands among the most influential Christian thinkers in history. His writing and thought have probably had more influence upon Christendom and Christian theology than any other individual in history. Thomas Aquinas was a student of the philosopher, Aristotle. He transformed much of Aristotle's philosophy into the foundations for Christian theology.

Instead of arguing from the nature of being as Anselm did, Aquinas found evidence and reason to infer the existence of God from the natural world order. Anselm looked within and said that the idea of God implies the existence of God. Aquinas looked without and said the world at large implies the existence of God. Therefore, his arguments are called "cosmological." "Cosmos" means world or order." *Cosmos* is the Greek word from which we get the word "cosmetics." "Cosmetics" provide order or structure, symmetry, balance. The creation of "world" is the creation of "order." Creation translates chaos into "cosmos."

Aquinas offered five such arguments, the first of which is taken from observing motion in the world. Things move. Experience teaches us that every moving object has been moved or propelled by some force. Things do not simply move on their own. The world, in this sense, operates like a row of dominoes. There is no movement unless the first one moves. In the world, we can account for movement only by reference to other moving things. Therefore, without asserting a "First Mover" that itself does not have to be moved, there would be no motion at all. Without a Prime Mover, God, there would be no motion. Clearly, we live in a world of motion. Therefore, the Prime Mover must exist. In the language of faith, the Prime Mover is called God.

Other arguments from Aquinas are similar. The presence of cause and effect assures the existence of a "First Cause" that itself does not have to be caused. From the experience of degrees in nature, such as *good* and *better*, he argued for the existence of Perfection. Perfection makes sense of all degrees of perfection. We call perfection God.

For me, the most impressive argument comes from the idea of contingency. Aquinas argued that the existence of contingent beings requires the assertion of Necessary Being. Put differently, the world obviously is composed of limited, finite objects. All of these objects can "not-be." Their existence is conditional and limited. I exist because my parents existed. The chair on which I am sitting exists because someone made it. Everything that we know exists because someone or something else exists. Everything is dependent for its being on something else. Aquinas concluded, therefore, that unless there is some being whose being is not dependent on other beings, nothing would exist at all. God is the Necessary Being that precedes and makes possible the merely contingent existence of everything else in the world.

Aquinas added one other kind of argument to his arsenal. He asserted that the evidence of design and purpose in the world implies the existence of a Supreme Intelligence. God is the Master Designer, the Intelligent Architect of the world order. The design and workings of such things as the human body and the starry heavens is stunning. Order is not the product of chance. Order implies an ordering reality behind the universe.

Clearly, arguments for the existence of God do not belong exclusively to Christians. Many non-Christian thinkers have offered similar intellectual defenses for the existence of God. They are products of reason and observation. Our speaking of God inevitably resorts to the mind to say what we mean. The mind does not provide every answer, but without thought, our beliefs have no voice.

Philosophy is a friend of faith. It never displaces faith. It does not even justify faith. Rather, philosophy provides a systematic and coherent effort to make sense of the world. It helps us sort through the important questions. Philosophy means the "love of wisdom." The ways of philosophy can teach us that the good life does not come from adopting easy answers. Life cannot be lived with rhetoric alone. Wisdom is more likely bred by facing up to and wrestling with the difficult and challenging questions of life. We face questions that are too large to be answered once and for all.

Philosophy, at its very best, drives us up against life's most genuine and awesome mysteries. Faith begins with mystery.

Belief versus Argument

Our speaking of God should acknowledge the historic traditions of faith and reason. Believers can be thoughtful, and thoughtful people also believe. Arguing for God's existence leaves most people cold and unpersuaded. We do not believe in God because our mind has taught us to believe in God. Thought, for most of us, brings us to the brink of asking better questions. Our many arguments do more to pose the question of God than to answer it. They end more in mystery than answers.

The mystery reminds us that belief is inevitably more than an enterprise of the mind. The question of God is really the question of connectedness. It is the question of our ultimate roots. The question of God is more personal than intellectual. We want to know what our being here means. People and things come and go. People and things grow and decay. We live up against the abundant temporariness of our life and all that lives around us. There is a dreadful impermanence to what we see. There is also disorder that we find disorienting and disconcerting. In the presence of disorder and impermanence, we wonder what our being here means, if anything. In the face of these actual experiences, it really does not matter much about the intellectual proposition that "God exists." Arguments leave us unsatisfied. What we still want to know is whether we have a reason for being here.

Thought's answer to the question of God may not generate life's belief in the reality and presence of God. We have confessed that in everyday, ordinary experience we chase after many gods. We long to know, even to believe, that God embraces us despite the many gods that consume us. We yearn to know the reality of God that transcends all of our words about God. We build mountains of doctrines. Much of our speaking of God turns to nonsense. Our words lose their power to persuade. When it comes to creating a god, we have a vivid imagination. We want God to be on our side in war and to take our side in our human and religious disputes. We call God Father, inferring that God possesses gender. God has no gender. God is neither male nor female. Our language betrays us. Whether we refer to God as Father or God as Mother, God is still God.

The truth is that all our intellect and speaking generally bring us to the edge of silence. When the mystery of God finally overtakes us, we enter the land where God can speak to us. God speaks to us mostly in the language of relating. The God we yearn to believe in is not the God of abstract thought. That God is interesting but not sustaining. The God that sustains our belief must be the God that relates to our being here. Believing is inextricably bound up with relating. Above all, believing in God means relating to God.

Chapter 8
Meeting God

We are coming nearer the heart of the matter. God is not an idea to conceive or a concept to accept. The truth of God is to be found only through relating to God. The focus of our thinking must shift. God is not an idea to be grasped. God is spirit to be embraced. We know God by meeting God.

For too long, we have been inclined to capture the essence of God in our ideas. Our doctrines are frail. Relating to God cannot be replaced with proper doctrine. We should not substitute "right-believing" for "right-relating." Relating to God is the center of faith. Our religious doctrines are skewed by our preoccupations and the character of our relationships. The development of Negro spirituals is a telling example of how the life of slavery and oppression was reflected in the faith and music of the slaves. Our vocabulary for speaking of God is shaped, in part, by the language of the religious culture in which we live.

As a majority religion, Christianity is a noisy, busy religion. The noise of religion can drown out God's voice. Meeting God has a language of its own. It requires solitude and devotion to the life of the spirit. Instead of being deafened by our talk of God, genuine spirituality is borne of disciplined listening. Meeting God begins with utter silence.

Our willingness to meet God means becoming vulnerable to the spirit of God. Though we are not all religious, we are all spiritual. Both the secular and the religious blind us to the spiritual. In our secular lives, we make it our business to stay busy. Staying busy is a sign of success. We work until we are weary, and when we are not working, we worry about all of the industrial-size "ifs" that could beset us: What will we do "if" the contract doesn't work out? What will we do "if" the value of the dollar falls? What will we do "if" we lose our job? What will we do "if" inflation becomes double-digit? What will we do "if" sales decline? What will we do "if" we get sick and can't work? . . . We worry.

Religion also distracts us from spirituality. We have to be concerned with meeting the requirements of our religious commitments. There are classes to teach, services to attend, committees to manage. In short, we have to help the church succeed. The budget must be met. The pledges must be counted. The newsletters must be printed and fellowship supper prepared. Spiritual nurture gives way to the requirements of religious success. We worry.

Meeting God creates a new center of gravity for our lives. Meeting God is an inward event of coming to terms with our own spirituality. The deepest lesson of life is that we are people of the spirit. The affirmation that we are spiritual means that when we have learned all about ourselves that we can learn from evolution and genetics, there is far more yet to learn.

God lives within us—within everyone of us. We mostly conduct our affairs without reference to God. We like to live on the open plains where we can see what is coming. We dread the deep valleys and the steep mountains. We dread the terrain where we cannot see our way clear. The gospel is that God is present within us in the plains where we do not need God, and God is present in the valleys where we are often too frightened to wait for God to lead us through. We are people of spirit, and only by waiting and opening ourselves through disciplined devotion can we meet up with God in ways that are transforming and hope-giving.

Beyond Time and Space

We are confused by the notion of spirit. We are more at home with the material. We grow up developing a bias toward what we can see and touch. Because of our bias toward materiality, we are put off by the call to spirituality. When we describe God as spirit, we are not meaning to depict God as a ghost-like thing in the world. God is not a vague, shadowy existence that floats about us.

A large measure of our confusion is natural. It springs from the excessive weight we give to time and space. Time and space can easily come to be regarded as our principal realities. A person is somebody because he is somewhere. We measure our lives in days and months and years. We are born on a certain day, and that day is a day to celebrate throughout our years. We measure life by counting the years: She lived to be eighty-seven. Learning to define our lives by a meaning other than the number of our days and the place we live is a serious challenge.

The human spirit and God's spirit have no reference to time or space. You and I cannot be defined by *where* we are or *how long* we are there. Where we are and how long we are there bear real importance, but the Christian faith is not about changing where we are. The Christian faith is not about a change of pace or a change of space. The Christian faith speaks to regaining the spiritual center of our lives. The spiritual center provides us a means for understanding the time and space in which we work and live. Space and time is about clothing and shelter and food. The clock ticks. We get hungry and tired. We must manage time and space, but time and space will not sustain us. Food and water can only sustain us for a life in time. In time, we want to find a life that endures.

Jesus said, "You should first seek the Kingdom of God." He was saying that the heart of life is meeting God. Managing time and space will fall into place if we can ever shift the center of gravity for our lives from the world that comes and goes to the spirit that endures. We should not conclude that the worries of the world—food, clothing, work—are wrong or illegitimate. To the contrary, they are vital ingredients for living. Only meeting God, only seeking first the Kingdom, teaches us that they are not the center of life. The daily necessities will not yield fulfillment or well-being. We can never do enough or acquire enough or gather enough food in our silos to make us feel good or safe or secure. Our life in time and space will never be secure.

Our hope lies in meeting God. Our highest calling is to sense the reality that breaks through the boundaries of time and space. Our calling is to come to terms with the spiritual character of our lives. Only faith gives us light beyond the borders of time. Only faith will give us hope beyond the limits of where we are and how long we last.

Meeting God does not begin by asking "where is God?" Someone might say that God is not anywhere or that God is everywhere. The truth is that "whereness" does not apply to God, and, at the center of our souls, "whereness" does not apply to you and me. We place far too much weight on what I call a "region of behavior." When it comes to people, what you see is not what you get. What you see is a region of behavior. We call that "region" Bill or Don or

Judy or Stephanie or Raleigh. To know a person requires more than describing what we see.

What you see when you look at somebody is, at best, a region of behavior. I can see what you do and how you look. I can observe your size and shape and physical demeanor. I can see your actions and your reactions. But getting to know a real person requires more than adding up what we can see. We are who we love. We are what is important to us. We are our thoughts and our worries. We are the children we raised and the parents who raised us. We are what we think about and long for. We are what we worship and the values we embrace. As a mere organization of chemistry and matter, you and I are strictly passing phenomena. We are not defined by our chemistry. We are spirit. Spirit is not vulnerable to the passing conditions of time and space. Spirits grow; they do not age.

The Hebrew word for spirit is *ruach*. It means breath. The Greek word is *pneuma*. Breath is a good image for trying to distinguish a person or God from being conceived as a particular thing in a particular place. Breath conveys vitality and life. Without breath, life ceases. Yet, breath cannot be placed as a spatial object. Because desks, chairs, tables, and trees can be seen and touched, our inclination is to say they are real.

Spirit cannot be seen or touched. Our inclination is to say that it is unreal. It is what the philosopher, Alfred North Whitehead, called "misplaced concreteness." We are prone to call real those things we can touch and see. For a child, it is much less so. For a child, a mother's embrace is as life-giving as a mother's milk. An embrace is not a thing to be placed in a corner. An embrace is an experience to be felt.

Either we need to grow up enough or become childlike enough to learn that reality cannot always be seen or measured. How do you measure an embrace? How do you weigh hope? God is not an object in the world that is defined by volume and weight. God is spirit, and describing God as spirit means that all of nature, and every person in nature, bears the presence of God.

The creation story teaches us that the fish of the sea, the fowl of the air, and the cattle of the fields are here as an act of God. We will not learn that truth from genetics or evolution. Their being here is a part of the purpose of God. They are the product of God's hovering and brooding over the chaos. They are a part of God's order. The creation story also tells us that God took hold of the mud of the earth and shaped a person and breathed into a person the "breath," the spirit of life. God bestowed spirit upon the earth. The creation story enables us to see that we are spirit at the core of our being. Without the spiritual factor, we are nothing more than the mud from which we were formed.

Spirit also means that God is present in every situation of life. We cannot escape God's presence, and we cannot escape our own spirituality. It is popular to assume that God is present only in the high and holy moments of worship. Or, God is present when we call on God in prayer or in those intense experiences in which we seem "to feel the spirit" and experience the "coming of the spirit." It is true that God is present in the high and holy moments. It is also true that God is present when we cannot seem to find God anywhere.

We should never allow our experience of God to become a test for God's presence or a test for another person's experience of God. Our road is never the only way to God. When you and I begin to elevate our religious experience as having superior religious value, we are close to claiming that we possess God in our experience. That is sheer folly. In the heights of joy and in the depths of emptiness, and every place and time in between, God is present. No act or decision will move us outside the intimate presence of God. God is our enduring companion.

A Personal God

Meeting God is often described in personal terms. The biblical descriptions of God and our own descriptions of God usually resort to the image of person. The power to relate is the key to understanding God as person. God is not a person in the sense that we are people. Personal is perhaps better than the term person for describing God. The Christian interpretation of the nature of God as personal should avoid the easy but erroneous expectation that God is some mythological super-person. God should not to be confused with the Olympian ideas of Zeus. The conception of God as personal need not be construed into this kind of crude, anthropomorphic image.

Personal, on the other hand, is a profoundly important symbol for conveying God's presence in the world. Our most definitive understanding of God comes to us by means of a personal, historic event. We meet God in Jesus. Looking to our ordinary experience, we speak of God as personal as a way of saying that our meeting God is shaped by the presence in history of this person we call Jesus. We are persons. God is the heart and soul of our being persons, and we cannot know ourselves fully until we know God. God is present in us, and in Christ we see how God's presence in a person redefines the character of being a person.

Meeting God means discovering that love is life's only enduring reality. God is love. In this simple, disarming statement, the ultimate meaning of God's nature and ours is put into words. You and I were created to love, and only when we get in touch with our capacity to love, can we be set free to live out the authentic power of our lives. Love is the only reality that can sustain. If we love, we live.

We have said already that the language of love has a way of losing its persuasiveness. The act of love never does. Nothing possesses the power of loving and being loved. Our language gathers barnacles. It gets confused with sentimentality and pity on the one hand, and lust and abuse on the other. Language suffers grave limitations because love is a human word. That's why Jesus came. A human word cannot convey the power and presence of God. Words will not do. Love is how God meets us because love is how God relates to the world. Love's definition cannot be merely verbal because love, at its essence, is relational.

We have said it before. All real living is relating. Relating at its highest is loving. Relating, whether relating to one another or to God, is always a spiritual event. Making someone's acquaintance may not be a spiritual event, though we should say that every occasion of becoming acquainted is an opening of the spirit. Meeting is always spiritual. It means becoming vulnerable to one another's presence. It means sharing space and time. Meeting, in the sense of authentic relating, is an event of the spirit. To say that God is love is to say that relating in love conveys the ultimate meaning of the world and the ultimate meaning of our being in the world.

The Christian's affirmation that God is love is not a verbal proposition to be accepted. To be Christian does not mean to accept that God is love. God's love is not a doctrine to be accepted; God's love is a way of meeting to be followed. In the presence of Jesus, love takes on flesh and blood. You and I are able to see how love acts and decides. Therefore, when I face into the responsibility for living in time and space, I face the prospect of relating as God relates. I am facing a change of heart. I am called upon to reorder my living in the light of God's presence at the center of my soul.

When God speaks most clearly to us, God does not choose the language of words. God visits us. God's visit should remind us that the faith we live is far more important than the faith we speak. We cannot substitute saying, "I love you," for caring. To identify the Christian faith with words is to miss completely the richness and vitality of God's ultimate truth. Jesus' life and being cannot be caught in language. To understand him, we must follow him.

Christian love should not be confused with being nice to everybody—not that being nice to people should be discouraged. The faith of Jesus does not require that we resolve to like everybody. Its demands are far more exacting. Christian love calls upon us to act for the good of those we like and also the good of those we do not like. Love means caring for people we don't like and wrapping the wounds of people we don't even know. Love affirms the worth of other people. Love transforms each person we meet into somebody. Love takes every person seriously, understanding the ultimate oneness of that person with God. Love does not love for the sake of being loved. Love is God living through us.

Love as we know it is always mixed. You and I are, at once, both loving and unloving. The motivation for the way we relate often remains obscure. At best, we could describe ourselves as learning to love. Our relationships are only beginning to be lived in the light of love. But I believe that God is present in every human relationship. On occasions, unconditional love breaks through. Our meeting is transformed into caring. God can speak through any relationship, and where a relationship exists, there exists the possibility that God's spirit will change the way we meet. Only the absence of relating excludes God. God lives among us, and God's presence gives us hope that we can learn to love.

I have sometimes been reminded that wrath is also an act of God. I believe that we will understand the meaning of wrath only when we see wrath as another face of love. We should not learn to love wrath. Wrath that does not operate as an instrument of love cannot be identified with the character of God that we know in Jesus. God's love is holy. Love begets love. Speaking of God's wrath, or even of divine justice, should keep us from changing the

idea of love into a sentimental figure of speech. Love includes justice, but it never stops there. Love requires that we be just, but it
demands far more than justice alone can deliver. Love believes in
the ultimate integrity of the people who are loved. Love acts for
their well-being, even when loving brings personal pain. Love
draws no boundaries and keeps no records. God's love is unconditional and acts without reservation.

Walking away from God never affects God's love. You and I are
more accustomed to reciprocity. Not so with God. God's nature is
neither capricious nor unpredictable. God's love is clear and vulnerable; it is open and unrestricted. We may choose to live as if God is
not present in our lives, but our decision in no way affects God's
presence. God's love will endure.

The only important witness that we can bear to God's love is to
love as God loves. Our calling is to love people whether they are
Christian or not, whether they will ever become Christians or not.
Christian witness is not a matter of getting other people to agree
with us. People are not waiting to hear that God loves them. They
need something more telling; they need to be loved. The most compelling witness to God is not to tell about God's love but to love as
God loves, freely and not possessively. When we say possessively,
"I love you," what we may really mean is, "I love me and want
you." In contrast, love does not grasp. It sets people free.

Meeting God in the World

Meeting God changes how we live in the world. The world is alive
with God's presence. Albert Schweitzer was right to teach us that all
life deserves our reverence, for indeed, all creation is of God. We
divide the world up into categories. We describe the world through
complex classifications of animals and plants, stars and galaxies of
stars. It is a way of trying to understand the world and to manage
our knowledge of the world. The temptation is to take our classifications seriously. When we do so, we can miss the wholeness of the
world and its oneness with God. We, too, are members of creation.
Our purpose is to meet the world in God's name. When we abuse
the world, we abuse God. The human destruction of the earth rails
against God's presence on and in the earth.

In the language of faith, we speak of God's relation to the world
as creation, judgment, and redemption. We should wonder whether

it is even useful to recover this kind of language for ordinary conversation. If we are to do so, we will have to work at bringing these ideas down to earth. Creation is not a remote reference to an event that took place some thousands or millions of years ago. Creating is the way God relates to us and to our world. The more compelling meaning of our faith is not that creation is a long-ago event. Creation is a present ongoing event of which you and I are a part. Creation is not something that got finished. The world is being created.

The process of overcoming the chaos is very much alive. You and I are either a part of the chaos, or we are a part of the creating. We are either participating in God's creation, or we have cut ourselves off from God and have become a destructive force in the world. Creation is the continuing act of God. Meeting God and being embraced by God's presence means becoming an instrument of God's creative energy in the world.

Even more than creation, judgment has become mired in the rhetoric of official religion. Judgment is what happens when we sever the world or ourselves from God's presence. Living as if we are self-sufficient carries consequences that are self-destructive. Abusing our environment bears consequences that should properly be described as judgment.

Perhaps ironically, people seem to love judgment. We want everyone to get their just desserts. We want God's wrath to be visible. Acid rain is God's visible wrath. We are prepared to mete out God's punishment and take the sinner to the gallows. It is our love of judgment that should worry us. Judgment does not mean getting even. Our instinct to get even should not be confused with God's holy judgment. God's judgment is always in the service of redemption. If we meet God, our eagerness to condemn will be transformed into a plea for mercy.

God does not judge in order to condemn. God judges in order to redeem. When Jesus met the accused woman almost to be stoned, he lived out the difference between judgment as condemnation and judgment as redemption. God meets the world with mercy and loving kindness. Our self-destructive, abusive behavior carries weighty and woeful consequences. The tragedy of human destruction carries within it the call to meet the world and to see ourselves as God's creation. Meeting the world in the light of God's presence is the beginning of redemption.

This remote-sounding language of creation, judgment, and redemption may be rescued best by reclaiming the notion of the providence of God. The providence of God does not mean that God runs about the world fixing what is broken. Providence means that God is present in the broken places as well as the whole places. We can never, through our free and capricious decisions, move the world outside the orbit of God's presence.

Our human behavior can be tragically evil. We kill and destroy, sometimes in the name of progress, sometimes in the name of right, even sometimes in the name of God. Wars, genocide, capital punishment, the Holocaust—all are evidences of our living unto ourselves, separating ourselves from our brothers who are the children of God. We act toward one another with tragic consequences. We confirm the chaos. Yet, in all our sin and contempt of God, we can never move history outside the boundary of God's grace.

Providence means that God is always at our side—when we are at our best and when we are at our worst. God is with us. Even when we abandon the world and cripple our relationships with one another with bitter words and hateful actions, God is with us. That is the meaning of grace, and grace is the meaning of providence. God is light for us, waiting to meet us at the end of the deepest night. Providence means that God is with us both now and forever.

Chapter 9
Being Human

When we talk about God, we tell a lot about ourselves. Honest. The ability and need to speak of God signal that there is more to being a person than what meets the eye. Even before we try to frame the words, we sense that we are more than the dust. The poetry of Genesis teaches us that everything has its origins in God. Without God, nothing would exist—only emptiness.

If we let the message of Genesis break through, we may be startled to realize that in all creation, only man and woman talked back to God. When it comes to creation, people are different. They are the kind of creatures that speak of God and speak to God. They wonder about themselves. They seem to possess a moral sensibility. They make utterances such as "ought" and "should." Even more telling, they feel their deep responsibility to join hands with God in taking care of the world.

From Genesis we learn that people are awakened from the clay by the breath of God. While being molded of the earth, they are formed in God's image. People are different. We are told that they are to name the animals—more a sign of responsibility than authority for the world. We name and continue to name the species. There's a lion, a mockingbird, a butterfly, a deer, and a raccoon. There's an amoeba. There's a streptococcus. Naming means taming. The naming persists because the taming of the chaos is God's work and it is ours.

God's work is not done. God works through these beings called people, brooding over the chaos with microscopes and telescopes, with experiments and tests, brooding over the teeming constellation of matter and energy, bringing order and dominion "over the fish of the sea, and over the birds of the air, and over the cattle, and over all the wild animals of the earth, and over every creeping thing that creeps upon the earth" (Gen 1:26). Creation continues.

The splendor of being human is that people are like God. God has made people into a special species among all the creatures in the world. God said, "Let us make humankind in our image, according to our likeness" (Gen 1:26a). We are like God. God creates, so people create. Humankind is a species that takes on the holy stewardship of creation. But there is more. People stand apart also because amidst all the things God creates, God engages people in conversation. People raise the question of God. People raise questions about what makes everything "tick." People want to know what it means to be here. While gentle winds blow and the cattle graze on a thousand hills, people are restless inhabitants of the garden.

All our talk about God begins with people, because the question of God is a human question. It falls first from human lips, and the question reveals our story. Our contentment is bounded by discontent. The world is composed of the starry heavens above and the living things below, but humankind inquires and probes the nature of God and the inner workings of the earth.

It is not enough that we walk about and enjoy the world's bounty. We are restless. The mysteries of the universe haunt us. We wander across the earth and mark our place with monuments and outposts. We want to know where we are and what lies beyond the horizon. Our wondering defines us. We are more than a body that must be fed and rested. Humankind is also mind and spirit. We belong to the earth, but we also study the earth. We transcend the earth. No mere physical description of a person will ever exhaust a person's character. There is in us a likeness to eternity that cannot be fully bound by the claims of time.

The questions we call religious—man, woman, life, death, eternity—are born of the human spirit. No mere fragment of clay would ask such questions. They have to be thought of more as spiritual questions than religious ones. Religious questions can be taught. We are taught the right questions and answers. The questions that underlie the life of belief are rooted in the innermost depths of the human spirit. They are not questions that can be taught. They are questions that reside within us. They are questions that break out like sweat on a runner. Humankind would not be contained by the borders of Eden. Our questions are too far-flung. We could not rest in the garden of contentment. We want to know it all.

Our talk of God inevitably drives us to ask deeper questions about being human. What we believe about God has serious implications for what we think of ourselves. What does it mean to be a person? Or, in its more personal form, "Who am I?" Is my being here fanciful and insignificant, or is my presence here of some ultimate importance? Such questions might wedge their way into academic conversations about the earth and the people who inhabit the earth. There we would intend to explore such issues with dispassion and remote eloquence. But questions of what it means to be here are rooted in a more primitive experience. These kinds of questions arise when we wake up one day and discover that "I am here." There is not another "I" in the world. Everyone else is a "you." There's you, and there's me. We wonder who we are and what all of these other people are doing here alongside us.

The question of being human is not brought to us from outside. The question rises like a geyser within us. It cannot be held back. It rumbles through our being and will not be quieted. To be a person is to ask human questions. And human questions never stay answered. They are answered throughout our journeys. When we have finished our course, being human will have meant something. We will either have been worthy stewards of our humanity, or we will have given up a measure of our humanness. Persons are not only here; they wonder why they are here. They are spiritual to the core.

Human Spirituality

The ability to raise the question of our humanity is the most primitive evidence of our spirituality. It is a testimony to the reality of human self-transcendence. Spirituality is not a vague notion of some indeterminate and undisciplined state. By referring to person as spirit, I mean to underscore three specific dimensions of being human that distinguish humankind from the rest of creation. First, we have said that being human means the ability to raise the question of God. It is more about raising ultimate questions than about having clear and precise answers. Even such questions as "What should I do?" or "How ought I to behave?" are questions that grow out of the question of ultimate reality. Inevitably, when we plow the fields of "ought" and "should," they lead us to the edge of the question of God. The question of God is a peculiarly human question.

Second, spirituality points to the essential connectedness of our lives. The bond among us is more than verbal. It is spiritual. That is why loneliness is so painful. Humankind was created to live in community, and our life together reflects that we connect to one

another in ways that are beyond our physical and verbal relationships. Our spirits touch. We are bound together as spiritual beings.
When we are isolated from our connections with others, we become
less than human. No punishment is more severe, more dehumaniz-
ing than isolation. Joy can only be found together.

Third, I mean by referring to human spirituality that we, like
God, cannot be defined by the space and time we occupy. You cannot define a person by when and where he lived. We define our
lives by episodes and events, by happenings and occurrences. Our
lives are not a collection of minutes. They could better be described
as a collection of moments. We are defined by events such as birth
and marriage, divorce, and devastating losses. Lives are defined by
a war that rips away the life of someone we love. Lives are defined
by a fire that burns treasures and collections of our history. Lives
are defined by episodes of painful rejection and embracing affec-
tion. When we look back on our lives, it is not the minutes that we
remember. It is the moments. We remember relationships and
losses. We remember sights and sounds. We remember tears that
would not seem to run dry, and we remember laughter that was
deep and left our spirits lifted. Being human is spiritual. We are
more than the mere passing of days can ever capture.

Spirituality does not refer to the level of our religious activity.
Spirituality refers to our capacity to transcend what we do and what
happens to us. We are not objects of history; we interpret our history. We rise above our history, finding meaning and significance
from what happens to us. More important than being data of history, we create history. We interpret where history has been and
where the years ahead may take us. We bring our intentions, blessings, and curses to history. We change the prospects of history.
History records more than our physical journey. History comes
alive because of the convergence and conflict of the human spirit.

The Genesis language is telling us that humankind is spirit. Persons cannot be defined by their embodied presence alone. People
are creatures who love and hope. People are shaped not only by
what occurs to them but how they interpret and respond to what
happens to them. They bring intelligent will and reflective transcendence to their living in the world. To describe humankind as spirit is
to convey that people's lives overlap. My being here impinges on
other people's being here. Whether I regard them with respect or

malice, with love or hostility, affects what they and I can become. I am not only what I do; I am what I intend to do. I am how I relate. I cannot define myself in isolation or independence from others. My spirituality points toward my relatedness to other persons and to all creation. As spiritual beings, you and I influence the course of history and shape the character of our human life together. Our lives overlap.

The Truth of Genesis

The story of Adam will be misconstrued entirely if we read it like a source book for human genealogy. The point of Genesis is not to trace human history back to Adam. The message of Genesis is to trace human history back to God. The early chapters of Genesis are poetry and parable. They use metaphor and myth. Genesis is myth in the sense that your life and my life are myths. Saying they are myths does not say they are untrue. It is saying that our lives are more than a collection of facts. Obituaries can be brief because they recite only the bare facts. My life as myth includes both the facts and how the facts are lived out in actual experience. To know any person really means to know the values they embrace, the passions and fears that compel them. Myth and parable point us to the depth of our life and teach us that we can never understand our world's history until the story of creation includes God.

The richness and power of the creation stories should not be lost amidst misguided efforts to make the truth of Genesis coincide with a recitation of the facts of history. Genesis sets before us the table of truth and meaning. Historical data should be sought in other forums. Look to archaeology and scientific analysis to tell us about the facts of history. Look to Genesis to tell us the truth of our being here. The writers of Genesis put us in touch with the spirituality of humankind. Science cannot do that. Science can bring us to the edge of spirituality. Revelation must take us the rest of the way.

We should acknowledge that Christians have sometimes felt threatened by scientific inquiries into the origins of human life. Theories of evolution have been especially bothersome because they seem to cast shadows on the biblical account of human creation. We have watched as certain Christian advocates have sought to have "creationism" taught alongside evolutionary theories in school. Though I do not doubt the conviction and fervor behind the desire to teach these "creationist" accounts, these efforts grow out of an unfortunate misunderstanding of the meaning and character of the biblical stories.

Scientific assessments and confessions of faith should not be confused. Scientific propositions do not threaten the power of biblical revelation. The biblical revelations about humankind and all of creation have no standing as science. Science is about truth with a little "t." Biblical revelation is about truth with a big "T." Truth with a little "t" changes as our scientific inquiry moves forward. Truth with a big "T" speaks of the meaning of creation that endures beyond the boundaries of any scientific investigation. Science teaches us timely lessons about the world. Genesis teaches us ultimate truth.

The creation stories tell us something about creation and about being human that science can never teach us. The writers of Genesis give us a deep and abiding insight into the nature of our being here. We learn that we are kin to God. Where science concerns itself with the temporal origins of things, including humans, the book of Genesis looks at the world's beginnings through the eyes of faith. The eyes of faith will always tell us more than can be seen by the eyes of a scientific observer alone. The scientist is allowed to bring only his mind to the analysis. The person of faith brings her spirit as well.

Any coincidence between what is seen by scientist and prophet is merely superficial. Their work is driven by different purposes. The scientists want to know what is the case. The person of faith wants to know if whatever is the case matters. Two different frames of reference condition their questions and answers. We are doing an injustice to the biblical writers when we press upon them the expectations of science. Even more important than the injustice, however, our arguments and fears cause us to miss their message entirely.

When the Genesis writer says, "God created humankind in his own image," he is again more poet than analyst. The "image of God" is not something you find in a cadaver. The Genesis statement does even sound scientific and measured. Nevertheless, the statement is weighted with meaning and impact for understanding our place in the world. This simple affirmation of Genesis conveys to us that our lives are rooted in God. When a person pushes back the history of the universe, such as Stephen Hawking does in the

History of Time, he or she is inevitably driven to the boundary of the question of God.

Faith crosses the boundaries of time, enabling us to see what our telescopes can never fathom. The eyes of faith enable us to see that our lives have their origins in God. Disregard the reality of God in understanding ourselves, and we lose the vitality and ultimate energy of being human. The writer of Genesis is saying that without God, we cannot account for anything. God is the author of our being and all being. Our place in nature and our responsibilities over nature are derived from God. No microscope will ever reveal it. We know it only by the light of God.

The notion that "God created" also gives us a new assessment of human character. That we are born of God provides the foundation for affirming that people are essentially good. The affirmation that people are good can be viewed as a starry-eyed, naive way of looking at other people. Certainly a mere objective review of the human scene will give us no clear and definitive answer as to whether people are good or evil. We see persuasive and telling examples of both good and evil in the annals of human history. It is hard to tell from history alone. It takes a clue from Genesis to be able to see.

That is the point of Genesis. History alone does not give us a definitive insight. Genesis enables us to see what history alone will not reveal to us. Our creation by God means that the essence of our being is good. People's lives are grounded in God. At the wellspring of their life, people are good even when they do evil. When people's actions are evil, they are acting against their essential nature and their deepest purpose for being here. They are not only hurting others, they are destroying themselves. Genesis tells us that persons were created by God and for God. The Genesis story also tells us that humankind turns away from its origins. History shows people tragically seeking to shape their histories without reference to God. Even so, revelation teaches us that we never elude the reality that our lives have their origins in God.

The statement that "God created humankind" also tells us that our lives are finite and limited. Our being here is contingent and conditioned. We live between the "not yet" and the "no longer." There was a time when we were not yet here. There will be a time when we are here no longer. If we had no beginning, we would not be asking why are we here. The philosopher Martin Heidegger would say that the most basic question is "Why is there something rather than nothing?" The reality of God is the only answer, and it is the answer that comes more by faith than by analysis. Everything is a process, events cascading upon events. Why is there anything at all? Why are we here?

Clearly, we have not always been here. Even a long while has its limits. A thousand years is but a day. There was a time when we were not here. The Genesis story tells us what we cannot see with our limited sight. Genesis enables us to see what only humans can see. Other creatures in the garden of creation apparently did not even wonder. Adam wondered and probed. Adam plucked the fruit of every tree. While we did not choose to exist, we do wonder why we exist. Genesis enables us to see that even though our existence is finite, it is not dangling or unattached. God is the fountainhead of our being here. Genesis teaches us that we are the offspring of God.

Genesis adds this wonderful, elusive phrase that humankind was created "in the image of God." No words have ever supported so much theology. They have, no doubt, carried a greater burden for theological explanation than the writers of Genesis ever intended.

On one fall afternoon, I was driving home from work, coming down one hill and approaching another on which I lived. As I came nearer my home, I saw that a car was stopped angularly, and in another moment, I could make out that a child was lying in the street. By that time, I was near enough to stop, only to realize that the child was my five-year-old daughter, Erica. A few steps to her side seemed like a country mile. She was alive and conscious, dazed and frightened. In a moment, I gathered her in my arms, and her mother, Joan, drove us to the hospital. As we anxiously waited in that sterile, medicine-scented anteroom, beyond the doors where they examined and mended what turned out to be mostly only superficial injuries, I learned the meaning of *imago dei* in a new and compelling way. Erica was more than a child, more even than a daughter. She was God's nearest presence to me. She was God's image for me. She mended, and my heart recovered from its fright, and I knew as I had never quite known that when you love some-body, you are as close to God as you will ever come.

The point of this rich description of Genesis is that when we have described ourselves as creatures of the earth, we have not told the whole story. We are, indeed, creatures of the clay, but we are more. We are not only of the earth; we know our earthiness. We know that the clay does not fully define us. We are not just creatures; we are creators. We, too, govern the earth. We, like God, bear a special responsibility over the earth and everything that moves upon the earth. The earth is God's sanctuary, and it is ours. Dust will never be enough to define us.

Our calling is to be like God, brooding over the dark side of life. Our calling is to bring order and hope from the chaos that threatens and disrupts the earth. People bear the likeness of God. Our calling is to be human, and we cannot really be human without carrying out God's work. Being human means to take God's likeness into account in the structure and priorities of our living. If the dust is the only measure of our lives, we live toward futility. Living toward hope requires becoming centered upon the spiritual character of our lives. To become really human means knowing that we are of God. Because our origins lie in God, we cannot live fully until we live in the light of God's presence.

Chapter 10
Becoming a Person

O ur talk of being human, even of belonging to a humankind created in God's image, can seem abstract and distant. The fact is
that we experience our lives as individuals, yearning to be free
while being uneasy about the choices we have to make. We keep
bumping into one another, watching each other out of the corner of
our eye. About the time we are adolescents, we begin especially to
sense our unique place in the world.

Adolescence is often a painful episode for children and parents
—parents feeling shut out, children feeling misunderstood. It is an
awkward process of letting go and holding on. Individuality and
freedom translate the abstractness of being human into the concreteness of being a living person who bears a name. Much of our
personal history is shaped by how we come to understand ourselves
as individuals, how we handle our sense of being free and whether
we ever achieve a sense of being genuinely connected to others.

Being an Individual
There is an individuality and a singleness about being human that is
hard to escape. In the daily course of our lives, we are thrown
together with many other people. Still, it becomes apparent, sometimes even frightfully clear, that no one stands exactly where any
one of us stands. No one sees what I see. They do not hear precisely
what I hear. There is a solitariness and an individuality about being
a particular person that will not go away.

Taking seriously our individuality requires us to come to terms
with ourselves. The struggle for self-identity lasts a lifetime. One
component of that struggle is whether our character and identity
flow inside out or outside in. Is our identity directed from within, or
is it directed from without? Do we hammer out our identity, or do
we simply become what someone else wants us to be? In truth, it is
both. We are defined both by what lies outside us and what lies
within us. Our chief difficulty is this: The rush of the external
forces upon us—family, work, position, professional responsibility,

civic duty—can consume us totally. There are plenty of claims for our attention and allegiance. The external voices, worthy and unworthy alike, are relentless.

We should say again that the external relationships play an important role in shaping one's individual character as a person. No person can achieve precisely what you can achieve or bring to the order of things exactly the gifts that you as an individual can bring. The issue is whether we as individuals can maintain any sense of our personal character beyond those insistent and external calls for our time and devotion. Our challenge is to match the abundance of external claims with some measure of personal transcendence.

The identities that grow out of all our external relationships should not become the only identity we know. Insofar as it is, we become many people, chasing after many faces, seeking to meet everyone's expectations. At the end of the day, we will have been many people, and we will have done many things. Only death will prove unifying; because when the busy self dies, the whole self dies. All of the activity generated by all of the external relationships stops. Death is very personal.

All of this is to say that the search for genuine individuality cannot be conducted solely on the streets. Becoming an individual person with a distinctive identity that we can call our own must include making a long journey inward. Dag Hammarskjold said that "the longest journey is the journey inward." The journey inward is about searching out our own strengths and probing the unique gifts that reside within each of us.

Two experiences early on seem to move us away from taking up the inward journey. One experience comes from our parenting. The most difficult responsibility any parent faces is to set a child free. We, as parents, are inclined to make our children into instruments of our will. Children represent another chance to achieve our unrealized dreams. It is easy for children to become possessions by which parents extend their own identities. The less inward the sense of worth for a parent, the more apt a parent is to try to control the identity of the child. Parents often resist the responsibility of permitting their children to come into their own. The real gift of parenting is not only to permit but to empower your children to come into their own.

The inward journey usually begins when a child first finds the courage to begin to put us aside as parents. It is often awkward. It is rarely a transition that is not full of bumps and bruises. Nevertheless, if the child is to become a person, she or he must move beyond where I stand and what I think. She must cast off my clothing and put on her own. It is the continuing process of birth. Our children must take their place in distinction to us, sometimes even over against us, before they can take their place beside us. One must become two. Then and only then can conversation really occur.

The second experience that inhibits the inward journey is not especially associated with children. It plagues us all. It is the urge to seek the center of meaning in the universe of things. After all, things are quantifiable. We can count them. In general, we treat the world this way. Unless it is countable, it is unimportant. We measure the meaning of human existence in numbers. If a financier, we are measured in assets. If an athlete, we are measured in yards gained, runs batted in, or baskets made. If a preacher, we are measured in baptisms and church additions. If a district attorney, we are measured in indictments returned. If a college president, we are measured in dollars raised or students enrolled. It is easy to come to believe that our meaning and worth can be measured by our quantifiable performance.

The capacity to take our measure by an inward journey is something like the distinction between soul and body. The body represents the quantifiable aspect of human life. It can be tested, analyzed, and summarized. The notion of soul speaks of the non-quantifiable dimension of life. We will miss the powerful imagery of "soul and body" if we construe the soul as an entity within the body. When we do so, we are trying to make the soul into something we can count. The soul is not some "thing" some "where" in the body. The apostle Paul made a similar distinction between "flesh" and "spirit."

Living "according to the flesh" describes a point a view for interpreting life. It is a point of view that identifies life with sensual experience. The objective, quantifiable becomes the focus for our choices. Living "according to the spirit" suggests an alternative means for understanding our being here. It is a point of view in which the non-quantifiable values such as peace and hope and joy become the focus of our choices and decisions. Lust can be counted; love cannot. Envy can be counted; grace cannot. Lust, envy, and hatred objectify. They make objects of other people. They use and abuse people for their own goals. Grace, peace, and love relate to another person as subject and spirit. The goal of relating to other subjects is to meet, not to prevail.

The search for our own identity and character can never find fruition except through the disciplined journey inward. We are far more at home in the outward fray. We are even uneasy when we are alone. The inward journey requires purposeful aloneness. It means being alone not because no one is there, but even though people are there. We are distracted both by the noise and demands outside us and the private thoughts and worries within us.

Focused, deliberate solitude means working at freeing ourselves from the distractions and finding the discipline to be silent and open to the spirit within. It means getting to know and coming to appreciate the gifts we bring to the world. The slow process of being deliberately and thoughtfully alone, of listening to the inner spirit, enables us to grow toward becoming a person whose name bears its own character. It is good and proper to listen to voices from beyond our lives, to listen to friends and companions. But listening to the voices beyond will never be enough to settle us. Becoming a person also means coming to terms with ourselves.

Being Free

No discussion of what it means to be a person can stay away from the issue of personal freedom. When it comes to freedom, we both desire it and dread it. We want to be free of control, and yet we often eagerly yield our freedom to others. Going along is a way of getting along. As a result, the notion of freedom is confusing, and in some cases, controversial. We have been prone to claim too much for the idea of freedom, and, as a consequence, we find it difficult to define what we mean and difficult to defend the significance of freedom in human experience. We have no basis for believing that we are always free. No one is unconditionally free. Reason does not require it, and experience does not support such a conclusion.

The confusion surrounding the idea of being free is created, in part, by the fact that we use the same word to describe very different experiences. For example, we can mean by being free that we do not live under external constraints. Constraints may be physical, social, or emotional. Some constraints are reasonable and prudent, while others are unjust and immoral. For example, the constraint of a prison cell for a person who pathologically kills or abuses seems entirely just. The social convention of a traffic signal that permits some persons to move forward while others stop is a reasonable and prudent constraint.

Some constraints are imprudent and even immoral. The physical and social constraints of slavery and apartheid are wrong and unjust. The emotional constraint of certain forms of religious fundamentalism whether it be in Christian, Muslim, or Jewish clothing is wrong. At the same time, we regularly submit to conventional expectations in virtually every aspect of our lives. We do what is expected. In effect, we conform to external forces that mold our behavior by granting approval or conveying disapproval. In these cases, the loss of freedom relates to external constraints, and the achievement of freedom means gaining a greater measure of independence from these external forces.

Beyond the absence of constraint, a more important aspect of the meaning of freedom lies in the possibility of choosing between alternatives and the capacity for self-determination. If the election ballot provides no alternatives, we could reasonably conclude that we are not free to make a choice about who leads us. Voting without alternatives is meaningless. The willingness to face and to choose among alternatives lies very near the heart of human freedom. Take away our capacity to choose, and we will cut away a large measure of what it means to be free.

Alternatives create dilemmas. It is often easier to "go with the flow." If alternatives do not exist, or, as is more often the case, they are ignored, freedom is affirmed in theory and denied in practice. Alternatives do indeed create dilemmas. Dilemmas give rise to frustration. We either embrace the frustration with its freedom, or we avoid the frustration and discard our freedom. There are no shortcuts to being free. Either we face the alternatives, or freedom is denied. The dread of freedom in everyday experience is certainly as powerful as the tug toward being free.

The idea of freedom within Christianity goes even further than freedom from constraints and the freedom to choose. Perhaps the most moving and memorable of the speeches of Martin Luther King, Jr., was the speech shortly before his assassination when he spoke of black and white children being able to live and worship together. He completed that address with the dramatic words carved now into his tomb: "Free at last, free at last; Thank God Almighty, we are free at last."

Segregation was a dreadful problem of society. It brutalized the human spirit. People were "kept in their place" on the basis of something as superficial as color and heritage. But the real freedom for which King marched was ultimately far more than social freedom. It was more than the freedom to vote and the freedom to ride. The real freedom he sought was "soul freedom." Both black people and white people were in bondage. Segregation and racial discrimination enslaves not only the victims of prejudice but the authors of prejudice as well. The march to end segregation was as surely a march to end the bondage of whites as the bondage of blacks.

The bondage of the spirit is an awesome force—far more difficult to crush than prison walls. In 1964, a full ten years after *Brown versus Board of Education*, my wife, Joan, taught music to young black children in a Head Start program in Marion, Alabama. The program was held at the black Baptist church on Main Street, and she was the only white person who offered to teach in a program where the funding then required an integrated faculty. The outrage was shocking and frightening.

The mayor's job was part time. He was my colleague and friend. He was incensed and angered because of the trouble Joan was stirring up. Bitter words were hurled like firebombs of resentment. Late-night calls of anger and vile rhetoric—still, she taught music. One evening at dinner, we heard shots and screeching tires, only to see that someone had wounded our dog in the front yard of our home. The children were frightened, and so were we. Sadness, depression, and uncertainty were heavy in the air. It was the rain of rage born of the bondage of racism. The truth is that they, whoever "they" were, too were afraid—frightened of change, frightened of the loss of control. They were themselves victims of racism. We all needed to feel the hope of soul freedom.

The Gospel writer John said, "If the Son shall make you free, you shall be free indeed." Speaking of human freedom in the context of Christian faith has a different ring to it. Freedom is not merely the absence of external constraints or even the willingness to embrace alternatives. Freedom is more. Freedom constitutes a new vision of life. Our ordinary lives are bound by mortal fear. We become victims of greed and envy and hatred. We are possessed by our possessions. We are controlled by our prejudices. We are driven to know enough, be powerful enough, or even be good enough to stand on our own. We want to make our own order and to create our own hope. As a result, when we are overcome by ignorance or weakness or human failure, our inability to manage the outcome of our lives leaves us hopeless.

The Christian faith turns the notion of freedom upside down. In ordinary parlance, to be free means to be independent. In faith, being free mans regaining a sense of our ultimate relatedness. Being free comes from knowing our connections to God. Our relentless quest to live as though we can make it on our own leads to our being victims of fear and dread. We fear other people because we are never quite able to control them. We dread the boundary condition called death. Death is a barrier we cannot overcome. So, being free means more than simply having choices before us and escaping the rigors of physical restraints. Freedom springs from having a reason for being here. To be free means to have found the larger meaning of being human.

Real freedom is soul freedom. It means defining our lives not only by their temporal and physical boundaries but by God's presence within us. The Christian understanding of human life affirms that following Christ sets us free to become the persons God created us to be. Otherwise, we are living beneath our highest calling. The ultimate freedom is the freedom of God's embrace. The truth of our being is that we belong to God and that we can never experience the peace of being a person until we replace our efforts to assure our own security with the freedom of God's embrace.

The Gift of Community

Our yearning to be free as well as our serious and responsible understanding of human individuality should not be permitted to overshadow the reality that we essentially belong to one another. Our lives overlap. No understanding of personal life can be achieved without including our interpersonal life.

American culture has consistently underscored the significance of individual initiative. The culture in which the Christian faith was born was far more a shared culture, a society in which the values of a community took precedence over the priority of the individual. In my view, individuality and community are simply two different perspectives on the same reality. The world is what it is and is not ultimately defined by how we see it.

The key to our understanding both individuality and community is the nature of relatedness. Our individuality can be viewed as a unique collection of relationships. An individual is one opening onto the relationships that ultimately constitute the entire world. Everything in the world is related to everything else in the world. Nothing stands alone. There is "no-thing" in the world, absent the relationships, that makes that thing possible. That is why the philosopher Alfred North Whitehead would describe all things as "events."

Every time we identify an object in the world, we are, for the sake of convenience, cutting it off from what made it possible and what flows from it. Everything is related. Relatedness predates the existence of any particular thing in the world. God's creative relating, described as "hovering over the dark abyss," made the world possible. Every individual is a constellation of relationships. On a human level, we call that constellation "community."

To speak of our relatedness means to acknowledge that our interpersonal relationships do not simply color our lives. Relationships do more than influence us. In the most elementary way possible, we must affirm that our lives belong to one another. We cannot live well, while living solely unto ourselves. We cannot, in good faith, go our own way. Our interdependence is an essential component of our being here. Take away our human connections, and nothing really human is left.

Obviously, some relationships have more immediate impact on us than others. We could view ourselves as the center of a set of concentric circles. The inner circle is made up of those relationships that reverberate at the very pulse of our lives. They are primary relationships—parents and children. Other relationships are slightly more remote—chosen but standing with intense commitment. Those may include marriage or devoted friendships. Still others are more distant, for example, our relationship with the butcher or a regular co-worker. Then, there are those relationships that are fleeting. We do not know their name. They come across on the scope of our experience for only a short time—a salesperson or a chance meeting on a trip.

These latter relationships would seem, at first blush, to have no bearing on us at all. On second thought, reflection will show us that we often react personally to the way in which others are "with us" even in a fleeting encounter. My point is that all relationships— those that are close and valued, those that are remote and unfocused, and those with persons we do not even know or much less care about—affect our being in the world.

When we understand our essential connectedness as persons, the Christian admonition to love one another takes on more dramatic significance. The failure to respect another person reflects the failure of self-respect. The admonition to love is not an admonition that we go out and create relationships. In most cases, we have relationships aplenty. The command to love speaks to how we engage the relationships that constitute our lives. Hatred is self-destructive. Learning to love is God's ultimate gift for those who yearn to experience the highest meaning of being a person.

Chapter 11
Coping with Chaos

Life hurts. The tragedy of evil and suffering, along with the human failure we call sin, shapes the contours of every person's story. Interwoven among all our separate ways are strands of pain and moral decay that breed chaos in our world. Some of the trouble seems beyond our control—even unfair and unwarranted. Some of the trouble is of our own making. Whatever the source of our troubles, we all know what it is like for life to come undone. Our living together gets out of joint. Despite our differences, anguish makes us brothers and sisters.

While related, the tragedy of evil and the failure of sin are distinct. Evil and sin are very different issues. It is wrong and misleading to try to account for some painful and dreadful tragedy as being God's punishment for personal wrongdoing. It is appealing but wrong to describe a devastating earthquake as God's act of judgment on an evil generation. It is immoral to account for the HIV infection as evidence of God's wrath toward gays.

The reason we reach for such associations between God and human suffering is because we long to explain it somehow. We want to make sense of that which makes no sense. We want to give reason to the bombardment of the irrational. Describing such tragic conditions as a consequence of human sin is an easy rationale that takes everybody off the hook for explaining the unexplainable. We are like the friends of Job, always wanting to give a ready and neatly-reasoned explanation to suffering. Our words are hollow. We should resist the alluring path of easy judgment. The simple truth is that the rains of suffering and pain fall on the just and the unjust alike.

If our confessions of faith are to be able to stand under the light of God's grace, we cannot confess God to be the cause of the global evil or the personal tragedies that beset us. Human sin and global evil are related but not as cause and effect. Both sin and evil are expressions of the chaos that remains untamed and loose in our world. A person's sin may and often does precipitate tragic and dreadful consequences. But we should not reach for the converse conclusion. We cannot and should not suppose that every tragedy can be traced to a corresponding human misdeed. Such an effort to draw a necessary relationship is fraught with treachery and abuse. It confuses the human inclination to get even with God's character.

Evil and Suffering

Evil and suffering are the problems that give rise to all of the world's religions. One of the difficulties facing any world religion, including Christianity, is the inclination to focus more on evil and suffering than upon the light of revelation. The Christian understanding of salvation is more about the revelation of God than the escape from suffering or the escape from the consequences of sin.

Nevertheless, before we speak of sin and salvation, we should provide some context for understanding evil and suffering in human experience. Pain and suffering abruptly confront us with the reality that we are frail and vulnerable. We feel trapped by tragedies that invade and leave us wondering why did that happen to me.

My son-in-law, Dave, battles with a brain tumor. The event was startling: Stephanie shared a quick sandwich with her husband, Dave, before going to a graduate class. Suddenly without warning, he fell into convulsions—no history, no prelude. The panic yielded to enough calm to gain help. The diagnosis was numbing and frightening. An astrosartoma was doing its bitter work. Surgery could only partially dislodge its fury. Stephanie and Dave are afraid. We can but wonder why this awful evil should threaten his life while he is so young and vigorous. We do not stand beside them to explain it. We have no explanation. We are there to walk alongside them in the midst of an illness that seems maliciously out of control and frightfully unfair.

This story belongs to everyone. There are accidents that kill and maim. Senseless wars and violence destroy our neighborhoods. Evil is a terrible fact of life. Our confessions have no easy, doctrinaire way of explaining it. When we are leveled by evil winds, we are left weeping and bewildered, empty and frustrated, angry and resentful. Life hurts. The hurt is real and near and dreadful.

We desperately need honest talk about pain and suffering. God is not the omnipotent one, coldly looking down on our trauma and pain. There is a higher truth. God is the suffering one who creates new worlds within our pain. The notion that God is the all powerful, the high and mighty principal of heaven and earth should be laid aside. God suffers. God is the creative and redeeming power within heaven and earth, and within our souls, enabling us to move beyond the power of suffering.

God does not abolish evil and suffering because God cannot abolish evil and suffering. "Cannot" may seem like a difficult word to use when we speak of God, but it is a word that we must have the courage to say if we speak honestly about God's suffering. God suffers with us, and the mantle of suffering becomes the power of a new creation. Miracles are not the abolition of evil. Miracles are the creative energy that flows from the power of grace.

The issue of faith is how shall we cope with these real and present tragedies. We cannot pretend they are not there or that the hurt and fear do not matter. In our confessions, we must cope first by confessing that we do not understand. Our fear is genuine and intense. We are without answers. We cannot make sense of the evil. Evil is haunting and irrational.

Our confessions do not offer easy explanations. Our confessions do not make light of the suffering or pretend that it will go away. Our confessions do not have a veil for us to put over our suffering. Our confessions meet us at the edge of suffering. And there at the edge, the word toward which we stumble is hope, and hope is more an embrace than a word. When life comes to pieces, no amount of explanation will fill the void.

In part, we cannot explain evil because it is evil. Evil is our head-on confrontation with the disorderly, chaotic side of life. No amount of talk and no volumes of explanation will make everything fit. In the face of the tragic, authentic faith provides us not with answers but with a reservoir of hope and encouragement. Our faith enables us to experience that our lives are deeply intertwined. Our faith gives us the courage to face the suffering with the conviction that evil and suffering do not constitute life's final word. Hope and grace provide the only final redemption from suffering. All our medicines and all our interventions provide temporary reprieves.

Our faith gives us a clue for defining our lives so that while we struggle against the realities of suffering, the ravages of evil do not become the measure of our lives. The gift of faith is that we live beyond the boundaries of suffering. Suffering is never the final word. While suffering is real, it cannot destroy us because it does not define us. Only faith can enable us to live beyond the limits of the present moment. If we define our lives solely by present experiences, we are left to joy or despair depending upon the experience. Faith enables us to understand our lives beyond the boundaries of birth and death. Evil is real, but the confession of faith is that evil will not ultimately prevail. The ultimate Word of God is grace. God's grace is our only hope to cope with the forces of evil.

Dave and Stephanie continue their battle with the chaos. But amidst their struggle, they are sustained by the light of hope. They wrote to their family and friends:

> The year 1995 is coming to its close. Life has played hardball with us this year. There were days we thought we would collapse from the pressure, the pain, and the fear. Somehow we found the strength and the courage to face each day. Some of those days were hopeful, and others desperate. We have experienced every emotion to its extreme, except for loneliness. All of you—our family and friends—have ensured that we have never felt alone in our trials. You have been like a warm blanket on the coldest night.
>
> As we celebrate Christmas and the coming new year, we have a task to complete. It is time to put away past suffering, cherish what we have learned, and look forward with fresh hope. The season affords us that time—to close the door on the pain, yet always remember that we are stronger for having lived through it together.
>
> Christmas is so much more than the traditional exchanging of gifts. It is a time to step back and realize how very lucky we are to have life. Too often we take each other for granted, and forget that without each other, life has little meaning. Our wish for you this Christmas is that you cherish those you love, and remember that the past has no power over us, the present is a gift, and the future holds hope and joy.
>
> We look forward to 1996. The new year promises renewal of strength to fight our battle with cancer. We have learned that together we can achieve anything, and together we have nothing to fear, and together we have the power to overcome any challenges put before us. You have stood behind us with the great force of love, ever-present and encompassing us. You have our deepest gratitude for your diligent support and endless encouragement. God has blessed our lives with people like you who have held us in our times of need, and laughed with us in our times of joy. We carry all of you with us in our hearts daily.

The Evil Called Sin

Beyond the irrational that bedevils our lives, we bring suffering upon ourselves. The Christian faith affirms that our lives are rooted in God. Apart from our participation in God's being, we cannot understand ourselves or even begin to live authentic lives. If all real living is relating, sin describes our failed relating. It is relating gone astray. Sin is the mis-living of our lives. At its heart, sin springs from "wrong-living" and "wrong-relating."

The character of sin is too often chiefly defined as "wrong-doing." Sin is more serious than wrongdoing. Sin means that we have defined our lives the wrong way. We are driven by the wrong values. We have become disciples of untruth. Sin means staking our lives upon a center that cannot and will not sustain us. "Sins" or "sinful acts" are signals or symptoms of our twisted and misdirected living. So, we should distinguish our use of the word "sin" from the word "sins." The essence of sin cannot be captured by a list of prohibited behaviors, no matter how long. When Jesus sought to sum up all of the commandments, he gave his disciples not a set of prescriptions but a way of relating: "Love the Lord your God." "Love your neighbor as you love yourself."

The real human dilemma is not that we do "bad" things. The problem of sin lies in the distorted living from which we need to be free. Our sins, the unholy acts, betray our dislocated lives.

The confession of our faith is that we are the offspring of God. Sin means living as if this were not so. Sin is living our lives, making our choices, as though our relationship with God does not exist. This effort brings chaos and tragedy into our lives. The attempt to live as independent, self-sufficient persons is doomed to failure and fraught with consequences that are truly judgments on our sin.

The issue of sin is prominent in both the Old and New Testaments. The prophets and the writers of Genesis struggled with sin in ways that are profoundly instructive for our own struggle. We should try to sense the context in which they wrote. The Old Testament was the testimony of a people who understood themselves and their history as the children of God. God had brought them out of Egypt "on eagle's wings." It was from this sense of being a people of the covenant that they looked back at their beginnings. The scriptural probings of sin in the Old Testament reflect the desire of the Hebrew people to understand their own tragedy.

Their writing grew out of their own mourning. As they wandered in the desert's wilderness, uncertain of where they were going, uncertain of their survival, they wondered about what went wrong in the journey with Jehovah. Consumed by bitterness and bickering, they wrestled with their own failures. Reading the Genesis stories enables us to sense the intensity and imagination with which the Hebrews saw and understood the depths of the human problem. Genesis gives us a vivid and dramatic account of human sin.

The human predicament grows out of the reality that all of creation, including our individual lives, has its origins in the will of God. "In the beginning, God created heaven and earth." Heaven and earth—that's all there is. The initial condition is described as a formless, watery abyss, a sea of chaos, churning, without meaning, wreathed in disorder, dominated by darkness. God hovered over this chaotic darkness, and out of the chaos brought order and calm and light. God formed human life, and humankind became God's partner in creation—having dominion over the earth, naming the animals, and dwelling in Eden.

The human drama of life in Eden described humankind as having access both to the "tree of life" and the "tree of the knowledge of good and evil. The story of the garden was hardly conceived as some heavy, dense theological account. Nevertheless, it is weighted with truth and light of God's ways. If we are prepared to listen, Genesis will teach us not only of Adam but about our own situation. The story tells us plainly that a full and rich existence is possible for us here on God's earth. We can pick the fruit of the "tree of life." We may eat freely. We can know God, talk with God, and experience the good life while dwelling with and talking with God. The trees of the garden also make clear that we face real moral responsibility. We are not only of the earth. We bring to the earth a measure of freedom. A part of our freedom includes the real possibility of living for our own sake—choosing what is good to the eye, choosing a course where we live without reliance upon God.

The Genesis insight tells us what we already experience, namely, that we prefer the garden without God. Adam and Eve were attracted, even enamored, by the prospects of living as gods. The Genesis storyteller sets before us the very heart of the human problem. It was Adam's problem, and it is our problem. We do not wish to be dependent, finite creatures when we can eat of fruit that enables us to shape our own world and to be our own masters. The fruit of the tree of knowledge of good and evil will enable us to know enough and to be wise and good enough to live unto ourselves. We can manage the garden without God. Curled around the core of Adam's problem lies the urge to place himself at the center of the garden called Eden.

Adam is every person. His problem is my problem. I want to become my own god. Surely I can be god of some garden—the university or a church or a house or a family. Enough of being a mere participant in the garden—I prefer to be god. So, like Adam, I fall prey to both an intellectual and a moral error. The intellectual error is to think that I am the center of the universe; I am not. The moral error is to behave as though I were the center; I should not. The Genesis story shows us that our perverted, distorted, sin-filled lives grow out of our efforts to live in the garden without reference to God. God asked Adam, "Where are you?" The answer is that you and I are nowhere without God.

Sin means living in the universe as if God is not present. It is the attempt to live unto ourselves, seeking to center both order and meaning within ourselves. The outcome is that we wind up living outside Eden, back where the chaos is less tamed. In effect, we choose to plant our own gardens and harvest our own fruit. We wander aimlessly, trying to create our own purpose. The whole biblical picture reiterates again and again that God does not leave us alone in our wandering. Even east of Eden, God pursues and probes. Genesis depicts us as fugitives from Eden, but we always remain God's fugitives. In the final analysis, God is our problem. We prefer to make it on our own. We want God out of our world. We are quite sufficient unto ourselves.

Our confession of faith should not require us to try to account for human sin by means of some intricate doctrine of the devil. The figure of Satan serves as a powerful and dramatic symbol of the presence of pain and temptation in all our experiences. The idea of Satan does not serve us well as a principle of explanation. The persistent notion of Satan simply underscores in a dramatic and symbolic way that irrationality and chaos are unyielding parts of the world in which we live. The language of Satan should not become a means of escaping moral responsibility. The notion that "the devil made me do it" is nonsense. Becoming whole does not mean we have eluded the grasp of Satan. It means the "power of Satan" has been overcome. Despair has yielded to hope. The problem of sin is not that we want to follow Satan. The issue of sin is that we want to live without limits. We prefer the garden without God breathing down our backs.

Human sin is possible because we are both limited and our future is open. That is the meaning of human creation. In our human situation, we feel free and bound, limited and unlimited, strong and weak. We feel the boundaries of the garden, and we know that we are free to live beyond those boundaries. Like Adam, while being very aware that we do not live forever and that we do not know everything, we try to obscure those limits by asserting more than we know and claiming more power than we possess.

On the one hand we are contingent—cut-off, as it were. When we look back, there was a time when we were not here; when we look ahead, we cannot be sure about our future. We face squarely into a time when we will not be here. We face death. We sense profoundly the contingencies of our being here at all.

We are also free. That is to say, the future seems genuinely open. We are at risk. We are continually called upon to make choices that radically affect our lives. We must choose between diverse and distinct alternatives that harbor very different consequences. We cannot do away with risk and uncertainty.

Experiencing both being limited and being at risk creates within us genuine anxiety. The anxiety of life is real and present. Worse than being scared of something in particular, we often feel uneasy and threatened. To be human means to live with this inner tension. A poised turmoil and a quiet unrest characterize our lives. This dread, or *angst*, as Soren Kierkegaard called it, is not sin. It is what theologan Reinhold Niebuhr described as the precondition of sin. Worse than being scared of anything in particular, we are filled with dread and uncertainty.

Given this state of affairs, we are tempted either to deny our limitations or to discard our freedom. Abandoning our freedom, as we have already seen, can take many forms. In any form, it means giving unlimited devotion to limited values.

The rise of Hitler to authoritarian control was a reflection of the call to abandon freedom in favor of uncritical devotion to a compelling leader. That herd instinct displayed in Hitler's rise to power usually delivers the very sense of comfort and security that displaces the terrible anxiety that accompanies being free. Some counselors say that sexual exploitation and sexual abuse often go unreported not because of fear but because of the sense of security that the control and possession provides. The security is worth the pain. We will trade the perils of being a person with all its uncertainty and frustration for the tragic comfort of being a non-person, owned and possessed by any master who will provide even a make-believe haven of security.

Seeking to escape freedom is only one means of coping with the inner contradiction of feeling free and feeling limited. We also cope with that contradiction by denying our real limitations. Our ambition to be something is always partly prompted by our fear of being nothing. We seek to overcome our limitedness by stretching ourselves out in power, or knowledge, or wealth, or even virtue. We claim more power or more knowledge or more virtue than we can live up to. We can only hope that our claims will disguise our doubt and misery. Martin Luther was right: "The unwillingness of the sinner to be regarded as a sinner is the final form of sin." The final proof that we do not know God is that we do not face up to our own estrangement.

It is this inner tension between being limited and being free that lurks as the underlying issue of sin. We wish either to escape our freedom or to claim more for ourselves than we are. Our denial of freedom and our claim of power are played out in every context in which we live—political, religious, and personal. Even our drive "to establish" the Christian religion can be simply another form of greed and power. Religious power plays are no more seemly than political ones. They are all expressions of human sin.

Chapter 12
Walking on the Edge of Darkness

In "Coping with Chaos," I focused mostly on the meaning of sin and evil both as a condition of our living and a general predicament of human experience. In all candor, these kinds of conversations about sin are more convenient because we can keep our talk of sin at arm's length. Intimate conversations about sin are delicately avoided. Speculations about God make good table talk. Speaking of sin, on the other hand, is rarely appropriate for polite conversations.

The plain reality is, of course, that the actual drama of sin in our own experience gnaws and grates within us. We feel its appeal, and we get sucked into its vice-like grip. In ordinary experience, we walk along the boundary between light and darkness, often uncertain whether we are being pulled by the attraction of good or evil or some combination of them. Sin is easy enough to recognize when we see its work on the dark and seamy side of life. When sin stuns us in the form of devastating violence and rage that rips at the very moorings of civilization, we can call sin by its name. The horrors of murders and the stench of drugs prompt us to point our finger with passion toward the dreadful presence of sin in our experience.

Most of us do not dwell at the center of the dark episodes of violence and abuse. At the same time, however, virtually all of us are affected by the deadly darkness around us. Moreover, we all contribute more than we ever wish to acknowledge to the strength and persistence of the darkness. We like to think of ourselves as children of light even while we find ourselves nurturing the darkness. We live somewhere on the edge of darkness, darting into the shadows, grasping for enough joy to make us feel good. The shadows have great appeal. In the shadows, there is enough light to see our way, yet the light is not so bright that it blinds or binds. We especially do not want the light to be binding.

Jesus didn't seem to shape many parables or preach many sermons about the siren call of sin. Rather, day by day he brushed up against people who were crippled and paralyzed by the residue of sin in their own experiences. Sin is a part of who we are. We walk along the edge, trying to keep our balance. We don't want to be called a "do-gooder," and we don't want to be judged as a reprobate. Sin, for most of us, is neither pharasaism—a kind of holier-than-thou view of life—nor decadence—a kind of living that discards the sanctity of human life. We make our way, instead, closer to the boundary of darkness where one of the chief evidences of sin lies in the pretense that sin does not apply to us.

The message of Adam and the lesson from the dramas of Scripture are that we are all children of darkness. Person by person we make our way toward being the center of our universe with the world orbiting around our own priorities. We keep other people's need at a distance so that we can focus on our own. We juggle to keep everything in order until we can juggle the world no more, and the weight of living by our own lights comes crashing down upon us. We come undone, trapped by our own self-imposed order that crumbles into disorder. When life crumbles, we drift into the cold shadows. There, we become vulnerable to God's presence. God has always been there, walking along the edge of darkness with us. God has not come to judge and condemn. God has come to help us limp toward the light.

The Legacy of Sin

Human sin causes enormous pain and grief. The darker side of our experience can be found in every arena in which we live. It can be found at work, at leisure, at home, at worship. We doggedly determine to order the world by our own rules. The grasp for security and power and wealth is relentless. The outcome is this: No person ever possessed enough security to be safe. No person ever possessed enough power to be invincible. No person ever possessed enough prestige to remain unchallenged. No person ever possessed enough wealth to be content. We cannot make it on our own.

A principal reason for trying to understand the meaning of sin is so that we may face up to it more honestly in actual experience. Our real situations of pain and grief bring us to the brink of asking important spiritual questions. From down underneath where we struggle with the dark underbelly of life, we run into the most significant questions of faith. Questions of the head are easy. Even abstract questions of sin are easy. Making sense of our lives is difficult. When our inner content begins to corrode and our relationships with one another become confused and distorted, the light of faith has a chance with us.

For most of us, there is an enormous chasm between where we are and where we long to be. We find ourselves where Jesus found people—bodies broken, spirits depressed, insides knotted. We find ourselves causing hurt and being hurt. We feel lonely and afraid, even trapped. The precise course of human pain is always personal. The contours of our paths are different. We never need to conjure up a confession of our sins. Individually, we are fractured and frustrated. We are sinners.

Only the brokenness of sin can make sense of the wholeness of salvation. The most compelling aspects of salvation rarely relate to some remote notion of heaven. Our struggles with sin are more immediate. The idea of salvation takes on intensity and passion when it addresses the real pain that gnaws within us. No one had to arrange a crowd when Nelson Mandela spoke of freedom from apartheid. The painful sin of apartheid was not imagined. The pain was real and close up. Hope was not a message of an ultimate "sweet by and by" in which sin would be no more. Hope and salvation as an honest and passionate experience meant being free from the demeaning rule of apartheid. Sin and salvation are not remote theories. They are rooted in real-life experience. Look for the traces and consequences of sin up close. If you want to know what salvation means, look at where you hurt.

Doing and Relating

Moving beyond sin as a concept and facing up to our experience of sin, we find sin's impact in three dimensions of our character. First, we do not understand ourselves as related to God. We fail to see or acknowledge the spiritual underpinnings of our lives. Second, we do not recognize the value of others to our own worth and achievements. We act as though other people are to be used as means to achieve our own ends. Third, we want to conceive and create our life in the world without reference to God.

The biblical metaphor of estrangement is often used to help describe our human ways. Actually, estrangement sometimes comes across as a rather cold, medicinal word like the latest strain of a flu virus. The Bible is brimming over with stories of the great divide between ourselves and God. The expulsion from Eden, the deadly hostility between Cain and Abel, the confusion of language at Babel, the Babylonian captivity, the crucifixion itself—all are graphic portrayals of alienation. We have always been good at building barriers and drifting off into the far country.

Our experience of alienation and estrangement in everyday living is more mundane. We know estrangement as moving out, burying ourselves in consuming preoccupations, even arrogance. In countless concrete ways, we break away from God and each other. Breaking away is where our experience of sin comes to bear on our living and relating. Because we are sinners, we behave in hateful and crushing ways.

We can never come to grips with the experience of sin unless we take into account the profound connections among us. Sin is not simply a personal problem. Looking at either sin or salvation as chiefly a private matter is itself a part of the human problem. In the Christian faith, both sin and salvation are thoroughly relational. Sin is not a solitary problem. Adam and Eve left the garden together. Salvation is not a solitary event. We must find hope together. Indeed, the preoccupation with personal salvation can itself become one more illustration of human sin.

The biblical narratives describing our sinful behavior focus always as much on the way we relate to one another as the way we relate to God. The reason is clear. Our relationship to God is formed primarily in the cauldron of our relationships to one another. Our "wrong-being" cannot be understood or addressed as a private problem. Regarding sin as a private and personal dilemma misses the real significance of the human tragedy. Sin means that our relationships and social structures are corrupt. Sin twists the way we deal with each other. Our relationships are where sin confounds us and where love eludes us. The place where you and I are most likely to face our sin against God is the interpersonal traumas between each other.

We will never be able to address the living human tragedy of sin without confronting sin as a social phenomenon. Sin creates wars among nations, flesh and blood killing flesh and blood. There are no holy wars. Sin sustains feuds between friends. Sin causes us to build protective walls, to go our own way, and to ignore our brother's misery. We shut each other out. We craft class structures and define racial lines to distinguish us. We classify and categorize people by power and wealth. All these artificial boundaries become expressions of human sin. We create exclusive groups. We do it in the church. We do it in society. We identify ourselves by the people we exclude.

Our experience of sin is rooted in fear. Fear and fear alone causes us to be ugly and hateful and destructive. We hurt people because we are afraid. Fear is a powerful force in our lives. Afraid of our limitations and afraid of our own freedom, we try to establish our reality over against the reality of others. We deny our reliance upon others and stand tall alone in order to show that we are safe and sufficient. The truth is that our meanness is a child of fear. We are afraid to love because we do not really believe that we are loved.

Sin and the Law

In interpreting the meaning of sin, law is a very important notion within our Jewish and Christian heritage. The Hebrew word for law is *Torah*, which comes from the verb "to throw" or "to direct," and later "to instruct." Living under the aegis of God's presence is described in the Bible as living in covenant with God. In the Old Testament, the people of God are called Israel. In the New Testament they are called the church.

The law helps us to understand what it means to be a person whose primary life-reference is God. The Torah spells out the implications of being the people of Jehovah. In this law we are able to see what being God's people requires in ordinary, everyday life. It is a very easy step from regarding the law as God's instruction to regarding the law as a test of whether we are acceptable to God. The essence of sin does not have to do with breaking the law. We break the law because we are sinners. The law is a gift of God. The law is not intended to make life difficult or to construct certain hurdles that we must scale in order to win God's approval. The law tells us how living unto God causes us to behave. For example, it means respecting other people as the creation of God. It means respecting property and life. It means looking beyond ourselves to God for our ultimate strength.

The law is God's instruction concerning how "living according to the spirit" will work out in everyday experience. When we want to know what to do, the law serves as our teacher. Our faith should not transform the law into an abstract tyrant. The law does not determine what is right or wrong. The law guides us in making those determinations. Morality is not prescribed, it is chosen. Our lives are not so simple that we can use the law book or the Bible as a rigid code of behavior.

Determining what is right is a continuing process. The responsibility rests with you and with me. We have to discover what it means to be good. Right actions come from right-being and right-relating. The law may spell out for us what living under God's will involves in our daily behavior, but determining in our lives what is right must occur in the daily process of coming to know and to follow God's will. The law is a gift, but doing good springs from relating to God. Goodness does not flow from an abstract allegiance to the law.

Sin and Guilt

In seeking to understand the meaning of guilt, we need to distinguish between guilt as an objective reality and the sense of guilt that becomes a weight upon our life of faith. Frankly, guilt has become an enormous burden to our interpretations of faith. The ambiguity of our references to guilt has caused confusion and misunderstanding. As an objective reality, guilt describes the distance between where we are and where we ought to be or between what we are doing and what we ought to be doing.

The distinction between guilt as a descriptive fact of having acted wrongly and guilt as an inner sense of being unacceptable is crucial. We have described sin as "wrong-being" and "wrong-relating." In our wrongful relationships we are indeed guilty. If I treat my neighbor unfairly, I am guilty of that wrong. The only proper response to my guilt is to face the wrong and seek a better way of relating to my neighbor. This "turning around" may be as simple as an apology. In other cases, it may involve a complex set of reparations for the wrong. In either case, guilt refers to the actual state of affairs in which I have made a wrong decision. In that sense, guilt is a part of the objective reality of our lives. The experience of guilt can become a productive and dynamic force in our faith. The reality of guilt calls us to come to grips with our wrong.

In addition to this meaning of guilt that is clear and constructive, we very often use the term guilt to refer to the inner feeling of being unacceptable either because of what we have done or what we want to do. In this context, guilt really becomes a means of turning our backs on ourselves, of meting out self-rejection. But the truth is that our sense of guilt, no matter how dreadful, does not and cannot solve the problem. Guilt turns the problem inward.

Guilt is a powerful dead weight upon our lives, dragging us down, leaving us often with a twisted perception of reality. While a seminary student, I served for a time as pastor of a small village church in Norwood, Louisiana. Hardly any experience bore more enduring friendships or enabled me to get to know good people up close than these years in Norwood. From "Tedo" Jelks and Jimmy Reynolds, I learned of joy and self-reliance. From Harold Jelks and Fletcher Rollins, I learned of responsible stewardship and the holiness of laughter. One by one, simple and straightforward people taught me how to recognize God when God showed up in "overalls." In that place, I also saw the dreadful effects of guilt—people who sometimes could hardly let themselves believe God's genuine and unencumbered forgiveness.

One summer's evening a rainstorm came up—what my grandpa would have called a "gully-washer." Thunder roared and rain came down like sheets of water rushing to heal the cracks in the dry earth. The rain was cooling, a refreshing close to a hot summer day. Dusk was coming. I walked out on the covered porch that wrapped around this large frame house where the preacher lived in the summer months, only a stone's throw away from the stately white frame meetinghouse called Norwood Baptist Church. I was startled. Standing at military attention in front of the house in this downpour was a young man—college age. He lived next door. I called to him, "Billy, come in the house." He came. Joan was about to serve supper, and Billy sat down at the table and began to eat and to talk. Much of what he said was incoherent, nonsense, almost babble. As I strained to listen, I realized that Billy was speaking as though he were Jesus and that he believed that he had chained the devil behind the post office in a neighboring village.

After supper, I walked Billy home next door. The rain had sub-
sided. I spoke haltingly with his parents and left to prepare for a
Wednesday evening service for which the church bell was beginning to call the townspeople.

We assembled in the church, a small remnant of people gathered for singing and praying and studying the Scripture. Actually,
being together more than learning or worship prompted their persistent presence. Their days were filled with difficult labor, and for
most of them weariness had set in by sundown. As we began to
sing, young Billy came in the church carrying a small, lighted candle. As he came in, he switched off all the lights within the church.
In the night dark, the small candle was larger than life. People were
astonished, stunned, silent. I asked a young high school student to
turn on the lights.

As the lights came on, Billy arrived at the front of the sanctuary. He gently placed the candle on the piano and abruptly turned
and lurched with fire in his eyes to assault me. Just before his
attack had reached its target, he was restrained by a friend who did
not typically attend midweek meetings but who had come this
night, at my request, to make a report to the church. Safely subdued,
Billy was led from the sanctuary into the night air—with his daddy
weeping "don't hurt my baby boy" and Billy whistling "The Love
of God." During Billy's recovery, I spent many hours with him and
learned what the dreadful and destructive baggage of guilt can do to
the human spirit.

The Christian gospel is often eclipsed by our dreadful sense of
guilt. The gospel is that our sins do not make us unacceptable to
God. It is selfishness and a faith gripped by fear that cause us to try
to justify our wrong actions by punishing ourselves with a load of
guilt. The sense of guilt becomes a way of brooding upon our
wrong actions. The Christian gospel is that God assumes responsibility for our guilt. Our Christian confession calls for us to walk
free of our guilt. God accepts us in spite of our sin, and God's
acceptance becomes the energy for redirecting our lives.

God's Relation to Sin

God's relation to our sins is governed by God's nature and not our
own. That is to say, God's will toward us does not vary depending
upon our actions and decisions. God's love and forgiveness are

unchanging. In every way we are children of God's grace. The truth of our faith is that God sees us the way God sees Jesus. Sin does not distort or diminish God's love. The simple, freeing, unfettered affirmation of the Christian faith is that God forgives and accepts us—no conditions. Sin is our immodest effort to demonstrate that we are quite sufficient unto ourselves—strong enough, knowledgeable enough, even good enough to stand alone. We claim to be our own gods. We are wrong. The fact is that we are broken, limited, and afraid. We are sinners. Yet, in our brokenness and limitedness, indeed, in our fear, God waits for us. God loves and forgives us. God lets us leave, but God never lets go of us.

The compelling confession of our faith is not that God will love us or forgive us if we will repent our sin. The truth of the Christian gospel is that God loves us and forgives us already—no conditions. That affirmation is hard for us to believe because it is not our way. We, more typically, make our love and forgiveness conditional. But you and I should resist imposing our ways upon God. What we see of God in Jesus proclaims that God's love is free and unencumbered by human treaties. We need only the courage to live in the light of God's forgiveness. Grace, not sin, is the final word of our faith.

Chapter 13
The Heart of
Our Confessions

The heart of our confessions of faith is that this person called Jesus is God's light for our lives. Confusion frequently reigns when it comes to thinking about Jesus. Our faith does not claim that Jesus has either said something or done something that you and I must accept or reject. Meeting Jesus is not an emotional or an intellectual transaction. Through the disciples we can see the essence of the matter. Following is the heart of believing.

If we don't get it right, we will get it wrong. Jesus is not a god to be worshiped or the founder of a world religion to be admired. From all that we can discern about Jesus, setting up a new religion was the last thing on Jesus' mind. Replacing the Jewish temple with the Christian church was simply not the focus of Jesus' ministry. Jesus' message was much nearer to where people lived. Jesus was a friend to ordinary people and became, for some of them, the principal event by which they knew God. Jesus turned their world of believing upside down. The temple became peripheral. Jesus came to the center and soul of their life.

We are tempted to conceive of Jesus as a formal act of God, calculated to save people from their sin. It is Jesus, the carpenter's son from Nazareth, who stands at the center of the Christian faith. Much of our talk about Jesus has little reference to our actual experience. We lose touch with Jesus as a person. Instead, he becomes a larger-than-life religious figure.

We develop elaborate Christologies that confuse as much as they clarify. We devise complex theological theories that transform the life and work of Jesus into a cold and distant mechanism of redemption. All of these weighty theories prevent us from meeting Jesus as God's word of light and truth for our difficult and painful situations. Our theologies and Christologies become a way of keeping Jesus at a distance. If we are to meet Jesus up close in the street, we should be prepared to lay aside much of our religious rhetoric. Jesus is not a legend. Jesus is God's word to us, a person who comes to us on a human scale. Jesus is God with us.

Recentering Our Faith

If the center of our faith is Jesus himself, it means that the Christian faith is not chiefly about Jesus' ideas or his deeds or even his death. Jesus, the person, is the focus of our faith. The disciples, no doubt, first listened to Jesus with considerable skepticism. We can imagine how they must have felt about this stranger approaching them with words about God's Kingdom. They were templegoers, but the language of the temple belonged to the Sabbath. They were more focused on fishing—making the day's catch.

Typically, we hear of Jesus a long while before we follow him. Like the disciples, we at first only give him a glance. We hear a word. Our hearts are centered elsewhere. Yet, we cannot quite escape his grasp. His spirit resonates with our spirit. At last, we look up from our labors to listen more intently to this person called Jesus. We put down our work and walk a little nearer. Amidst all the noise that floods our lives and the difficulty that dogs our steps, Jesus' presence sheds new light here that causes hope to well up within us.

Our decision to follow is not very different than the choice of Peter or Matthew or John or countless other nameless followers of Jesus. For them and for us, Jesus becomes a radically new center for thinking and living. Their belief and our belief in Jesus is mixed with disbelief. The disciples were sometimes bold followers, while on other occasions they retreated quietly into the shadows. Our devotion is sometimes explicit and eager, sometimes reticent and reluctant.

We live with this mixture of belief and unbelief. On most days it seems that our Christian commitment is mostly formal, having little to do with our everyday choices. Christianity seems to be more about worship than life. In the daily run of things, our convictions give way to more weighty encumbrances that eclipse the centrality of Jesus. Our confessions would not be honest without acknowledging this eclipse of the centrality of Jesus. However, honesty also causes us to confess that sometimes we have nowhere else to turn. When those of us who believe and half-believe are driven either by the absolute weariness of work or losses that are too heavy to carry, Jesus becomes the only point of reference we have for recentering our lives. Jesus becomes light for resolving the conflicts that confuse and devour us. In the midst of competing forces that clamor for our attention, Jesus becomes a resting place.

If we are to speak plainly about the place of Jesus in our faith, we should begin with where we find him. Jesus is a person of history. His address was RFD, Nazareth. We make Jesus into such a "divine" and unapproachable person that we find it difficult to meet him where the disciples met him. What we first find in history is not the Christ of faith but a person who has all the marks of the human condition. Indeed if Jesus were not a real and "honest-to-goodness" person, his relevance to our lives would be seriously compromised. Unless he has been where we have been, he cannot speak persuasively to our problems.

Our confessions should not require us to view Jesus as a half-god disguised behind a mask of humanity. For Jesus, the turmoil and pain of existence is not a mask. The historical Jesus is one of us. Let there be no question of his real humanity. Jesus lived among the people of the street with the same needs and uncertainties, the same fears and doubts to which you and I are subject. Jesus was a person who walked alongside the disciples in their time and space, flesh and blood to flesh and blood, spirit to spirit. Our confessions of faith should not diminish that Jesus was born in history and lived beside us in our kind of world. Whatever else we say of Jesus, it should not obscure that Jesus is one of us.

The Christian faith goes further. Our faith affirms that through this particular person in history, Jesus of Nazareth, we are able to see God clearly and definitively. It is a radical assertion. On the face of it, the claim appears bizarre. Can it be that this faith has the audacity to assert that within the whole frame of human history, God was uniquely present in this particular person?

All world religions have important persons who play central roles for interpreting the meaning and character of the world. To say that Jesus is God's word is not to say that Jesus is God's only word. For the Christian's faith, Jesus has defining and ultimate significance. These events of history serve as the hinge upon which all of history comes to be understood. This event in human experience becomes the integrating center for all human experience. So, in the Christian's experience, Jesus is neither a prophet nor a god. Jesus is the center of our revelation. In Jesus, we see what God is like, and we see the meaning of our history. Jesus is the person in our history that enables us to make sense of all history.

Both the historic presence of Jesus and the real humanity of Jesus form the heart of our confessions of faith. The precise contours of Jesus' historical existence cannot be easily confirmed. While our ability to reconstruct his historic life is limited, the impact of his presence is boldly evident. The relationship of Jesus with his followers was a relationship of extraordinary power. It is not surprising, therefore, that the significance of Jesus' life began quietly to overshadow his simple historical presence.

This historical person to be followed was soon changed by his followers into a divine figure to be worshiped. This transformation is largely a mistake. The focus of the Christian faith should not be reconstructed into the worship of Jesus. The earliest church knew Jesus as a simple and plain person who brought the reality of God down to earth. For us, Jesus tends to become the beautiful and wonderful object of religious belief. For the disciples, on the other hand, he was first of all a person and a friend. In their relating to him, Jesus became the Christ.

The Virgin Birth is more truth than fact. Facts are historical and mundane. Truth transcends the ages. The truth of the Virgin Birth is that God speaks to us through this event in history. Jesus is the historical event. The idea of the Virgin Birth is a way of describing the event. It is like a trumpet blast before a grand entrance. It tells us that something dramatically important is happening here. Jesus' coming is like the windshear of history. The Jesus-event is a cultural and religious "shear." He represents a radical shift for our religious consciousness. We were not expecting to meet God in this fashion—human and ordinary. We expected fanfare and majesty—an entrance that would seem to befit God.

Focusing on the Virgin Birth instead of Jesus is like focusing upon the trumpet blast rather than the grand event that it heralds. The Virgin Birth is used by Luke and Matthew to signal the radical character of Jesus' presence. Its status as an actual historical fact is unimportant. Clearly, there are many records of so-called "virgin births" in history. It was certainly not a novel image to denote an extraordinary event. The preoccupation with this virgin birth as a doctrine based in "flesh and blood" distracts us from the truth of the

Incarnation. Mark and John make no reference, and the apostle Paul never speaks of the Virgin Birth. When we focus on defending the facts rather than conveying the truth, we are making more of the notion of the Virgin Birth than the earliest records made, and we are making less of the importance of the truth that God is with us.

Confessing Jesus to be the Christ

That Jesus is the Christ is a confession of faith. Jesus asked of his disciple-friends, "Who do people say that I am?" They replied that some people think you are a prophet—Elijah or Jeremiah. Jesus pressed the point, "Who do you say that I am?" Peter responded, "You are the Christ, the Son of The Living God." Peter confessed boldly that Jesus is the Christ. Peter's boldness was often a coverup for his caution.

Over against Peter's confession stands the fact that many people, indeed most people, knew Jesus without making this kind of awesome, mind-boggling assertion about him. After all, Jesus looked and talked as an ordinary person. No mere review of historical evidence is ever likely to lead someone to conclude, "Thou art the Christ." Flesh and blood will not reveal it. This high confession that Jesus is the Christ stands only by faith. We do not believe it because we know it. We know it because we believe it.

The disciples did not visibly see God in Jesus and thereby conclude that he was the Messiah. It was in and through their relationship to this person Jesus that they came to the overwhelming and defining conviction of the presence and work of God through Jesus. Our feeble attempts at historical research to validate the deity of Christ will always fall short. Faith reveals it. The deity of Christ can never be more than a confession of faith, and it shall never be less. It is not a claim that can be demonstrated in some objective or scientific manner. The search for the historical Jesus is largely in vain. To confess the deity of Christ is to assert that our understanding and our relationship to God have been defined in an ultimate manner through this person called Jesus. In that confession, the historical Jesus becomes the Lord Christ.

In truth, we have to let this confession stand within us with all of its risks and vulnerability. There can be no historical or logical proof. We are children of faith. The Christian faith is not about doctrine. It is not even about a book. The defining mark of the

Christian faith is our confession that Jesus Christ is Lord. After all, hardly anyone, Christian or non-Christian, wishes to diminish the wisdom of the teachings of Jesus or the importance of his life. The confession, however, that Jesus is the central event through which our history is to be understood is another matter. That confession can only be made by people who have decided to follow Jesus. Without following Jesus, the confession is empty.

Each of us makes confessions from the context of our own history. Some persons are strangers to the church, and the sounds of confessing Jesus as the Christ are unfamiliar. Still others actually grew up in the church where the language of religion is abundant. There, the confession of the centrality of Jesus can become lost amid the debris of church busyness, church politics, and even church hostilities.

In all candor, the dysfunction of the church has made it very difficult for some persons to embrace a clear affirmation of faith. The poison of distorted and twisted religious experiences have blocked out their vision of the simplicity and wonder of the gospel. Breaking through that residue of resentment toward bad religion is often a difficult challenge. Our capacity to confess becomes buried under a load of unhealthy religious experiences. Before we can find the courage to confess Jesus as a centering power in our lives, we have to find a way to confess our confusion and disappointment with the tragedies of our own religious experiences.

I can hardly recall a time when Jesus was not a conscious fact of religious experience for me. Even now, I still recall when a modest woman of faith in the quiet solitude of her home placed before me the reality of God's grace in Jesus in a persuasive and compelling way. I recall the unfolding of my own belief under the instruction of a schoolteacher, John Youngblood, who helped me and countless young people discover that faith could have a constructive and intelligent bearing on life. I have learned that our convictions grow. They change. Honest confessions do well to stay in touch with our genuine convictions. It is easy for what we say to run ahead of what we actually believe. Our faith does not settle into a state of molten stability or a glassy pool of certainty. Our faith provides continuity and strength while it represents a changing and growing understanding of reality.

Living, dynamic confessions of faith constitute the difference between a religious adherent and a disciple. Every religion has adherents. To be an adherent means to accept somebody's system of belief. In contrast, being a disciple requires a leap of faith that no amount of historical verification can ever quite justify. The early disciples followed Jesus despite the counsel of the authoritative "men of God" that they should not be so foolish. Believing as an act of following was a profoundly personal event that took them out of step with conventional religious wisdom. Following Jesus made them uneasy. They were often unsure of the implications of what they were doing. They were bound to be full of doubt and uncertainty. After all, they were young and uninfluential. Who were they to be taking on the ruling class of religious and community leaders?

Being a disciple meant knowing Jesus as a person and believing him to unveil the character of God. The disciples could embrace their belief, but they could not demonstrate it. They were committed to what they could not prove. It would be more appealing if faith carried no risk. But our actual situation is this: "We see through a glass darkly." We cannot demonstrate Jesus to be the Son of God. We cannot claim objective, scientific validity for our confessions. We confess our faith, and we leave our confessions open. We leave them open to grow, open to new light and open to others who must embrace convictions of their own.

The Jesus Event

The meaning of Jesus for the Christian faith can only be understood in terms of the total event of his life. We like to analyze people and events and reduce them to manageable parts. Some people are more interested in Jesus' teachings. Others focus more on Jesus' death. Still others are more captured by his mighty works, miraculous acts. While we may focus from time to time on some particular aspect of Jesus' life, we should be clear that the meaning of the Jesus experience cannot be reduced to any event or episode within his life. Jesus was a person. We can be interested or intrigued by a particular episode in his life, but no person can be properly understood through the lens of one important episode. The converse is true as well. No episode can be understood apart from the whole person.

At some considerable peril of misunderstanding and distortion of the meaning of Jesus' presence in history, the Christian church has frequently made the crucifixion of Jesus into the primary symbol of our faith. The cross is everywhere. It stands atop steeples and is carved into windows. It is worn as a lapel pin and bedecks dashboards. The cross is the most universally-accepted and recognized symbol of Christianity. The problem only arises when we take the step of regarding the crucifixion as the essence of Jesus' life. The crucifixion is not the saving act of God.

I will speak of the cross and its significance in a later chapter. Here I wish simply to say plainly that when we confess the centrality of Jesus to our faith, we are speaking of the whole person, Jesus of Nazareth. We are not speaking only of the cross or only of the resurrection. God's presence in Jesus cannot be adequately understood if the life and ministry of Jesus is viewed in fragments. Jesus, the whole person, is the revelation of God. Attempts to reduce the meaning of Jesus' life to a single event or to a certain body of teachings are foolish. Such reductions lead to a treacherous misunderstanding of the Christian faith. God is disclosed in history through the event of Jesus who lived and walked among us. Any other view of revelation winds up turning the gospel into an artificial means by which God manipulated human history.

Jesus' life is full of passion and pain. He was caught in the web of religious conflict and political dissension. If Jesus bears God's word to us, he bears that word as a whole person who lives and works in a world that is overcome with human turmoil and conflict. Jesus lives in our kind of space as our kind of person. We must reckon with the whole person if his life matters as a reference point for our own.

As a young seminary student, I recall hearing an evangelist who came to preach to preachers about preaching. His words were bizarre. His topic was "Ten Ways to Close Them Out for the Lord." His message consisted of ten illustrations that would hook listeners into saying "yes" to Jesus. The idea was that you had to clinch the sale. The absurdity of this twisting of the gospel was overshadowed by the poverty of turning salvation into one person's manipulation of another.

Jesus was not a religious pied piper. The goal of faith is not to get people to say "yes" to Jesus or to adopt a system of beliefs.

Following Jesus means living in the light of God's unconditional and enduring love. Love will set us free and enable us to walk beyond a life of fear toward a life of grace and hope. The proclamation of the gospel is not about getting our religious hooks into people. Proclamation is the confession of God's grace. Grace sets people free through the power of God's unencumbered forgiveness. Jesus as a whole person embodied the grace of God. We are able to see how life's priorities and responsibilities become changed when a person walks in the light of God's grace.

We can only relate to Jesus as an event in history. Christianity is not about accepting the fact of Jesus' death or pledging to be faithful to his admonitions. The Christian's faith has to do with relating to Jesus as a follower. We may be inspired by Jesus' tragic death. We may be counseled and persuaded by the Sermon on the Mount. But the abiding issue of Christian revelation is that Jesus enables us to see history in a different way.

Jesus embodies among us the character of God, and his complete life becomes our primary reference for seeing the meaning of our lives. Jesus should no more be equated with certain of his words or with certain episodes in his life than should you or I. We know Jesus, and we see ourselves as a constellation of episodes and words that reflect the heart of our being. The person of Jesus is the event in history where, for those of us who call ourselves Christian, God comes to us. It is the event where God's unconditional acceptance and embrace of us is lived out in history.

The heart of our confession is that Jesus Christ is Lord, which means that in Jesus we see the light. God's love and grace become forces in our world where confusion and trouble reign. Grace does not pretend that our trouble is unreal or that it is less painful than we think. The heart of our confession is that God's love will prevail beyond every barrier of chaos and failure. The heart of our confession is that our hope rests in God. Jesus' presence teaches us that God is not remote and far away. Jesus teaches us that God is near and will stay by our side even in the darkest night. Jesus means that God is with us. Being Christian means following Jesus.

Chapter 14
A God Who Speaks

The history of God is the history of God speaking. God speaks, and the worlds come to be. God said, "Let there be light." And God said, "Let the waters bring forth swarms of living creatures." And on another day, God said, "Let us make humankind in our image." A word from God sparked creation. God's presence was like a "wind from God swept over the face of the waters." God speaks, and the light breaks. From Genesis 2:1 we hear, "Thus the heavens and the earth were finished and all their multitude." So, all of creation is a word from God.

In the garden, God looks for the hidden Adam and says, "Where are you?" As Cain slew Abel, God said, "Where is your brother, Abel?" Surely, God knew the whereabouts of Adam and the fate of Abel. God's speaking creates. God's speaking judges. God's speaking redeems. The Bible is the story of God's speaking. It is the story of God saying to Abraham to leave his father's country. It is the story of God's speaking to Moses from a bush in the desolate desert. God speaks in the epic of Job and the hymns called psalms. The prophets thundered forth the oracles of God. And in the misery of Babylon, the people wondered why the Lord seemed to be "silent when the wicked swallow those more righteous than they." God answered, "The righteous live by faith." "Write it down," Jehovah said, "write it down so that any runner could read it." "The righteous live by faith" (Hab 2:4).

God speaks, and the world churns out of the watery chaos a remnant of order. God speaks, and Adam suddenly senses that he is alone and naked. God speaks, and the shackles of Paul's prison cells fall away. God's speaking creates. God's speaking judges. God's speaking redeems. Only as we understand that God is a God who speaks can we begin to comprehend the power and presence of Jesus as the speaking of God. Jesus is the Word of God. Those who follow him are saying by their steps that in Jesus they have heard the voice of God in a clear and decisive way. When God speaks most clearly to us, it is not from the whirlwind or a burning bush; it is through the living presence of a person who moves onto our neighborhood street.

Jesus as the Word of God

Words are the currency of our being together. We relate mostly by speaking. Words become our instruments for reaching toward each other. Speaking is a way of letting our inner thoughts and feelings flow into the consciousness of another. When we speak, we expose our inner being to those who listen. Those who are listening quickly lose interest when it seems that the words have no relation to who we are or what we really believe. Hollow sounds leave us disinterested. We want to hear words that connect us with the person who is speaking. Wisdom flows from the connections for which the words are only symbols.

Words convey God's creative presence. They present how God connects with humankind. When people speak honestly and openly, they are laying themselves open. They are making themselves vulnerable. When God speaks, we see God's purpose and character. God becomes vulnerable to us. God speaks even while Adam prefers to live beyond the boundaries of the garden. God speaks even while his people create other gods and pursue other loyalties.

In a world where people characteristically seek to chart their own paths and create their own destinies, God continues to speak. The history of history can be read as the history of God speaking. People often listen with only one ear. The other ear attends to all the other sounds that consume them. The children of Israel wandering in the wilderness wanted more than words. They wanted a god they could see and touch. They longed for a golden calf that they could cherish. That way they could keep their eye on their god.

We are like the wandering Israelites. Jesus is our word. Like Israel, our first temptation is to make Jesus into an icon of devotion. We want to see God, touch God, clutch God, and make sure that God belongs to us. So, we make Jesus into an object of worship. Let us not make Jesus into a magic fetish. Jesus is God's speaking to us. Jesus is not God. Jesus is the Word of God. Jesus is the speaking of God. Every other reference to the Word of God, such as referring to the Bible as the Word of God, should remain secondary to Jesus himself. All religious orders love their holy books. The Bible as the Word is subordinate to Jesus as the Word. Word is a telling and enduring image of the presence of God. The goal of faith is not to possess God. The goal of faith is to hear God and for the Word of God to change the center of our lives.

Creation, judgment, and redemption are all described as the speaking of God. It is a way of saying that God speaks to us in every condition. God's words pierce the walls that separate us. God's word overcomes the distance we call estrangement. God's speaking enabled a frightened Jacob to meet a hostile Esau, and they wept together as brothers. Words tear away the barriers that keep us apart. God speaks, and there is light. God speaks, and there is hope.

When the Gospel writer John describes Jesus as the Word made flesh, we are confronted with the simplest and clearest description of what it means for Jesus to be in the world. Words can be mightier than armies. Neither the written nor the spoken word, however, can ever fully capture the import of God's presence. In Jesus, God comes to us in flesh and blood. Jesus is the living word bringing the ultimate meaning and the enduring reality of the world before our eyes. Because of Jesus' life, God is no longer Olympian and remote. God is near to us as the words we speak. God steps into the stream of our history.

In Jesus as the Word of God, we see God's kind of life. We see what life is like when it is lived on God's terms. We see who Adam was created to be. We see God's kind of love and forgiveness. In the speaking of God embodied in Jesus, God's word is not an idea to accept or a doctrine to believe. The Sadducees had plenty of doctrine to believe. In Jesus, we hear and see God telling us something more important than religious doctrine. God's truth is translated into a way of engaging life. The reality of God becomes intimate and personal. We see and hear God up close. In Jesus, God speaks our language.

This new language of God called Jesus upsets all our comfortable ways of knowing God. In following Jesus, we are not chasing after a persuasive preacher with a new idea. We are not enamored by the founder of a new religious movement. Our way of seeing ourselves and our place in the world is overturned. Jesus gives us a new look at creation.

Life is not about getting; it is about giving. Life is not about winning at any cost; it is more about having the courage to lose.

Jesus speaks of life where ordinary values are reversed. Giving may
be gain. Losing may be winning. The established ways of the world
are in for a tumble. God reshapes how we deal with one another.
Jesus redefines self-fulfillment. God's presence in Jesus gave the
disciples the courage to claim the freedom to love even when they
were afraid to love. God's presence enables us to see the good in
people we don't like and to affirm the worth of people who offend
us. Jesus teaches us to enter life through a different door and to
conceive our history on a different plane. Forgiving instead of getting even means living with each other on a different plane.

Hearing Jesus as the voice of God should also teach us that
Christianity should not be conceived as an abstract philosophy of
life. The Christian faith takes very seriously the contours of our
actual living. This person, Jesus, lived where we live. He knew fear
and uncertainty, affirmation and rejection, applause and derision,
pain and joy, celebration and isolation, wedding parties and lonely
sojourns. That's why Jesus can serve as God's authentic word to us.
He didn't live an artificial life. Jesus' life stays in touch with our
own honest predicaments. All of the nouns and verbs of our vocabulary cannot convey the reality of God with power and persuasion.
Only a person who lives here in our corner of the galaxy can help
us to understand the being of God.

The effort to reduce the essence of Christianity into a compact
and neatly-packaged set of religious truth remains forever futile.
Some years ago, a Christian fundamentalist layperson visited my
office. For an hour, he would spin out discrete and familiar religious propositions, asking me to agree. I finally had to confess to
him my conviction that all of his propositions were of trivial importance. They posed interesting words for conversation and even
debate, but they had little to do with Christianity. He had caught
me. I did not believe his words. Plainly said, Christianity is not a
yarn to be recited and agreed to. The Christian faith is a way of
relating to God and to one another. Jesus' presence transforms how
we act together.

When we seek to reduce the Christian faith to a complete and
final set of speakable doctrines, we work in vain. The speaking of
God in Jesus teaches me that the words of God are not a message to
affirm but a new, transforming way of entering into life. The doctrines of the church are for instruction. They are always changing.

They express what the relationships of faith mean, but the doctrines cannot be "substitutes" for the relationships. The speaking of God enables us to see that Christianity is not a set of beliefs to be adopted but a person to be followed. For the disciples, Jesus' life with them was more important than what he taught them. The words of Jesus gain validity through his presence as the Word of God. For the Christian, all other words about God and from God become subordinate to meeting Jesus as the Word of God.

Speaking as Incarnation

In Jesus, God becomes flesh. The notion that God would send a deliverer was not itself strange. The notion of God coming to the rescue of the people of Israel was deeply rooted in Jewish consciousness. The Old Testament recounts the acts of God where the Israelites were brought out of Egypt, delivered from the oppression of Babylon, and rescued from flood and famine. The Jewish expectation of the Messiah was that this "Prince of Peace" and "Suffering Servant" would be something other than Jesus. This "Coming One" was larger than life. He might appear as a person, but he would certainly not be one of our kind. He would be a "mighty king," searing the pages of history, righting the wrongs, and overthrowing the domination of evil rulers.

The Christian idea of the Incarnation belongs to this Jewish tradition of God's suffering servant but places a more radical emphasis upon God's presence in flesh. The idea of the Incarnation is not that God appears as a person. God became a person and lived with us with all the humiliations of being our kind.

Above all else, the Incarnation resolutely affirms the centrality of humankind within creation. The Incarnation is God's ultimate affirmation of Adam. It conveys powerfully that we are all of God. Each of us is God incarnate. Each of us bears God's presence. We are God's words in the world. So, the historical presence of God in Jesus indicates the seriousness with which God takes our being here. Historical existence represents no unfortunate state to be endured in favor of a more "heavenly" status. Our being here reflects the will and purpose of God, meaning life should be lived as a gift of God. We are God's words in the world, and each of us is the most important word of God that some people will ever hear. You will be the clearest word from God that some person has ever met.

Speaking of Jesus as the God incarnate does not imply that Jesus somehow became the passive recipient of God's spirit. The notion of the Incarnation is far more powerful. God did not violate the human personality of Jesus or Jesus' own responsibility. Jesus emptied himself. It was within his own freedom that Jesus became servant to the will of God. God was in Christ, but not without the living struggle and the decisive commitment of Jesus himself. Jesus could have chosen not to become God's word in the world. Jesus was genuinely free. Through his freedom, he was open and obedient to the presence of God. Only thereby can we sustain the real humanity and moral responsibilities of Jesus.

If Jesus could not refuse to obey and if Jesus could not walk away from the cross or disregard the hungering multitudes, he could not be one of us. Jesus was not an apparition. Jesus lived and worked in our kind of world, and he brought before us the possibility of a new kind of earth. Jesus empowers us to create a new heaven and a new earth. Jesus lived in our history the power of this new creation. The lofty God of the heavens becomes the patient and suffering servant who embraces human existence on its harshest terms. Jesus embodies in flesh and blood the truth that the only enduring reality in the universe is unconditioned love.

This historic and specific communication of God in Jesus becomes for Christians the defining reality within their individual and personal histories. By means of this historical event, it is possible to interpret all of history. In our defining connection with Jesus, we are able to see how we can face disappointment and how we can cope with anxiety and fear. In flesh, we see God's perspective on human successes. In flesh, we see how God sees religious arrogance. In flesh, we see God's way of responding to human hurt.

The faith that Jesus embodied was lived out amidst all the traffic of ordinary life and discourse. Frequently, religion becomes sterile and largely unrelated to where we live. If we think of Jesus as God's word to us, we might think of religion as our awkward and discordant word back to God. We have developed elaborate religious systems. We have disputed fine points of doctrine and have built churches into large business enterprises. The Christian church has become a huge success. We have developed wealthy cathedrals and high-rise executive towers. Churches own radio and television stations, satellites and all. It is best that we understand that religion is mostly a human creation. It is possible for us, as it was for the churches of Jesus' era, to be very successful in our religion and continue to live in spiritual poverty.

Jesus as the speaking of God does not come among us either to undergird or to tear down our religious structures. Jesus did not come to dismantle Judaism. He did not come to start Christianity. Jesus came to live God's grace in our presence. We will sometimes have to come out of the shadows of our complex religious systems in order for God's grace to become light for our path. Our future does not lie in the success of our words to God. The future of faith rests in the powerful presence of God's word in us.

Speaking of Other Religions

Christians seem to become remarkably troubled about whether Jesus is humankind's only savior. Is Jesus God's only word? The simple answer is "Of course not." But beyond a simple answer, the issue is largely a mistaken one. There are no right answers to wrong questions. The significance of Jesus for our own confession implies no limitations on the will and the history of God. For me as a Christian, Jesus is the defining revelation. This confession that lies at the center of my faith does not require an exclusivist position whereby I should feel compelled to deny every other person's claim to know God. I can say only that, for me, Jesus is the central event of history. I cannot speak for another. I cannot but bear witness to the light by which I live. At the same time, I should muster the courage to permit the one who listens to bear witness to me of the light by which he or she lives.

Insecurity in our own beliefs is the chief culprit that causes us to need to defeat the validity of another person's affirmation in order to sustain our own. The unique place of Jesus in my own life is clear to me, but my belief should not compel others to come to make my confession. Other people cannot live for long off the flickers of light that come from my path. They must see the light and become possessed by that light as the principal event that illuminates their life. While I speak from where I stand, I must leave every person to do the same.

I have always been uneasy with the alternatives frequently posed by evangelists that either Jesus was the Son of God or he was a madman. It is generally offered by someone as a means of saying that it necessarily follows that Jesus is the Son of God. I am struck by two haunting reservations. First, our agreement to the proposition that Jesus is the Son of God is not what is meant by Christian discipleship. We do not become Christian by agreeing to any statement of belief—even the statement that Jesus is the Son of God. Second, Jesus may very well have been both the Son of God and a madman, at least as far as society might define madness.

By all measures of normality, Jesus simply did not fit. He preached radical messages and pressed the unconditioned demands of God upon people. He announced that the Kingdom of God was not of this world. It could not be established by kings and armies. In order to find God's Kingdom, he said, we should begin by looking inward. Jesus' message was powerful and disruptive. He drew crowds. He incurred hostilities from the powers that be. Jesus repeatedly called people to a complete reorientation of their life and priorities. His preaching could reasonably be represented as a kind of demonic madness.

In all of his preaching, however, he showed no signs of wishing to destroy the Jewish religion and replace it with another religion. In fact, Jesus was a Jew. He was born a Jew and remained an active and practicing Jew until his death. The problems with Judaism were very similar to the pitfalls we face in the Christian religion. They had lost sight of the meaning of their own covenant promise. They were relying more on their religion than God's promise. Their spiritual journey with Jehovah had been displaced with a complicated, fine-tuned religious order.

Christians should take great care in dismissing their Jewish forebears. It is wrong-headed. What Jesus does is to pry open the covenant promise so that God's chosen people are not an exclusive club. God's covenant promise is open to all the peoples of the earth —even a Samaritan. Religion excludes; God includes. The irony of the Christian church is that we, too, have been guilty of seeking to define God's grace by those we exclude.

Jesus did not condemn the covenant promise; neither should we. Jesus' disappointment sprang from the failure of Judaism to listen to God as a spiritual presence in their life and culture. The Christian church runs the same risk. We remain perilously close to defining ourselves more by whom we exclude than by whom we embrace. Our calling is to take up the covenant promise as God's promise for all people and, with our Jewish brothers and sisters, to become a kingdom of priests.

Our need to establish beyond all doubt that Jesus supersedes all other religious seers should astonish us. We become frightfully pre-occupied with assuring that Jesus is the "only" name by which the "Father" can be known. It reveals more doubt than conviction. Our security does not rest in assuring that Jesus is the "only" name. Our hope rests in our belief in the name. For me, Jesus is the only name that stands at the center of my faith. My responsibility is to confess my faith. I have no responsibility to undermine the faith of others. It is a destructive and immoral turn of events when the source of our passion comes principally from defending the exclusiveness of our witness.

Our faith does not require that we believe that God permits no knowledge of God except through Jesus. This notion should run counter to what we know of God. We should not ever try to limit how God can speak. God acts creatively and redemptively in the world. We should let God draw the boundaries of creation, judg-ment, and redemption. I believe that our eagerness to draw those boundaries for God is itself a judgment on us. We need to get the religious lumber out of our eyes. Insofar as our affirmations of belief require us to discount or refute the earnest belief of others, we have rested the certainty of our belief upon their error. It means that I can be right only if you are wrong. Egocentric religion is no wiser than egocentric behavior. It is fear and not faith that causes us to reject others on the basis of their religious identity.

The question remains as how we are to think about other world faiths. As followers of Jesus, how are we to regard Judaism and Islam, in particular? These faiths have many devout followers. We have made clear one obvious choice already. We can maintain that the Christian religion alone is true. All other religions are pagan, and their affirmations of God are false. This alternative is appealing precisely because it is definite and clear. It leaves no doubt about the revelation of ultimate truth. We have the truth. Others are out-side looking in. Another alternative accommodates every religious perspective by saying that all world religions are relative. Each reli-gion serves its own people and reflects the priorities of the culture in which they were born. So, we begin with two alternatives. On one hand, we have an alternative that is exclusive. On the other hand, we have an alternative that is completely relative.

In my judgment, neither of these alternatives offers a Christian foundation for relating to the other religions of the world. The arrogant assertion that all other religious affirmations are pagan confuses our viewpoint with God's. We have no basis for such absolute judgment, and our judgments are unseemly. The witness of Christian missionaries has taught us over and over again that the Christ of faith has very often been known, at least in part, as God's light has broken through more primitive religious experiences. If we are to bear witness to our own faith, we would do well to accept where others begin with us. We confess the light we have received through Jesus Christ without requiring them to abandon all religious values or spiritual insights they have ever known.

Every world religion probably reflects some limited insight into God's revelation. We have absolutely no evidence that God speaks only to us. The truth of God in Jesus is not made more authoritative, and our commitment of belief is not made more honorable because we reject the truth of every other person's claim. Leading other persons to the affirmation of a living faith in Jesus Christ is not an exorcism but a conversion. Conversion redeems and enlarges the light by which they live and offers the light of Jesus as a clear and defining word from God. Let the light stand. Our mission is not to stamp out the light by which others live. Our mission is to confess the light of God in Jesus by which we live.

Relativism offers no better alternative than an uncritical exclusiveness. In relativism, there is no place for conviction. The Christian faith and most other world religions have a place for clear and explicit conviction. In the Christian faith, that conviction is not a hardened set of religious dogma. The Christian faith is driven by a defining relationship with the speaking of God we have heard through Jesus. A relativism that has no place for religious conviction offers us no basis for relating to other world religions. Unable to affirm any truth, a person is simply left to dismiss the value of belief altogether. If all religious belief is relative, it also becomes mostly irrelevant.

I believe that a more constructive view of relating to other world religions is possible. We should reject both relativism and exclusiveness. As Christians, we can affirm that Jesus is the ultimate and normative revelation of God, without denying that God's word has ever been spoken in other tongues or through other persons who have heard and embodied God's spirit. For the Christian, Jesus Christ is the central revelation of God by which every other claim to know God is measured. In Christian witness and Christian missions it is our responsibility to live and to proclaim the Word of God by which we live. We should respect the word that another has heard and respect the person who has heard that word. The fact that Jesus is not central in other world religions does not mean that we cannot affirm the worth of those persons who confess other faiths.

In our journey of faith today, we can confess that Jesus completes and enlightens the awareness of God that has come through all other religious perspectives. Our calling is to bear witness to God's presence in Jesus and to listen to those who follow a different way. They, too, are God's children. God's speaking will lead them and us, through listening to one another, to a higher and clearer vision of God. We now only see through the clouded eyes of humanity, but all of us are seen and understood and even loved by God without condition. The ultimate reality of God's love is the revelation of God in Jesus. We receive God's word without ever closing the window on God's light.

Our affirmation of God's truth in Jesus never requires us to reject others who claim to have heard God's voice. Neither does our faith require that we accept their claim. Jesus Christ is the measure against which we place every claim to have heard God's word. In personal terms, we are called, without exception, to love all persons. Our calling is to love them, whether Christian, or Moslem, or Hindu, and whether they will ever be Christian or not. Our call to love one another has no qualifications. Love defines the manner in which we are called to relate to those who follow other faiths.

Jesus Christ is Lord. When we have confessed where we stand and opened our own community of confession to the universal love of God, we can do no other. The light of God that has been revealed in Jesus is sufficient to enlighten the darkness of every world religion and to illuminate the shadows that linger within our own religious understanding. Our confessions should be tempered by the realization that the Christian religion is not the hope of the world. We must see beyond religion, even our own. Above all else, Jesus has lived out among us the ultimate truth that our hope rests solely and ultimately in God. Human religions will fail; God's love will prevail. Religions are born of human beings. Our hope rests in God.

Chapter 15
Amazing Grace

Growing up among Baptists meant that the soulful sound of "Amazing Grace" was early on embedded into my conscious-ness. I find that every time I hear its words, its melody embraces my emotions:

> Amazing grace! How sweet the sound
> That saved a wretch like me
> I once was lost, but now am found,
> Was blind, but now I see.
>
> 'Twas grace that taught my heart to fear
> And grace my fears relieved;
> How precious did that grace appear
> The hour I first believed!
>
> 'Thro many dangers, toils, and snares
> I have already come;
> Tis grace hath bro't me safe thus far,
> And grace will lead me home.
>
> When we've been there ten thousand years;
> Bright shining as the sun,
> We've no less days to sing God's praise
> Than when we first begun.

The hymn is sung in clapboard church houses across the coun-tryside and in stately, majestic cathedrals. It finds its way into the pop charts of country and rock stars. "Amazing Grace" seems to pull at the heart strings of almost every person who listens to its compelling sounds. It is music to our ears. I have wondered why it is so. We should take nothing away from the insight hammered out of the spiritual journey of its author, John Newton. The song res-onates within us, in part, because we long for its message to be true. It goes against the grain of a frantic religious atmosphere in which we busily try to cajole God into being on our side. We long and would even weep for grace to prevail, but, just in case, we make our own religious beds and hope and pray that God will come and lie with us when we feel alone in the dark night.

When it comes to trying to get our arms around the meaning of salvation, we are pulled in different directions. We sing about grace, and, at the same time, we construct elaborate processes to win God's favor. We make up plans for people to follow, in effect, cooking up our own recipes for salvation. In contrast to the labyrinth that we call the way to salvation, the Christian gospel is purely a proclamation of grace. Grace alone bears the burden of salvation. Enough of our systems and our plans, salvation is based solely on grace.

The reality of grace has been clouded in our faith largely because of the sterile and misguided theories of atonement that have been hoisted onto us. We have been captured by the appeal of being able to explain the mechanics of salvation. We wrap our minds around the idea of salvation and make it into a theory of our own. So, if the reality of grace is to come through in all the power of its plain simplicity, we will have to tear away the theological brambles that choke out the wonder of grace. Nothing is more tangled in our religious consciousness than our theories of atonement. If we can ever find our way out of that briar patch, we may be able to gain a better view of the crucifixion. Beyond the brambles, we can stand in the holy light of God's grace.

The Treachery of the Theories of Atonement

Theories of atonement are treacherous mostly because they divert us from the power and simplicity of grace. Atonement has been a principal thread in the fabric of Christian interpretations of salvation. If we have grown up in the Christian tradition, we have become well-indoctrinated in the language of atonement. In fact, atonement and salvation virtually become synonymous.

Several theories of atonement have competed for our loyalty. There was the view known as the "ransom theory." It was based upon a comment in the Gospel of Mark: "For the Son of Man came not to be served but to serve, and to give his life a ransom for many" (10:45). In this view, the death of Jesus is a ransom payed by God to Satan to "buy back" the people who were held captive by Satan. Since we are held in bondage by the power of our sin or the power of Satan, God acts on our behalf. In this case, one biblical word is used to explain the work of Jesus. Salvation becomes a great cosmic transaction with the principal actors being God, Jesus, and Satan. While this view takes very seriously the sense that we are trapped by our sin and depicts God's aggressive concern to help people in this tragic state, it also offers an unworthy view of God bargaining with Satan. This entire process seems to picture salvation as an abstract event in which the persons affected by the drama are largely unengaged with God.

Much of the same problem persists with the "satisfaction theory of atonement." Dating from the Middle Ages, this understanding of atonement is anchored by the belief that sin, above all else, violates the honor of God. Human sin deserves infinite punishment because it is sin against an infinite God whose honor is at stake. This notion of atonement suited up in the clothing of honor has all the ring of a Middle Age feudal culture. God's honor must be satisfied, and only Christ who is without sin and who deserves no punishment could satisfy the honor of God. Jesus accepts sin's penalty, and the dishonor of human sin is satisfied. Again, people are hardly involved. Atonement is an abstract transaction to satisfy God and put the universe back in order.

Closer to our own era, we have become far more consumed by what is known as the "substitutionary theory of atonement." It's simple. If you don't believe it, you are not a Christian. In fact, this doctrine is cited as one of the five beliefs that fundamentalism requires in order to meet its criteria of being Christian. In this analysis, the focus shifts from satisfying the honor of God to meeting the penalties for sin. Sin brings death. Jesus serves as our "substitute" in paying the mortal penalties for sin. Assuming our guilt, Jesus accepts a punishment that he does not deserve. He is a stand-in for us in taking on sin's dreadful consequences.

This notion of substitutionary atonement leaves us with the irony that God's chief concern seems to be to keep the books balanced. Over against one side of the ledger that records our sin must be another side that says the penalties have been paid. The books must be balanced. This theory, again, gives us a picture of God that looks more like a judgmental tyrant. It winds up making God responsible for Jesus' death. God is a God who must get even. Sounds a lot like the way we do business. It has the idea of reconciliation working the wrong direction.

The presence of Jesus is not an event that reconciles God to people. God does not sulk, waiting to be coaxed into loving people again. It is not God who needs to be reconciled. Reconciliation is born of God coming to us. Atonement is not something God has done for us in the sense that God has made Jesus take our place so that the books would be balanced. Atonement is something God does within us. The "substitution" is not an abstract act of making sure all the debts are paid. The "substitution," if we are to use that word, must be done in our own lives. We must "drink of his cup" and be "baptized with his baptism." Jesus does not come to pay off the heavy penalties for our sin. Jesus' word is that God loves us in spite of our sin. God's grace is unfettered.

The Death of Jesus

If we are to recover the power of grace in the meaning of salvation, we must come to grips with the meaning of Jesus' death. The crucifixion remains today the dominant image for our faith. In truth, however, we have celebrated the cross for so long and held this event so high in our interpretations of faith that we lose our capacity to see how awful the crucifixion really was. Look at what people did. We can only be shocked and dismayed. The death of Jesus was betrayal and rejection. People murdered Jesus.

On the human scene, we can only look at the cross as pure tragedy. Jesus did not have to die. The decision of the local government and the crowd wanting blood was grotesque and ugly. It shows us how far people will go when they are afraid. The cross demonstrates the distorted priorities that overtake both our political and religious lives. The goal is to win. Our political and religious positions must prevail—at any cost. The end justifies the means. In the crucifixion of Jesus, we see ourselves and our culture mirrored in the fear and the blindness, the malice, and the deceit that took hold of ordinary citizens.

Through this tragic decision, the cross sets before us people's relentless effort to make everything right on their own. No one was required to betray Jesus. No one was forced to hang him from a tree. Look at the human situation in which these people felt caught. It sounds familiar. Good people, the upstanding respected community leaders, the "best" people in town were trying to protect the society they loved. Jesus was confusing everyone. He was upsetting established traditions, even speaking to Samaritans as equals. Something had to be done. Crowds were beginning to follow him. People were terribly uneasy. They could see their orderly world coming apart. Someone had to do something.

Jesus was disrupting the entire religious and social order of things. He was calling people to new and revolutionary priorities. He was challenging the most deeply held religious traditions, and people were beginning to be diverted from the true and faithful way. Those persons who acted to nail him between two thieves were not really interested in "hurting anyone." They were simply frightened. They were gravely concerned to protect their church and society. Crucifixion seemed the only sure way. Let's be rid of our problem.

While the cross makes clear the values and priorities of a scared community, it also reveals the heart of Jesus' life. The actions of the scared run up against the power of the sacred. Jesus was more than a mere victim of circumstances. Jesus chose to die rather than to repudiate his calling to love unconditionally. You can hear it when he said in the very midst of this incredibly painful death, "God, forgive them." He was saying, "God, don't hold this against them. They are doing the best they can." That's the power of the sacred. Or, in response to Peter who took up a sword against the arresting officers, Jesus lived out the command to love our enemies. He said, "Peter, do them no injury. These people, too, are friends of God." That's the power of the sacred. In his death, we see love in theory being put into practice in the worst of conditions. We see how far God's kind of love will go.

I believe that we can understand the cross only if we are willing to see that Jesus did not die to appease an angry God. Jesus did not die to satisfy some abstract penalty for sin. God is not a bookkeeper. Jesus died because people chose to kill him. The truth that redeems is this: Jesus accepted even death with all of its pain, rather than renounce the power and presence of love as the ultimate reality and meaning of life. Jesus did not seek death. His death was not a passion play. Jesus with anguish and grief accepted death. Jesus died at the hands of what we might regard as the worst of people, because Jesus was able to see them as good. Jesus could see even in these people the face of God. Our faith does not affirm that God loves us because Jesus died for us. Our confession is that Jesus died because God loves us, and Jesus could see people the way God sees them.

We can admire the cross, be inspired by it, and build theories of salvation around it. The death of Jesus, however, becomes "atoning" when it becomes a power in our own being. There lies the meaning of being "crucified with Christ." In Jesus, God has done something of ultimate significance. In Jesus, we are able to see God. In Jesus, God lives love among us. There are no limits on that love. It is unconditional. Living the salvation life means taking on the character of Christ.

The problem with all of our theories of atonement is that they have isolated the death of Jesus as the saving act of God. It is a serious and unfortunate error. The cross is not the central or final revelation of God. In Jesus' death, we are able to see, in flesh and blood, the unqualified and irrevocable character of God's forgiveness. We also see the depth of human fear and our human efforts to fix the problem. Without the resurrection, the cross would only be a testimony to the futility of love and forgiveness.

The resurrection is the real victory over the cross. Without the resurrection, the final word would have been tragedy. The resurrection completes the revelation of God in Jesus' life and death. The truth speaks out of the shadows. The tragedy becomes comedy. Life overcomes death. Light overcomes darkness. God's love prevails.

Grace, the Only Word that Matters

Jesus embodies God's word. The meaning of salvation begins and ends with the wonder of grace. Sing it again: "Amazing Grace." The simplicity of grace is disconcerting. So, we make up these elaborate schemes to enable God to accept us. They turn out to be empty, clanging buckets of nonsense. Grace makes all our religious theories unnecessary and undermines our neat and complex human plans for salvation. Grace is a resounding "no" to all religious and moral systems as providers of human hope.

Jesus did not come to tell us how to be saved. Jesus came to tell us that we are saved. Jesus came to tell us that we live in the arms of God's grace. The message of Jesus is not a new religion to be adopted. Jesus lives before our very eyes the astonishing truth of God's unconditional love and acceptance. "Grace and truth came through Jesus," the Gospel writer John said. The Christian faith is solely about the power, presence, and reality of grace. The Christian religion never saved anyone nor gave anyone life. The Christian religion should not be confused as the hope of the world. Our faith centers on grace. It was grace and truth that came through Jesus.

That God would come to us in such a modest fashion seems naive. To compensate for such an unlikely story, we have put together our own religious complexities so that we can interpret salvation. The simplicity of the gospel is too absurd. We work at making God's truth more palatable. We prefer to earn our way. The affirmations of sheer, unfettered grace seem foreign and even unjust. We want God to care about us, but surely that does not mean that God has to care about some of these rascals who make life so difficult. All explanations of grace and all efforts to hedge the power of grace confuse the meaning of grace. Jesus did not come to explain God's grace. Jesus embodies God's grace.

Our Christian confession seems too plain. Nevertheless, in its plainness, we confess: Grace is the basis, the sole basis of salvation. Any conditions, religious or moral, that preempt the priority of grace distort the radical simplicity of the Christian gospel. The church is not the basis of salvation. Repentance is not the basis of salvation. The good life is not the basis of salvation. Accepting Jesus is not the basis of salvation. Jesus came to say that we are saved. We are forgiven. God's forgiveness lies within us. We are loved. God's embracing love lies buried within us underneath a load of guilt and fear. No conditions, no prerequisites, no plans to follow—grace is not a conditional affirmation. Grace is the center and soul of the Christian faith. Without grace, the gospel is empty. Grace is the gospel. Grace is the Christian good news. Indeed, it is the only good news that ultimately matters. If we miss the centrality of grace, we have missed the heart and soul of the Christian faith.

Grace flows from the reality of God. Forgiveness and love are God's enduring nature. Grace is not the way we typically behave. Our relationships are generally based on reciprocity. Our mercy carries conditions. We forgive when a person apologizes. We rescue when someone calls for help. We respect people who respect us. We love when we are loved. We like to grant mercy on the basis of good behavior. We are inclined to define our religion in the same way.

The ultimate reality of God's grace means that love and forgiveness are not simply attributes appended to God's nature. Grace means that God is with us and will never abandon us. We should not think that grace denies or gently overlooks our inhumanity to one another. The human tragedies and deep scars of human suffering burden us. Grace means that God moves into this twisted human situation and becomes our only ultimate resource for overcoming the power of evil and suffering. Grace points us to God's hovering presence over the natural and personal chaos. God is beside us, changing and creating order, turning night into day. The essence of grace is that God's love and affirmation endure beyond all our sin and trouble.

For our part, violence rages in the streets. Senseless killings and brutal abuse tear through our human relationships. We double-lock our doors and set alarms to warn us that another person may be intruding. Our lives are governed by "dis-ease" and anxiety. We abandon each other for fear of being hurt. Even when we are wrong, even when we act with violence toward one another, God remains near to us. God's grace never abandons us. God waits to redeem us.

God's remaining near to us means that grace is unconditionally unilateral. Grace is who God is. Salvation is God's act, not ours. When theologians speak of "God's elect," they are underscoring that grace comes solely as the unmerited act of God. We do not do something to earn God's grace. The chief problem with all our doctrines of election springs from our effort to define whom God has elected. Just to make our doctrines complete, we create a "theology of the damned" to go along with a "theology of the saved." God's grace is not capricious. The idea of election should not be stretched in this way. The idea of the "elect" bears witness to the reality of God's commitment to people. Adam may try to plant his own crops, but God stays in the field with him.

Emil Brunner described Jesus as "the grace of God in person." In Jesus, the grace of God takes on human character, and we are able to see how God's grace lives and behaves in the ambiguities of ordinary history. The issue of salvation is whether we choose to live in the light of God's grace. By failing to do so, we do not affect the ultimate character of God's being. God is grace. God relates to you and to me as grace, like the prodigal son's loving father. God acts toward us with love that is unilateral and unqualified. God's grace is the gospel in all of its purity and simplicity.

God's grace never coerces. That would not be the way of grace. God's love and forgiveness are not conditioned on whether we live and walk and decide in the light of that grace. Even though we are children of God's grace, we may choose to live in the unreality of our pretentious self-sufficiency.

Choosing to live in the light of grace is what we mean by the act of faith. The Letter to the Ephesians is explicit: "By grace you have been saved through faith." Faith means living in the light of God's grace. Faith enables us to live as though God's grace is ultimate and real. Faith means the acceptance of God's acceptance.

Salvation is solely and completely the act of God. Our experience of salvation is another matter. Believing requires courage. For Jesus, it took great courage to say, "Not my will, but thine be done." It always requires courage to live in the light of God's ultimate love. In our experience of salvation, God's grace becomes personally central in the living of our lives. Experiencing salvation means that we hear the word that God embraces us, and God's embrace becomes the transforming power of our lives.

Our experience of salvation is the ultimate wonder of grace. Grace gives us the courage to receive grace. Grace means that we matter. It does not mean that God is going to be with us if we do right. Grace, amazing grace, means that God is with us, no matter what. Grace means that we can quit being afraid. People are terribly hateful to each other mostly because they feel threatened. When people are afraid, they either flee or they fight. They fight with words, sometimes with guns. Neither the piercing assault of words nor the brutality of bullets will ever match the power of grace to overcome hatred and fear. Bullets will not do it. Hateful words will not do it. Bitterness will not do it. Only grace will set us free to love, even when we are not loved in return.

Grace, God's grace, gives us the power to behave differently. The law gives us instruction along the way. On most interstate highways, the paved shoulders have grooves or ridges to warn us when we drift out of the traffic lane. Rules and laws are something like those grooves. The law helps us stay on track toward our destination, but the law will not make us better people. We should tuck this truth away. Only grace—not rules or regulations or laws—grace alone, will make us better people.

Grace means that God believes in the people who were created to tend the earth. Our actual lives, like Adam, are constituted by a series of victories and defeats. It is easy to begin to define our lives by the defeats. When we do, we fall into a descending spiral of depression, trying to climb out, trying to be somebody, trying to believe in God even when things are really tough. God's word of grace begins at another place altogether. The real hope of grace is not that we manage to maintain our belief in God. The real and enduring hope of grace is that God believes in us.

So, the word of grace, amazing grace, is that God is not far away from us. God is not hidden behind the walls of temples and synagogues. God is not hidden away in cathedrals and churches. God is here with us—in the kitchen, in the boardroom, at the teller's window, at the corner grocery. We can meet God in the eyes of our friends—and our enemies. God is not distant. Grace means that God is here with us. God receives us and accepts us as we are—no conditions, no plans of salvation to figure out, no doctrines to adopt. The call to salvation is the call to hear the simple call of grace. Be at peace, God is by our side.

Chapter 16
Images of Salvation

Scarcely any of us are thinking much about salvation in the heat of the race. Making a living? Yes. Getting along? Yes. Getting saved? No. Each day life in our world seems to be punctuated with some startling, unforeseeable trauma. A passenger train leaves the tracks in the Arizona desert. We wonder why. An entire office building is bombed, killing employees, children, and visitors who just happen to be there. The tragedy is numbing. Our daily discourse is consumed by running to get ahead and then having to make sense of the senseless. Salvation does not cross our mind.

This matter of salvation can burn into our consciousness when we hear a stirring sermon or be caught up in a moving religious service. In Birmingham where I grew up, it seemed that every evangelistic road show made a stop there. It usually produced a good count of "money raised" and "souls saved." In our town, religious passions ran hot like molten steel in an open hearth. As a youngster, I remember going with a friend to one of those large evangelistic meetings. The coliseum was packed with thousands of people. On stage, this large, garish-looking preacher walked about preaching, Bible flopping open as he pointed to text that none of us could see. He raised his arms, stirring the crowd into a frenzy of emotion. For more than an hour, he preached and sweated us into submission. When the invitation came, the border of the stage was packed with people wanting some relief from the conviction that God was going to get even for their sin. This was big-time evangelism—color and lights and tongues of fire. Before it was over, salvation was on everybody's mind.

As a younger lad, I spent every summer with grandparents who made their living the old-fashioned way. They plowed the earth and "put up" food for the winter. Shiloh Church was a part of their life's ritual. The revival services in that rural church were nothing like the festive, colorful, loud sounds of a "citified" evangelist. In that rural setting, every year usually just before harvest, a visiting preacher would come to Shiloh. He would visit the prominent sinners during the day and round them up to attend evening preaching. Preaching was long. Funeral fans kept cadence with the rhythms of the preacher's warnings. The success of the revival would be measured by the number of people who "walked the aisle" to accept Jesus. It was apparent even to this young boy that a "good" revival sermon meant instilling a piercing sense of sin in order to create a weighty need to be saved.

The preacher had to get their attention because salvation was not on their mind. My grandparents were worried about rain for the crops amidst the August dry spell. They were concerned about fixing the pasture fence to keep the cows out of the corn. They were busy gathering vegetables and peeling fruit, putting them up for the cold winter. They were worried about beetles and blight and boll weevils, about bruises and breaks, about pain and disease that would hinder the harvest.

Only our preoccupations have changed. Today, you and I worry about cancer. We are consumed with succeeding in our jobs. We are anxious about house payments and whether the car will last until it is paid for. We wrestle with unhappy marriages, careers that get cut short by downsizing, and children who dust our values from their feet. Concerns about salvation, much less "getting to heaven," are placed aside for more immediate pains.

Aside from the cares of this world, we are also immobilized by recurrences of depression and anger. Frustration and feelings of inferiority lurch upon us. In the face of discontent, we submerge ourselves in busyness. We run to one more sale at Belk's, purchase one more thing in the hope that the good feeling will last. Concerns about religion remain at a distance. I do not need to understand salvation. Salvation is too heavy to think about. I need someone to hold me. I need someone to walk with me when I am alone. I need some relief from anger, and I need to find my way back from depression. I need time for the bruises and blisters to heal.

Evangelism usually is too full of talk. It aims to frighten and manipulate. It adds one more burden to an already overburdened life. For too long, we have proposed salvation as an artificial solution to artificial problems. If we listen closely to Jesus, we will always find him meeting people where they are. Jesus met people in their real troubles—people who were blind, people who were confused, people who were hungry, people who were grieving because their brother died. Jesus met people when they were scared to death in the middle of a stormy sea. The Christian word of hope is not that we should forget our troubles and turn our attention to God and "getting saved." God's word of grace comes to us in the honest and broken condition where we live.

Salvation as Healing

Salvation comes from a word that means "to heal." We do not need to be healed from some artificial, concocted hurt. If we want to understand salvation, we have to look at where and how we actually hurt. Salvation is not a healing for abstract brokenness. Salvation is a healing for the hurt that I experience in my own life. Salvation means mending what is broken and reconciling what has been estranged. Salvation is healing for our hurt.

Our experience of salvation, then, is related directly to how we experience the trauma of the human condition. Where the sin of life leaves scars of guilt, salvation means forgiveness. Hearing about forgiveness won't help much. Salvation means experiencing forgiveness. If the trauma of life is known as loneliness and isolation, salvation will only be the recovery of authentic relationships and genuine community. If the pain of life is felt in terms of being trapped and used, salvation can only be experienced as freedom, finding the light of self-worth and God's esteem.

Salvation, I mean to say, is not a well-honed theological concept, unrelated to where we live. Our experience with God connects to our experience without God. Our efforts to live without taking our connection to God into account finds specific manifestations in our lives. The meaning of salvation begins to make sense when it is related to the misery and wounds that tear at our souls. Grace for the prodigal son was not a theory. It was a waiting father who embraced him without conditions. Grace for the Samaritan woman at the well was springs of living water that would satisfy her deeper thirst. Salvation for the woman taken in adultery was stones falling from hostile hands and a chance to start over again.

Salvation takes on life and energy in the healing of the actual wounds that cripple. The images of salvation gain their intensity and power from their relevance to the real problems that paralyze us. Salvation is healing. For the blind, healing is sight. For the hungry, healing is food. Healing for the lonely is companionship.

Healing for depression is a listening presence. Salvation comes to life as God's grace makes a difference in coping with our hurt.

Salvation as Reconciliation

If all real living is relating, salvation enables us to step beyond our broken and bruised relationships. The closest relationship that causes us pain is with ourselves. The injuries we impose upon ourselves are staggering, and much of brutality toward others grows in the field of self-hatred. In psychology, a person who inflicts self-pain is said to be a "masochist." A masochist is a person who seems to have a taste for suffering and takes on suffering in some effort to purify his or her soul. The opposing problem is called narcissism. Narcissism is the habit of focusing only on one's self, making one's self the center of attention and devotion. Both forms of dealing with ourselves are destructive, and, at their heart, they are one and the same. The act of self-criticism, dwelling upon our own failures, is another face of unhealthy self-love. It is a lonely effort to cure our own problems, to burn the dross within our own soul.

I recall reading the minutes of an old church. It was the practice there that sinners would come to the altar, confessing their sins not only before God but before everybody present. Some names recurred. It was if certain persons sought favor with God by whipping themselves with public self-humiliation. The only avenue to self-respect was a convincing demonstration of self-disrespect.

Self-rejection and self-love are kindred spirits. In both, we are trying to recover our sense of worth. It is the sin of failing to see ourselves as God's creation. Self-hatred and obsessive love of self are ways of trying to create life on our own terms. We seek either to diminish or to build ourselves up as a way of securing the approval of others and even the approval of God. Meting out punishment upon ourselves is meant to cleanse our souls and make us acceptable to God. Self-centered devotion is the loneliest state of all. We cannot risk meeting or connecting with another. In order to avoid that level of openness, we arrogantly display our independence and pretentious self-reliance.

Salvation from self-centered devotion and self-rejection means risking ourselves to God's affirmation. Adam did not want to take that risk. He preferred to make his own way. Each of us has a personal story. Our being here has dimensions that belong to no one else. Tucked away behind the public stories we tell of ourselves, reside the incidents that make us cringe. Grace, the grace that is the reality of salvation, enables us to accept ourselves as children of God, despite the meanness that has been spawned from within us. Both harsh self-rejection and shallow self-love are deeply destructive. Salvation takes its first steps with our belief in ourselves that grows from the conviction that God loves us even before we have learned to live with courage and self-respect.

The burdens of sin also corrupt our life together. Our violence toward one another takes so many forms. We cannot even speak of holocaust. We can only drop our heads in despair. The slaughter at Srebreneza staggers our imagination as we watch humankind kill their own kind under the flag of "ethnic cleansing." Most of our violence is not so graphic or so staggering. It is violence nonetheless. We undermine the spirit of another. We are too busy talking to listen. We are too preoccupied with hawking our own achievements to be sensitive to the pain of another—especially if the other person is powerless.

Let us hear the truth of the gospel. God is not mostly present in the people we love. God is mostly present in the people we despise and ignore. Leo Tolstoy was right. We are far too busy in our trades and religious frenzy for us to see Jesus at our door. Whether it is global warfare in the Middle East or personal prejudice toward a gay Christian, every act of rejection is an act against God.

Grace, God's word of salvation to us, dismantles our structures of abuse. Grace calls to us of our interdependence. In the reality of things, our lives are intimately bound together. I cannot be whole apart from you. We are our brother's keeper because we are our brother's brother. The experience of salvation reconciles our fragmented and frayed relationships. Becoming church, the experience of genuine togetherness that replaces judgment with unconditional acceptance, represents the power and presence of grace among us. Our spiritual journey is never a solitary journey. Meeting one another, spirit to spirit, embodies the power of salvation.

Grace, God's word of salvation, means that God holds onto us even while we reject God's presence. God walks in the garden even while Adam is hiding. We belong to God. God lives deep within us. We may live as if God is not present. We may ignore the spiritual character of our being here and live as though God is not relevant to our lives. It is sin. Salvation means the recentering of our lives. God's presence within us becomes the defining reference point of our lives. We do not always live unto God. Salvation means that, even when we fail, God's grace sustains.

Recovering Old Images

Three prominent biblical images have dominated much of our pulpit talk about salvation. They are redemption, justification, and sanctification. Good words have a way of growing stale and musty. The only way to nurse them back to health is to bring them out into the sunshine. We have to let them breathe new life by taking a look at what they mean for our time.

Redemption. Redemption is not a word we use much anymore, unless we are talking about coupons or savings bonds. In its origins, it was not a weighty, distant word. It was quite specific and concrete, referring to the practice of "buying back" something that had been purchased or taken. In the case of a person held in slavery, it meant setting that person free. Exile, slavery, apartheid, racial segregation, and sex discrimination are sins for which the idea of redemption begins to make sense. Wherever people are treated like possessions or excluded from a club because of race or gender, the sin for which redemption is God's answer becomes clearer.

Grace, God's word of salvation, breaks down barriers of race and sex. We cannot dwell in the light of salvation and discriminate by gender. In Christ, there is no male or female. Control and discrimination are oppressive. The oppression of control and prejudice crushes the spirit of the oppressed. But oppression, in whatever clothing, also crushes the spirit of those who oppress. They, too, are trapped by the cycle of sin and evil.

The word of redemption is that God has taken on the whole debt, the debt of those who are oppressed and those who oppress. Controlling and abusing people are really the price people pay to make themselves strong enough, or right enough, or powerful enough, or enough-in-charge to warrant and demand ultimate respect and acceptance. It is the way humankind has ordered life outside the garden. It is a way of life that destroys and kills. In the ravages of war and discrimination, there are no victors. Everyone loses. The human way, outside Eden, destroys and maims in the name of establishing our way as the way things ought to be. We become trapped, chained, by the cycle of evil self-indulgence.

Redemption is God's word of grace in our human situations. God has set us free. When we let ourselves begin to hear that God has set us free, the chains of fear and control that have us trapped begin to corrode. Physical chains are never any match for spiritual freedom. The captivity of prison was no match for the freedom of Paul. The freedom of Nelson Mandela in a South African prison empowered the freedom of Mandela beyond the walls of prison. Redemption suddenly begins to make sense again when we face squarely into the walls that imprison us. We could be well-described as the "trapped generation." Everywhere people appear to be free, while they are trapped by their guilt, trapped by their greed, and trapped by the trying to gain more leverage through discrimination and abuse.

God's word of grace is that we are free. The announcement comes. Jesus himself is the announcement. Everyone who has lived in this awful state of being trapped has been set free. "Christ has set us free." At first, it seems unreal. We mostly continue to work and live as we have in the past. The experience of redemption means letting the power of God's grace take hold of our lives. You and I are not owned or possessed by any other person. We are God's children, and God receives us without conditions of race or gender or status. If we follow Jesus, that is to say, we take on Christ, our own chains begin to break away. They can no longer contain us. And there is more. This new freedom causes us to cast off the chains by which we keep other people, especially different people, in their place. The Word of God is this:

> As many of you as were baptized into Christ have clothed your-selves with Christ. There is no longer Jew or Greek, there is no longer slave or free, there is no longer male and female; for all of you are one in Christ Jesus. (Gal 3:27-28)

Redemption represents a different turn of events. We typically measure the world by who controls whom. The gospel offers a different measure altogether. The fulfillment of life cannot be found in controlling or being controlled. Grace sets us free. The shackles begin to fall away. With our new freedom, we are empowered to love.

Justification. A second image to be reclaimed is the idea of justification. Justification is used more frequently than redemption in
ordinary conversation. We are sometimes asked to justify a decision
or an action. We hear people speak of "justifying the margin" of a
letter or manuscript. A justified margin is one that is straight along
the edge such as the text on the pages of this book. Justification,
then, means to make things straight or to set things right. When
asked to "justify a decision," we are being asked to set it right, to
show how it was the right thing to do.

Sin can be described as a condition in which our lives are bent
out of shape. Sin twists and distorts. Sin corrupts our standing in
the world. Our lives get crooked and bent. To people who live
according to sin, the apostle Paul would say, "The just shall live by
faith." That Pauline statement set the soul of Martin Luther afire.
He could not stand still. Here in a religious tradition where people
had to buy indulgences and endure self-inflicted hardships to win
God's mercy, this light from God startled Luther into a transforming realization. A person can do nothing to secure justification. Not
by penance or indulgence can any person straighten out the edges
of their life. The "setting-right" with God is accomplished solely by
God's grace, and it comes to us by faith.

Justification is an act of grace. Our being made just or upright
will not be of our own doing. We will not be able to get the edges of
our life straight so that God will come over to our side. This word
from God goes exactly contrary to our way of making the world
work. We admire and salute people who pull themselves up by their
bootstraps. In the end, however, even they are exhausted and beaten.
The gospel does not admonish us to walk upright and thereby know
the power of salvation. To the contrary, the gospel is that God treats
us as upright, and the grace of God's treating us as upright gives us
the strength to begin to walk upright. It is a long journey. God's
respect for us is not based upon our respectability. Sin means that
our lives are crooked. We live in the land of wandering. It is not our
home. We lie and cheat. We indulge our senses. The truth is that we
cannot twist or cheat our way to straight edges and upright living.

The gospel does not begin with God saying to us, "Get it right,"
or "Justify yourself." Those are our sounds. We say to our misbe-
having children, "Well, what do you have to say for yourself." It is

our way of saying, justify yourself and you will be permitted back into my good graces. God's way is different. Jesus offered a different word that has a strange sound. Grace comes unencumbered. It is grace upon grace. God receives us as upright even while we are bent over with grief and despair. We are saved by grace. God embraces us, loves us as though we were just, in spite of our injustice. The act of faith, to which Paul referred, is the experience of accepting God's vision of us. That vision becomes the power and substance of a new vision of ourselves. That new vision enables us to do justice and to love mercy, to begin to behave as children of light instead of children of darkness.

Sanctification. The final image to be reclaimed is the notion of sanctification. Sanctification is the word that Christians have used historically to name the actual process by which God's grace and the power of God's presence become a force in our actual living from day to day. Following Jesus makes a difference in who we are and how we behave. Its implications flow from the inside out. Regaining our spiritual bearings changes the shape of our temporal decisions.

My son, Hunter, lives in Honduras. There he brings physicians and other health care professionals into remote villages of the back country who are cut off from health care that is a normal part of our lives. On one of his journeys, I went along with him into the dense rain forest area. In that dark and damp spot where we settled in for a few days, I was struck with the sounds, "Sanctus, Sanctus, Sanctus"—Holy, Holy, Holy.

Holiness is God being beside us in a remote forest or an urban street crowded with people and buildings gaping into the clouds. Sanctification or holiness is where God is. God may come in the hands of a physician who relieves pain or in the voice of a farmer who teaches someone how to grow corn. Sanctification is God's grace taking hold of our behavior, enabling us to see beyond the close boundaries of our own desires. Sanctification means bringing God's spirit in person to crippled and alienated people—even in a rain forest.

The reality and unconditioned character of God's forgiveness creates a new situation in which you and I live. Things will never be the same. Taking God's spirit into account and taking seriously our own spirituality makes a difference in our choices. Every decision and every relationship is affected by the power of God's presence and God's forgiveness. The experience of salvation is the beginning of a new creation. When God enters our work and our life, our religious vocabulary calls it sanctification. More important than vocabulary, however, is the spiritual reformation of our lives. If we follow Jesus, things are never the same. The real presence of God's spirit within us remakes life itself into a sacrament—a gift of grace to be lived for love and forgiveness.

Chapter 17
Disciplines of the Heart

The most basic lesson of faith is that your life and my life should be seen as sacraments. Whether we know it or not—and we often don't—we are solemnly bound to God. Each person is created to be a gift to the world, a particular instance of grace embodied in flesh and blood. You are one of a kind. The high and defining purpose of people is to bring order, not to contribute to the chaos. Devoting ourselves to a new reality of living in the world changes unalterably how we feel, how we see each other, how we behave, and who we are. Belief sets us on a path of a new understanding of ourselves and the earth on which we live.

Viewing life as a sacrament leads us toward the disciplines of the heart. These disciplines have been lived and taught by persons such as Saint Augustine, Saint Bernard of Clairvaux, Meister Eckhart, and Saint Francis of Assisi. In recent years, we have heard the call to disciplined devotion in the voices and writings of John Woolman, Thomas Kelly, Thomas Merton, Matthew Fox, Pope John Paul II, Richard Foster, and Henry Nouwen. Throughout the history of the church, the call to spiritual depth and commitment recurs as the greatest force for renewal and strength within the church.

The vision of God is the heartbeat of faith. The vitality of our life with God cannot be secured by programs and religious activities. God is spirit, and we are spirit. Only the deep and persistent communion of spirit to spirit can become a resource for keeping faith alive. The desperate disputes among Christian denominations that shield us from the mysteries of devotion are mostly an exercise in language. The practice of faith through disciplined devotion is, above all, a quiet conversation with God. They usually occur when no one is listening in on our personal longings. Our journeys with God are never complete. Our confessions can reflect only as much breadth and depth as the discipline of our devotion.

When I speak of disciplines of the heart I am meaning to point toward people's continuing struggle to keep their lives centered. The momentum of our lives usually leads us toward being persons who are carried along with daily currents. We are trained up to live by the calendar and to live by an agenda set by others. We schedule appointments even for leisure. Our daily logs include a miscellany of endeavors that dutifully consume our time and attention. Beyond the logs and schedules, when the quiet creeps into the room, we are apt to feel empty and unconnected. Without the frenzy, we become bored. The first thing you know, we discover that our joy comes from dashing here and there, trying to meet all of the obligations that have been pressed upon them. After all, that is where we live: professional lives, corporate lives, social lives, religious lives, political lives, family lives. We are lovers, parents, friends, employers, employees, church members, voters. The competing demands tear at us. Each vested interest for our time and attention jealously protects its interests.

If a person's relationship with Christ is described as a centering act, the disciplines of the heart refers to the process of tuning ourselves to that vital center. For Jesus' disciples and for us, following Jesus can shed light and give purpose to our everyday experience. The initial response of a person to the light of Christ is joy and worship. In the traffic of living, however, the complexities of religious and social activities cause us to lose sight of the light that, at first, lifted our spirits. We become focused on our careers. We become consumed by meeting the expectations that are heaped upon us. Our commitment to follow Jesus is obscured by the more insistent calls of the moment.

The discipline of devotion translates abstract worship of God into concrete discipleship. In his little book called *A Testament of Devotion*, Thomas Kelly describes the centering of our lives in this way: "Deep within us all there is an amazing inner sanctuary of the soul, a holy place, a Divine Center, a speaking voice, to which we may continuously return." The presence of the "inner light" or the "light within" uses the metaphor of light to speak of the influencing presence of Christ in our experience. The Christian faith does not rest upon a cold and disinterested affirmation of belief in Jesus. The call of the Christian faith to us is far more compelling. The Christian faith offers new light by which to find our way. The life of devotion offers us a resting place for our fractured and weary lives. In Christ, we learn what our being here is all about. The Christian faith calls us to center our lives "in Christ" and for the "mind of Christ to be in us." The Christian faith does not call us to some abstract acceptance of Jesus. Our faith brings us into holy communion with God as we set out on the pathway of following Jesus.

The practice of our faith through disciplined devotion cultivates within us the ability to listen for God's presence within us. That discipline will never be easy. We are accustomed to and more comfortable in our busyness. The discipline of devotion will require of us what feels like uncomfortable silence. In order to nurture the disciplines of the heart, we must be willing to take the awkward inward journey. That journey will require the courage to be silent. Only on that journey will we learn to hear the persuasions of God's voice. Disciplined devotion will teach us that we do not become certain of God's presence from our books and sermons. The surety of God's presence emerges from the intimacy of our own inward and personal experience of God.

A deepening sense of devotion also teaches us that the convictions of faith do not flow from getting our doctrines straight. Genuine convictions flow from the inward experience of God. The Christian's faith draws him or her aside from the daily preoccupations to find God's presence deep within. When we turn within, we will learn that the spirit of Christ is not far away in distant centuries gone by or lost in the remote heavens. Christ is in us. Returning to the center means finding the spirit of Christ deep within us. Christ's spirit will sustain our spirit. It will foster within us hope and encouragement.

Holy Obedience

Among the richest images of the inward commitment of the life of belief is the recurring theme of holy obedience. Being obedient, especially in the Old Testament, means hearing God—listening for the Holy. Connecting holiness and obedience conveys powerfully the meaning of God's grace in our lives. The essence of the meaning of salvation is God's grace taking hold of us, and God's grasp of us is the essence of holy obedience.

We have seen the Genesis picture of people hiding from God in the garden, as if being out of sight achieves independence. In human experience, we try to communicate strength by demonstrating that we don't need anyone. In our faith, the alternative to independence is not dependence but holy obedience. Assertions of independence ultimately crumble under their own weight. Holy obedience, on the other hand, looks to the affirmation of the Holy within us as the source of strength and enduring meaning.

Independence pretends that we always can provide for ourselves. Holy obedience trusts that sometimes only God can provide. Holy obedience teaches us to see life as a sacrament. Adam's claim to be self-sufficient left him aware of his nakedness. Clothing was not the issue. The issue, for Adam and for us, is vulnerability. When I claim final and ultimate responsibility for my life, I take upon myself all of the risks of being here. What I am and what I do are frail products of my own being. This vulnerability to failure is a weight that can drive me into the ground. The repudiation of God as Creator leaves us victims of our own reckless order. We are not victims of God's anger. God loves us anyhow. We are victims of the wasteland of our own creation.

The pretense of ultimate self-reliance is the forerunner to despair. The tidal waves of failure beat us down. We have to achieve life and well-being by winning every battle. Even if we defeat the external forces and assert our control, we wind up being defeated by our own sense of futility. When the sun goes down, we are left with no place to hide and no place to run. Our secure place will not hold.

Holy obedience turns our life in a different direction. The notion of obedience should be rescued from the murky waters of good behavior. Obedience is not principally a virtue of action. Obedience is a virtue of being. Obedience has more to do with being than doing, more with who we are than what we do. Obedience recognizes that our being here is a holy trust.

When it comes to obedience, our first inclination is toward external sacrifices. We want to keep obedience at arm's length. Burnt offerings, first fruits, and ceremonial fasting are transformed from an outward event to an inner truth through inward obedience. Our symbols should not be discarded. The power behind the symbol should be recovered. First fruits and fasting can be powerful instruments of faith. They should be redeemed. Fasting has a way of focusing people beyond the cares of this world.

In the twelfth century, Saint Francis devoted his life to living in poverty. He cared for lepers and outcasts, reforming the Catholic Church that had grown wealthy and influential. Sister Teresa received the call to serve the poorest of the poor in 1946, and she has devoted her entire life through the Missionaries of Charity that she began. Their community of faith is built upon prayer, forgiveness, being nonjudgmental, humility, truth, and total surrender to the Word, Jesus Christ. Sister Teresa calls it the Simple Path:

> The fruit of silence is Prayer.
> The fruit of prayer is Faith.
> The fruit of faith is Love.
> The fruit of love is Service.
> The fruit of service is Peace.

Saint Francis and Sister Teresa embody, in a time past and in a time present, examples of the meaning of holy obedience. For them, as well as for you and me, the essence of holy obedience resides in the devotion of the spirit. This commitment of spirit was represented in its purest and most classic expression in Abraham's sacrifice of Isaac. In that portrayal of holy obedience, the meaning of absolute, unconditional surrender becomes evident. The message of Abraham is that even our most priceless treasures should not be viewed as possessions. Through a long and difficult journey, Abraham had come to learn that life is a gift from God. All that he had, even his fondest dream, belonged to God.

The notion that a person could cut off a slice of the economic pie and go off to enjoy it alone is foreign to our faith. Holy obedience brings us into a relationship with God that can only develop into the practice of compassion and justice. There can be no discipline of the heart without a preemptive commitment to be obedient to God's will. It is a radical obedience. God is with us, and we are God's presence to countless people. Holiness is a simple and abiding duty. This call to absolute obedience should not be understood as a call for abstract allegiance. Such an interpretation makes holy obedience more a burden than a blessing. We do not achieve obedience by means of a sterile and abstract submission to follow God's will. We obey or disobey in the face of concrete choices before us.

When I reflect upon the life of holy obedience, my mind inevitably turns to persons such as Sister Teresa or Martin Luther King,

Jr., to William Carey or Albert Schweitzer—persons whose lives of devotion and singleness of purpose have been brilliantly self-evident. I also find them intimidating. The selflessness apparent in the life of Sister Teresa causes us to sense our failure to obey God's will so purely. This focus can distort the relevance and possibility of holy obedience for us, however. What we see in that distant saint is a pattern of decisions and actions that is made up of simple and discrete acts. The call of God is not for us to become obedient in principle. God's call is for us to take God's holy presence into account in the small, discrete decisions we make. Obedience is not a burden to carry; it is a resource to claim. God's presence is a new source of insight in the situations where we live.

Obedience is not a magnificent and grandiose posture of faith. Holy obedience emerges from the simple and unnoticed acts where God's grace influences our decisions. The call to radical obedience is not a weighty dictum that holds us hostage to narrow moralistic prescriptions. God's call to obedience means that the power of grace is enabling us to become persons for whom God's forgiveness and compassion are constant forces in our behavior. Obedience is a spiritual journey. It is not made up of large, earth-shaking steps. Obedience is made up of small, even unnoticed episodes of listening for God's presence within us.

Solitude

Listening brings us to solitude. Solitude is probably our chief resource for practicing the disciplines of the heart. Solitude begins with the simple willingness to be alone with ourselves, providing ourselves the space to listen to the God within.

Especially at first, solitude makes us uneasy. Busyness is our comfort zone. We are not quite sure what to do with ourselves without appointments to keep, books to read, letters to write, and phone calls to make. If all else fails, television is there to fill the void. Solitude is that first bold step toward opening ourselves to God's spirit. Jesus said, "Go into your room and shut the door and pray to your Father who is in secret." (Matt 6:6) The irony of solitude is that before we can embrace others, we must learn to be alone with ourselves.

Being physically alone will not be enough to achieve solitude. Solitude is not so simple as having no one around. Solitude means withdrawing ourselves from the occupations and noises of our lives to listen quietly for the whisper of God. It means clearing the mind of anxieties and worries about today's problems and tomorrow's challenges. Solitude means being present to ourselves so that we can listen to the deepest recesses of our soul.

We often resist. The silence is more than we can stand. We fear that solitude will make us lonely. Solitude does not mean to be lonely. It means to be alone. Loneliness springs from the sense of being isolated. We feel lonely when we sense that no one really cares what we are thinking or feeling. Loneliness should not be defined as being alone. The tragedy of loneliness is far greater. It means feeling forsaken. Loneliness feels like rejection. It breeds resentment and bitterness within us. Rejection and resentment create a spiral of defeat and depression. Loneliness is dreadful and devastating. Loneliness does not spring just from being alone. It springs from not being together. Connecting is the hope for loneliness. Solitude is the hope of connecting. We cannot be together unless we can first learn to be with ourselves.

Children are our best teachers. They ask difficult and compelling questions. They see light and touch joy long before we temper their senses with caution and unease. As parents bring their young to be our students for a season, I urge them to trust their investment in their children. I add another word. When they bring them to college, I ask them to reach for the courage to set them free, for if they will, these children becoming persons will come home as friends.

I learned this lesson from my oldest son, Raleigh, as he went away to college. Shortly after he left, I wrote him a long letter. The letter was probably more for me than for him, helping me to cope with his aching absence. Even so, I opened my soul to speak to him about what I thought and believed regarding issues that mattered to me and that I hoped would matter to him. I spoke of him making mistakes and changing his mind. I spoke of playing and being a friend. I talked of humor and forgiveness, of faith and doubt. I reflected on the goodness of life, the meaning of wisdom. Surely, I hoped that he could feel my unhindered devotion to him. I spoke to him heart-to-heart.

In that letter, I spoke to Raleigh about solitude and loneliness and said to him, "Do not confuse solitude with loneliness.

Loneliness springs from being afraid. Solitude means to know yourself, to know your own thoughts and your own feelings." In that same letter I spoke of relating. While I may have introduced him to relating as an idea, it was Judy, his friend and then his wife, and his own children, Lee and William, who taught him the real meaning of connecting. Judy's wisdom, more than mine, has enabled him to see that the gift of solitude gives us the power to relate soul-to-soul. Solitude and relating dwell together to nurture our spirits.

In the purported dialogue between Galileo and the priest Sagredo we have this exchange:

Galileo: "I'm not a theologian; I'm a mathematician.
Sagrada: "You are a human being! Where is God in your
           system of the universe?"
Galileo: "Within ourselves. Or—nowhere."

The focus of solitude is the presence of God within. If we are to know God, we must learn to meet God within, or else our awareness of God will remain largely a matter of the head. Inwardness teaches us of the true reality of God. Learning to listen for God comes by way of discipline. Our frantic pace is not simple make-believe. We do indeed live complex lives. There are people to see, shopping to do, children to carpool, and committee meetings to attend. Solitude enables us to meet the self that is hidden from public view. We meet the self where confusion, doubt, and uncertainty reside. In our solitude, we face our own hatefulness and greed. We face our own frailty. The threshold of solitude is not an easy threshold to cross, but only in the caverns of inwardness can we come to grips with the meaning of our faith.

The Christian faith is fundamentally an affair of the heart. The meaning of Jesus' presence would be lost as mere historical fact to be understood only with the head. Jesus reveals the depth of our being. In Jesus we begin to see the significance of our own lives. We see who we essentially are and what the image of God enables us to become. The power of Jesus' life is not exterior to our life. The real power of Jesus' life is that he creates a new reality within us. The voyage of solitude also carries us to an entirely new understanding of the meaning of prayer.

Unceasing Prayer

Prayer should not be confused with speaking words. Whatever else prayer means, the call to unceasing prayer is not a call to talk. Prayer calls us to listen. To "pray always" is an admonition to listen to God as a way of entering into life. We are told that the literal translation of the Greek words "pray always" is "come to rest." Solitude and silence form the basis of authentic praying.

Authentic prayer should be thought of as a condition of living. Praying means engaging our ordinary lives with ears that are sensitive to the sacred—the sacred in others, the sacred in nature, the sacred in us. The sacred teaches us to be reverent. Reverence frees us from the trivial conversations and mindless chatter that keep our focus on the mundane and temporary. Reverence enables us to step beyond the conversations of the world, so that the real worth of the people and the earth break in upon us.

Prayer means opening ourselves to God. In that opening, we expose all of our needs and wants and uncertainties. We confess our real condition, being prepared for God to see us the way we are. We cannot pray unless we are ready for that sort of openness. Otherwise, prayer becomes one more attempt to disguise ourselves before God. It is not that we do not want to speak to God; it is that we do not want to be naked before God. Prayer simply sets us before the presence of God with all our uncertainty even about prayer itself. It takes courage to pray with this kind of candor. We would ordinarily wish to put on our best face when we approach God. Prayer winds up shattering pretense. We face God as we are.

Prayer, then, means leveling with God. It means radical honesty. We are inclined to select our words with care. We craft a prayer that will warrant God's pleasure. Prayer is more likely to happen when we have given up on praying. Instead, we have turned away, unable to speak. Silence is God's tutor.

In the posture of unceasing prayer, we are able to see the world and ourselves as God sees us. Prayer is the first step of putting things in their right order. It doesn't put things right. Prayer puts things in the right order. When we level with God, we acknowledge our own weakness. We admit our own ignorance. We confess our own fear. The acknowledgment of weakness is the beginning of strength. The admission of ignorance is the foundation of wisdom. The confession of fear is the basis of hope.

Prayer is a discipline of the heart. It means approaching our lives with a stirring sense that God's presence is deeply embedded within us. Prayer does not change how things work. Prayer doesn't fix things. Prayer changes the meaning of the events of our lives. Prayer changes our relationship to what is occurring, and the power of that change can make a radical difference in how history happens as well as what history means. Whenever our awareness of God's presence becomes a factor in our decisions and relationships, the outcome of those decisions and relationships is altered. Prayer introduces our awareness of God's presence as a creative force in ordinary history.

Let me speak of miracles. When life really gets difficult and we find ourselves in a seemingly inescapable corner, we inevitably pray. When we are at our wit's end, we crumple up in prayer. We beg for a way out. Clearly, our words are not the most important dimension of these experiences. Each of us knows what it means to feel utterly helpless. The confession of our utter helplessness may be our most genuine prayer. We do not try to frame our feelings of despair in the right words. We do not even know the right words to say. Prayer exposes our deepest hurt and opens our vulnerable heart to God. We know nowhere else to turn.

The truth is that we long for a miracle. We long for some intervention in our trouble, some escape from being cornered by difficulty. Prayer has a miraculous word to deliver to us. Escape, cure, relief are what we want. There are indeed great moments of escape and cure. These mysteries should not be discounted. Our knowledge of human affairs, not to speak of human disease, is terribly limited. Prayer changes the character and meaning of the events of our lives. God is not capricious, sometimes listening, sometimes not; sometimes merciful, sometimes not. God does not dip into history on a whim and lift the veil of trauma like an arbitrary visitor.

Prayer represents a new creative force in the episodes of our lives. That force makes a difference in how things happen and, more importantly, how we relate to what happens. Prayer engages us as subject in the heavy traumas and simple decisions that shape our histories. So, miracles defined as the arbitrary intervention of a remote God whose fancy we catch is likely to leave us disillusioned. Prayer as honest confession becomes a creative force in the world, both changing how history happens and what history means.

Prayer is not a way of manipulating a particular outcome for our history. We long for a particular outcome. We want our way to be God's way. Prayer is a way of transforming our participation in history from victim to creator. That transformation sometimes means healing. Another time it will mean facing loss and death and tragedy with the courage to endure and a measure of hope that can redeem the loss into gain. Miracle is the intervention of grace in our lives. Sometimes grace heals. Sometimes grace gives courage to accept death. Miracle is not about facts or the perception of facts. Miracle is about meaning. Unceasing prayer tunes our hearts to God's grace, and God's grace always, always changes the meaning of our lives.

Chapter 18
Thy Kingdom Come

The church is our best evidence that the Kingdom of God is more than high-sounding rhetoric contrived to comfort us in all of life's troubles. Jesus' own confession of God rarely spoke of the church. Jesus talked about the Kingdom. If we are to understand the church, we have to come to grips with the Kingdom. The church is born when a community of believers takes seriously the calling to seek the Kingdom within. The church is composed of people who pray, "Thy kingdom come."

Tertullian, an early church father, said that there is no salvation outside the church. Before we discard what he said as being too foreign to our independent and Western ways, we should open ourselves again to his wisdom. If we will listen, Tertullian will teach us that we cannot claim in any persuasive way to be people of salvation unless we are born into a community of grace.

Among the most serious challenges of Christianity is for the churches to become church. There are churches everywhere—white frame meetinghouses and stately granite cathedrals. Church bells compete for ringing the noon hour. The slow traffic of Sunday mornings swell for a little while just before eleven o'clock. We climb the steps to the sanctuary, week after week, sometimes out of habit, sometimes because it is the thing to do, even sometimes because we need some help with our living and we don't know where else to turn. Everywhere there are churches. They belong to our culture. They influence our architecture. They soften our landscape. They gather us in their bosoms to mourn our grief. They stand atop hills, beckoning us to a nobler vision of what we can become.

Taking a step toward being the church is the challenge. This step does not call upon us to dismiss our meeting places as unimportant. We always mark where we meet, if the meeting really matters. Our memories ceremonially mark where we were during momentous events. The assassination of John Kennedy, the explosion of the *Challenger*, the end of World War II—places become monuments to events that change and shape our lives. Event is the key word. Before it becomes a place, the church is an event. Every place called a church or a synagogue or a temple signals some important events that lay behind the structures. Steeples never rise out of nothing. They are anchored in some telling encounter of the spirit.

The church is a believing community where Jesus lives in our time. In the church, Jesus is not mostly a fact of history. The church is where we meet Jesus in the flesh. The church is the continuing Word of God in the world. The Word is heard sometimes from the pulpit. The Word is heard and seen more often and more powerfully in how we meet one another. The church is the only living confession of faith where the gospel takes on life and energy. It embodies the gospel in flesh and blood and brings the gospel into our neighborhoods. The church is the dwelling place of believers and is the visible reality that our faith is not centered on the past. Jesus is alive, loving and forgiving in the life and work of the church.

The Vocation of the Church

The church is called to be the people of God. That calling makes it more an event than a place. The church is what happens when people take grace seriously. Like the people who dwell within them, churches do not have a steady, even life. The churches become preoccupied with their own success and achievement. They fill up their barns, and they build bigger barns.

I think of the Reformation as a good mistake. It was good because it represented an effort to recenter the church toward its holy calling. The gospel was being dragged down by the weight of a religious culture. The sound of the gospel was muffled by doctrinal systems and religious machinations that aimed to control people's lives. The church could hardly breathe because it was covered over with an avalanche of broken ritual. The Reformation broke down the barriers of this lumbering institution, enabling people to taste the fresh air of God's word. The Reformation was also a mistake, however.

We have used the Reformation as reason enough to splinter the church into countless dwellings, each competing for the claim of being the true people of God. In effect, we have done it all over again. We have created our own versions of religious hierarchy, established our own religious orders, and developed our own complex and cooperative programs that we defend with our lives. We have lost sight of the simple power of the gospel.

Our calling is to be the church. To be the church means, above all else, to embody Jesus' presence in our time. The church traditions and petty squabbles that inhibit our freely and deliberately living out the gospel turn our efforts at being the church into a side show. It can be fun and entertaining—and distracting. The church is called to live a new reality in our time and space. The power of the church is rooted in the power of belief. Belief, not doctrine, is the power of the church. Only our belief can shape our community of faith by taking seriously the reality and presence of God's grace and forgiveness in the world.

People come together and build communities for many reasons. We cluster together upon the earth in towns and cities, rural villages and distant outposts. We make our way together. People gather for worthy and unworthy purposes. They come together for holy and unholy reasons. The church occurs when the inner reality of having been forgiven by God and the inner sense of knowing God's unconditional acceptance become our common bond. In our coming together, the church breaks into history. When the church really happens, history is always changed. People are healed. The thirsty are given water. The blind are made to see, the lame to walk. The lonely are embraced. The guilty are forgiven. The despairing find hope. The world always changes when the church occurs.

Only God's grace can create the church. The people of grace are the people of God by whatever name they may be called. In Exodus they are called a Kingdom of priests and a holy nation. In the New Testament they are called the church. We have noted that we need to be cautious about defining God's people in exclusive terms. I have watched Baptists become so intense about being Baptist that you would think God was a Baptist—if you didn't know better. When people who call themselves the people of God begin to carry their calling around like a prized possession won at the last year's carnival in town, they inevitably set themselves against other believers. Before it is over, they begin to fight one another. Genocide and fratricide are common in the ranks of faith. We will do anything to be first in line with God, even it means throwing stones at those who are climbing the mountain of faith alongside us. We cannot resist the urge to win. Startling news—the Christian gospel tells us that the only way to win is to lose.

The people of God have no special status with God. They do have a special responsibility. They are called to be people through whom God can live and speak. The church is God's speaking to the world. The people of God become the people of God when they are not only "called" but "believe" their high and inescapable responsibility to live God's will and purpose in history. They become people of the covenant. The covenant simply points to a partnership between people who believe and the God of grace who empowers us to conduct ourselves in a new light.

In both Judaism and Christianity, the foundation for the life of faith lies in the initiative of God. We do not build churches. Churches are composed by the act of God, calling people out of the ordinary, humdrum of things to represent a new reality in the world. Grace is not theoretical. Grace is not hypothetical. God's act of grace is concrete and specific. It comes into the rough and tumble of a complicated world. In this kind of world, grace calls upon us to redefine our priorities. Believing is a concrete response to a visible act of grace. God's call and our vocation occur on the real stage where decisions are specific and where our relationships have faces and names.

For the people of Israel, the concrete, historical act of God's grace lying at the center of their history was the Exodus-Sinai event. For the Christian churches, the historical act of God is the Jesus event. In both cases, the community of faith has a clear and explicit historical point of reference. God's grace is not abstract. Grace is actual and historical. The people of Israel were charged to be a "Kingdom of priests," and the followers of Jesus were charged to be "light of the world" and "salt of the earth."

What in the world does a Kingdom of priests do? They are priestly. They minister and care. They take care of the earth and everything that is in it. They are God's people. They are full of grace. They care. And what of light and salt? They enlighten and make a difference in the quality of life. They are a force against darkness and decay. The real importance of calling people priests and salt and light is achieved when they become God's concrete acts of grace in the world.

The hope of the world does not rest in somebody's preaching of hope. The hope of the world rests in the people of God embodying hope. It is one thing to tell someone not to give up hope. It is another thing altogether to become someone's hope. Jesus teaches us the truth of God. Love in person is far more powerful than love in word. Saying I love you is the easy part. Caring, being full of a grace that takes us out of our way, is our challenge and our calling.

Jesus and the Church

Jesus didn't talk a lot about the church—so far as we know. The recorded Gospels only have two references, both in Matthew. We might conclude from the meager references that Jesus was largely unconcerned with the church. That conclusion would be overdrawn, but we should not ignore its measure of truth. Jesus was clearly not concerned to establish churches. Church planting was not in Jesus' language. Insofar as the Christian church has become another organized world religion, we should know that this outcome is more a reflection of how we need to carry out our mission than the specific aim of Jesus. Jesus' focus was upon empowering people to be the church. Building churches does not make our Christian religious establishment ill-conceived. Our higher calling is to build a church among our churches. Christianity remains servant to its calling of embodying grace when it gives birth to the real church.

If the Christian religion becomes focused upon its own success, it becomes demon-possessed. God's call is clear and rigorous. The church is called to be God's people. When we get our religious kicks from celebrating our institutional achievements, we are a long way down the wrong road. In a recent, large religious convention, I watched as a parade of bright colored flags was brought into the gathering, each with a blazing, triumphant message. There were crowns and stars, music blaring, lights flashing, flags waving. The audience stood and cheered, applauding, arms waving, tears flowing. There in this one hall was the triumph of human religion in all of its glory—gold, glitter, marching off to Zion. I could not but wonder what would happen if Jesus rode in on a mule. We would be embarrassed by the intrusion, shuffling him away, mule and all. The show had to go on.

Jesus' message was contrary to all of the ambitions to which even our own faith has become subject. The point of the Christian faith is not to replace the grandeurs of the temple with the elegance of a cathedral or the pageantry of Mardi Gras. The point of the gospel is to bring God's light simply and concretely into a world where people are rejected and families are broken.

The church as the continuing presence of God's spirit in the world was deeply important to Jesus. Jesus gathered around him a group of disciples whose calling was to embody and proclaim the gospel. The relationship of the twelve apostles to Jesus and to each other reflects the heart and soul of the church. The church is a community of followers who themselves take up the responsibility for living and interpreting God's good word. The church forms a new community of persons, a new kind of people of God. Being the church should free us from the encumbrances of a religion that has grown stale and doctrinaire. We are set free to be a new holy nation. Just as God's grace entered history concretely in Jesus, the purpose of the church is to live God's grace concretely in history.

In the life and teachings of Jesus, the meaning of the church is linked closely to his message about the Kingdom of God. Even though Jesus talked a lot more about the Kingdom than he did about the church, our talk has been just the opposite. We speak far more of the church than we do about the Kingdom. The idea of the Kingdom of God seems a bit remote and unfamiliar. As it turns out, an understanding of the Kingdom is the only thing that can give new energy to our understanding of the church. Without the reality of the Kingdom, the church ultimately makes no sense.

Taking hold of the Kingdom means seeing the world from God's point of view. The Kingdom of God is not a different world. The Kingdom of God is the world viewed differently. Seeing the world as the Kingdom of God radically alters the way we look at things. Insofar as the world operates like the Kingdom of God, the world behaves differently. Seeing people and things differently and behaving differently reflect the impact of a world viewed as the Kingdom of God instead of the kingdom of people. Seeing the world through God's eyes and behaving as God would behave change how history happens.

Let's use forgiveness as an illustration. Forgiveness, when it occurs, changes how people relate. Forgiveness does not mean forgetting. Forgiveness means remembering. It means remembering and moving beyond the hurt and bruises. It means creating a new relationship from the rubble of the old one. Forgiveness changes people's history together. "Thy kingdom come" would mean that the destinies of persons and nations would be changed when the power of grace is introduced. The Kingdom of God proposes a "new heaven and a new earth." The experience of the Kingdom reorders all our relationships from the perspective of God's presence. Grace changes everything.

Jesus tells us that we should seek first the Kingdom. Jesus' words to us represent a radical realignment of our priorities. The presence of God's grace will always, without fail, reconstruct our priorities. Seeking God's kingdom first is placed in contrast by Jesus to our need for clothing and shelter and food. There is no hint from Jesus that these matters were unimportant. They are identified precisely because they are universally important. Our ordinary experience finds us preoccupied by these overriding concerns. We label one another by our patterns of consumption. She is rich. They are poor. That group is upper middle-class. Much of our identities are defined by acquisition and consumption. The Fortune 500 lists people by how much they have acquired. Most mass advertising is aimed at managing what we consume.

Jesus never suggests that either acquisition or consumption is evil. Jesus speaks rather to the priorities that govern our lives. If we define ourselves first and chiefly by acquisition and consumption, we will finally be empty. Our consuming will end. Our capacity to acquire will run out. Jesus aims to refocus us on realities that are not so fragile. Seek first God's kingdom means creating a new order for measuring our lives. We are defined not by what we have or by what we consume but by who we are. We catch a glimpse of a person's purpose beyond our frame of time and space.

Debates about whether the Kingdom is present or future are largely irrelevant. Present and future do not apply to the Kingdom. The Kingdom exists wherever God is present. Jesus admonishes us to make the Kingdom a real and defining presence in our lives. The Kingdom is not far way. The kingdom of God is in our midst. Jesus says taking that word seriously and making the reality of God's kingdom the integrating factor in our living are exactly what we mean by the experience of salvation. Jesus embodied the Kingdom's kind of life. The church carries forward the reality and presence of the Kingdom. The church refers to people who embody, in concrete and specific ways, God's way of seeing the world.

The Kingdom of God is both within and above history. You and I are thoroughly historical. Everything we do and intend to do is bound by the framework of history. We are our histories. God transcends history in the sense that history is an event within the reality of God. History does not move alongside, quasi-independent of God. History is God's creation, and God risks the particulars of history to human judgment. The outcome is mixed. History records the story of our meanness as well as our nobleness. History displays our ugliness, and, on occasions, history records the light of grace breaking through our lives.

While history bears the scars and the triumphs of our freedom, we are never free to carry our history beyond the boundaries of God's presence. The reality and finality of the kingdom of God keeps before us that the ultimate ordering of the world belongs to God. History carries the wounds of human failure, but history does not move with reckless abandon. The reality of the Kingdom means that God is present even when our worst atrocities bring the veil of darkness crashing down upon us. The kingdom of God is God's ultimate answer to the frustrating and tragic ambiguities of our historical parade of war and peace.

Jesus said, "Seek first the Kingdom." The church as an event is the dwelling place of the Kingdom in human history. The church embodies that human community where new priorities prevail. The church represents that body of believers for whom the Kingdom has redefined their character. Whenever the church occurs, whether it is called church or not, the kingdom of God becomes present as a force for transforming history. The church changes the outcome of history. The church sets people free.

The church is too much a child of history to be called the kingdom of God on earth. Nevertheless, church enables the priorities of the Kingdom to come to light in human affairs. We do not expect that one day the offices of human governing will be wholly in concert with the will of the Kingdom. History is marred by trouble and sin. The reality of God's kingdom reminds us that we are not left solely to our own devices in determining the final outcome of human history. God's kingdom will prevail. God's kingdom will come.

Chapter 19
Speaking for God

The church is the continuing presence of Christ in the world. The calling of the church is to "speak" the Word of God in word and in deed. Saint Francis of Assisi caught this idea when he said, "Preach the gospel. Use words if you have to."

Voices claiming to speak for God are not hard to find. Television has made preachers into stars. Lights, makeup, cameras, directors—all the requirements of showbiz. We have grown accustomed to the scene. The church as theatre grows quiet, the music swells, the lights come up. The preacher enters. God's word is on its way. People will go anywhere, do anything, pay almost any price to see a good show; and they will double their money to hear God speak. Yet, when we turn off the television, we are left wondering which voice belongs to God. There are so many—male and female, black and white, sophisticated and down-home. Surf the channels and find a voice from God to your liking.

Our reliable sources for belief are the Bible, the church, and our own experience with God. None of us sees or hears a word from God with perfect clarity. We need to listen for God along with other persons who are also listening for God. I believe that we become better hearers when we are willing to devote ourselves to thoughtful reflection and the serious study of Scripture. The "drive-in, drive-out" voice from God will rarely be the ground in which our faith is nurtured toward genuine maturity.

The gospel is not a "fix." Preaching is not a feel-good dispensary for heavy-hearted people. Our faith, and our understanding of faith, grow and flourish best in the context of a community of believers. Our faith can grow only where the word is lived and not just spoken. Speaking for God arises most convincingly in a community of faith that listens for God. Where there is no disciplined listening, there should be no speaking.

Images of the Church

Our particular instance of the church embodies the Word of God to our particular generation. We are not responsible for every time or for every place. The calling of the church is to live the Word in the real time and space where the church actually lives in history. The New Testament helps us clarify the identity and work of the church as God's voice through three images.

Ecclesia. The first and most prominent image of the church is the Greek word, *ecclesia*, which is commonly translated into English as "church." It is helpful to look at the image that the word describes. *Ecclesia* refers to people who are "called out." The people who are the church are people who are called out to look at themselves differently.

Being called out does not mean that you don't go back in to do your work. For Peter, there was nothing wrong with being a fisherman. It was honest and honorable work. Jesus said, "I will make you fishers of people." In other words, "Peter, your focus has only been on catching fish; that is to say, you have been focused only on making a living. In addition to making a living for yourself, there are people to care about."

Life cannot be summed up as being simply about surviving. The center and soul of life is about caring. When we have been "called out," we gain a different take on what it means to be here. Life is lived differently. We decide differently. We behave differently. We relate differently. People who are "called out" by God are never the same when they go back in.

Whenever and wherever people come together in response to the voice and the word of God, the church comes into being. That is what it takes to be the church. The church is people who have heard God speak. Human life takes on a different character when we reconstruct our values according to the Word of God.

The church can be distinguished from other social gatherings only by this peculiar calling. People gathered at church look very much the same as people gathered at the Rotary Club. Both gatherings are cordial. Both gatherings are inspired by some worthwhile identity that binds people together. The churches are people who have been grasped by the power and imagination of the life of Jesus. For the disciples, this historical Jesus became the living Christ. The imagination and message of Jesus transform individuals into the people of God.

We should not become helplessly confused over this issue of whether the church is local or universal. The church is both. The church is born and comes to life in particular places where people come together under God's purpose. The church also refers to all people, in any time or place, who celebrate God's grace and presence in history. In our passion to preserve such ideas as local autonomy, we should not deny or even overlook the common life of people who follow Jesus. The splintering of the Christian faith into hundreds of sects and denominations is a sign of sin, not holiness.

The local church embodies the universal church in a given place and time. The larger church lives beyond the local church. For this reason, churches will do well to listen and to be attentive to one another. Our separateness is more history and sociology than theology. Common worship breaks down the historical barriers among churches. The more we listen for God, the more common will be our life of faith. No local church in history can claim to be the true "called ones of God." Through the broader community of faith, we can overcome the narrowness and self-exile that threaten the character and spiritual strength of churches. Christians of all persuasions should call out hope and encouragement to one another. Whenever we behave as exclusive religious groups, our sin is showing. Listening dismantles the barriers between us. Together we become the people of God—called out to recenter our lives in the light of Jesus.

Koinonia. This image of the church is usually translated as "fellowship." The compelling idea is communion. All people of faith share a common bond. The church as fellowship speaks to the realities of grace and love that bind people into a common community. The benediction of 2 Corinthians is familiar: "The grace of the Lord Jesus Christ, the love of God, and the *koinonia* of the Holy Spirit be with you." We can live separately, independently, as if people do not exist. When we do so, we are living only partial lives. In Christ, we are ultimately bound together. *Koinonia* seeks to capture this common spiritual bond that holds us together.

The formation of our common life springs from God's nature and character. We all huddle under the umbrella of God's grace. So the church is not composed of people who agree or even think alike. The church is not even composed of people who believe alike. The church is composed of people who dwell together in the light of God's promise. Our belonging to one another grows from the soil of belonging to God.

Unlike other human societies and clubs, the church is not based upon common values and interests. There is the Republican Club for that, or the Democratic Club, or the Press Club, or the Palaver Club. These clubs play significant roles in our life and business together. They provide a forum for exchanging ideas and debating social policy. The church is a different sort of place. The common life of the church is not ideas or policy or doctrine. The common life of the church is listening and speaking for God. Fellowship under the light of God prevents the fellowship from growing sentimental and undisciplined.

I am a member of a Rotary Club. In order to be a member in good standing, I must attend at least 60 percent of the meetings. I live on the edge of being in poor standing. Attendance provides a measure of discipline. The measure of the church is an altogether different discipline. It is the discipline of listening and caring. Listening and caring should always precede speaking. The reality of the church is not to be found in church attendance. The reality of the church is found in following Jesus.

Koinonia as an image for the church, then, helps us understand the common life of the church as more than the achievement of cordial, positive human relationships. Positive relationships build better social organizations. The church, on the other hand, is based upon a new vision of reality in the world. Jesus loved people the way God loves people. Our calling is to love people the way God loves people. When we want to know what that is, we look to the Word of God, Jesus.

The church lives together in *koinonia*. Fellowship is not an achievement of the church. Fellowship is a gift. Fellowship happens when the grace that Jesus embodied dominates the way we live together. In our "new being" with God, we are enabled to be with one another in a new way. A new community of the spirit is created among us. God's acceptance makes us new people.

The Body of Christ. The third New Testament image of the church to which I refer here is the church as the "body of Christ." The apostle Paul did not call the church a body of Christians but rather "the body of Christ." The distinction is significant. The church is not an association. The church, when it occurs, is nothing less than Christ's presence in the world. The church is itself a reality that the individual members cannot otherwise be. The church is not simply a meeting of people who claim "to be saved." Becoming the church belongs to the experience of salvation. Tertullian may have been right. Outside the experience of being the church, there is no experience of salvation. The church is the body of Christ.

When we say that the church is the body of Christ, we are saying that the church is Jesus present in our time. The reality of God that was unveiled for us in the historical event of Jesus lives now in the life of the church. The church is the living Word of God. It is the body of Christ in our particular world.

Insofar as churches become preoccupied with their disputes and differences, they can no longer claim to be the continuing incarnation of God. Indeed, they cannot claim to be the church at all. They become empty altars. When we say that the church is the "body of Christ," we are saying that the church is Jesus living and acting, walking and talking, loving and forgiving in our present forum. The church is God's speaking. The church's living and proclaiming God's grace become God's voice to the world.

The Christian faith is not focused on the past. The church, for our world in our time, is the most important and visible meaning of "God with us." The presence of the church teaches us that the revelation of God in Jesus is not buried in the ruins of history. Through this body of Christ, Jesus continues to live and love and forgive.

People do not pay attention to mere words. They will only believe what is lived. People will believe that God loves and forgives only if the church embodies that love in a concrete and specific way. The calling of the church is not to love everyone. The calling of the church is to love someone. The church does not proclaim the gospel to the world generally. The church lives and speaks the gospel to the world that lives next door. Unless the church lives the reality of Christ, Jesus is not alive in our time. He is a mere relic of antiquity. The church, for our time, is the Word made flesh.

The Voice of the Church

The reason the church does not speak more clearly and persuasively for God is because it bogs down in its own sin. The chief sins of the church are narrowness, exclusiveness, and institutional success. In order to recover the voice of the church as the voice of God, we must first acknowledge that the church as the people of God and the church as a human institution are distinctly different realities.

The church as an institution is of our own making. It is a human organization subject to all of the difficulties and deficiencies that human organizations face. The human church errs. The human church falls victim to greed and envy. It becomes victim to the urge to acquire and the pleasures of consumption. The church becomes political and arrogant, enamored by its own progress, captivated by its own success.

The humanness of the church can cause us to be cynical. Sometimes, the church is not a pretty sight. It can be a troubled, confused, messy organization. Churches can be unforgiving, far more fond of judgment than redemption. Yet, while subject to all the ambiguities of existing in history, the church bears a least a clouded image of a new order that has entered our life together. These human organizations called churches are places where the self-destructive forces in our history are overcome by the power and presence of our life in Christ. We should neither worship the church as a human altar of faith nor abandon it. The local churches where we worship can become the context for becoming the church in our place.

The denominations of the church—Baptist, Methodist, Presbyterian, and all the rest—are only monuments to our fragmented vision. Even though the church as the people of God has no denominational boundaries, the churches of history are likely to be plagued by continuing human divisions. These divisions mirror our fractured understanding of faith. These boundaries become most destructive when they become exclusive.

The denomination defeats itself when it presents its own version of truth as the only avenue for God's grace. When narrow exclusion occurs, the churches of history serve as one more example of the towers of Babel where people's destinies were corrupted by their self-centered ways. Denominations can remain servants of the church only if they remain genuinely secondary. When the church happens to us, the boundaries of our historical churches break away as unnecessary chains and we are free to live together as children of God.

You and I experience the church in our time as a worshiping community, as a proclaiming community, and a community of caring. We know the church most directly as a worshiping community.

Worship is not an activity. Worship is a sense of the Holy breaking in upon us. We attend church wrapped in all our busy ways, distracted by work to be finished and personal lives that are disordered. We regularly attend religious services with our minds and hearts somewhere else. Worship is not a place where we lay hold upon God through our liturgies and episodes of singing and praying. Worship appears in that quiet moment when we let down our defenses long enough and loosen our grip on all our intense cares that God can take hold of us. God's presence meets our presence. God's spirit meets our spirit. Worship occurs when we find courage enough to open ourselves to the Sacred. Though worship is a deeply personal experience, it is never a solitary experience. Worship is communal. You can't worship for long by yourself. Worship always brings us together. When you meet God, you always meet one another in a new way.

The church is also a proclaiming community. The community of faith confesses. It can do no other. The church proclaims the Word of God. The inwardness of worship cannot be kept inward. Whenever people's lives and relationships have been reshaped by the inward presence of God, it changes how they meet those beyond their community. The church is thoroughly missionary. Whether we choose to do so or not, we always communicate who we are and what we believe. We cannot do otherwise. Both our actions and words belie the compelling passions that guide our lives. The church being the church is the essence of proclamation.

The chief problem of proclamation is that the gospel gets confused with our own cultural expectations. It is always a danger. We are rarely ever able to eliminate all of the cultural barnacles that attach to our life of belief. These distortions inhibit us, but they should not paralyze us. Our speaking for God by embodying God's presence should be undertaken with a listening ear for our frailty. But even our frailty should not cause us to fall silent.

The work of the church as the voice of God is focused most clearly when we see the church as a caring community. The calling of the church is to love and forgive. Saint Augustine described the church as a community of love. We become so protective and defensive about all our differences. Christians are a diverse lot. Whenever the church as a caring community occurs, all our differences of ideology and race and status fall away. Insofar as we quibble about differences, we are postponing our life as the church. The reality of the church does not eradicate our differences. The church defines our lives by a new measure of what matters.

The church as a community where love is the compelling reality should not be confused with sentimental romanticism. The real power of love and forgiveness is not that it ignores the hurt. Love acts in spite of being wronged. Love cannot be coerced. No level of hostility will ever create peace. Hostility breeds hostility. Bitterness breeds bitterness. Love will breed love. The Christian community of faith is, above all else, a community of love and forgiveness.

The church through its simple, even ambivalent, acts of caring speaks of God's presence in our world. The church happening in our midst is the clearest revelation of God that the world has today. The church makes God's grace an actual force in addressing the troubles of our times. By living God's grace, the church becomes the community of salvation. As children of grace, we are the children of the family of God.

It is true that the churches of history become victims of their own history. They become focused on being right and perpetuating their own kind. It is all folly. It distracts us from the family of faith. Any particular church or denomination may die. Denominations always die. Sometimes they exist after they have died. But the church as a community of belief and devotion will endure. The church breaks through the ambiguities of history and lives through the experience of grace that redeems the moment.

The church is Jesus living in our time, speaking for God, stumbling on its own words, and being lifted by grace to speak again. The most powerful word we speak is caring for someone's hurt. The gospel is not very glamorous. It does not live most clearly in the bright lights and loud sounds of glorious religious celebrations. The church lives when we pick someone up who is broken down. Feeding, healing, visiting, and listening ring true as the caring voices of God. The caring voice is the birth of the church.

Chapter 20
The Ethics of Confession

What the church does inevitably speaks more loudly than what the church says. I learned of the ethics of the church first during my seminary years in New Orleans. New Orleans was, in many ways, strange terrain for me as a young seminary student. I lived half a city away from the main seminary campus. The religious atmosphere of Seminary Place ran thick and slow like new sorghum syrup. I could taste the aroma of the hallowed grounds as I arrived on the campus each morning. My quarters—remnants of a dormitory where the old Baptist Bible Institute had once dwelled—stood among the upscale houses of the upper crust of New Orleans. We lived there on the street with the world-famous Commander's Palace Restaurant and houses that would put monarchs to shame. We were definitely uptown.

Between where I lived, the Garden District, and the sacred terrain called Seminary Place was the enchanting New Orleans French Quarter. There were faster routes home everyday, but I tried only to accept rides with students who were errant enough to want to drive home through the Quarter. Tony's Pizza House and Al Hirt's Club on Bourbon Street became familiar landmarks. In the evening it was only a ten-cent fare and a short ride on the St. Charles Streetcar to romp in the streets of the Quarter. It was a far cry from Seminary Place, and, during our six-year stay, I learned lessons from both quarters.

The intensity and passion of Bourbon Street had a lot in common with the intensity and passion of Seminary Place. On one end of the city were preachers talking loud and fast about Jesus. On the other end were barkers opening the doors for a peek at dancers luring those of us who were passing by wanting to be lured. We gazed through those open doors until the passions ran sufficiently high that even a closed door was only marginal restraint. In our case, the real restraint was neither closed doors nor moral resolve. It was being broke. You had to pay money to get more than an urgent glance. My mama felt okay about sending funds for the seminary bills and even meal tickets in the cafeteria. Bourbon Street frolicking was another matter.

As my seminary years aged, I entered a graduate doctoral program—in ethics. Subsistence wages for graduate students were called fellowships, and the holders of those fellowships were called fellows. I was a fellow for one of the professors of ethics. At least majoring in his field seemed the proper thing to do since his generous fellowship was helping to put bread on the table. I was paid to grade papers and manage the class. Professors had better things to do than to get to know the students. We were middlemen. (There were no middlewomen. There were no women in the program. At that time, our seminary leadership had not heard that God could be a woman.)

During my duties as a fellow, I met a young man whose name had already become familiar to me. He called himself the "Chaplain of Bourbon Street." By that time, I was part of the street for which he was chaplain. I had seen it many times. He had a small storefront with a large, plate-glass window. Beyond the plate glass was a shiny red cloth crumpled like a storefront decoration. Light blinked around the edges framing the silhouette of a large portrait of Jesus. Like me, this seminary student had become familiar with the common life of Seminary Place and Bourbon Street. He could check his watch to see whether it was school time or show time.

One day on one of my regular visits to the Quarter, I was startled by the Chaplain's office. Lo and behold, things had changed. Instead of Jesus' portrait, there was the student's portrait—dressed in dark suit, red tie, and red Bible. This young man had hit the big time. He had become a star. Star dust was definitely in his eyes.

For him, I was simply a starry-eyed liberal; and for me, he was a student who knew opportunity when he saw it. We were both right. Actually, I always enjoyed hearing him make his pitch. He was good-looking, well-groomed, and articulate. He was most things that a good preacher needs to be. I had graded his papers and listened to his preaching and had concluded that down deep, he was shallow. The judgment was more arrogance than fairness on my part. I may never have heard or seen him on a good day. We all need a heap of mercy to cover our bad days.

Through the years gone by since the chaplain and I struggled with the shrunken worlds on Bourbon Street and Seminary Place, I have learned that we always find ourselves living on conflicting streets. Confession either must be made in this kind of diverse world at odds with itself, or it cannot be made at all. As a practical matter, the ethics of confession have to help us deal with the discord between Bourbon Street and Seminary Place. We soon have to get beyond the anemic rhetoric that Bourbon Street is bad and Seminary Place is good. Good and evil reside on both streets. Christianity as an ethic does not change the street on which we live. It changes how we live on the street. T. S. Eliot described Christianity as a condition of complete simplicity. That Danish individual, Søren Kierkegaard said, "Purity of heart is to will one thing." Complexities bear down upon us. We do not just live on one end of town. Christianity is a call to simplicity amidst the discord of conflicting streets.

Simplicity

The ethics of confession begin with simplicity. The ultimate poverty of human experience is not economic poverty. Economic poverty is wrenching and stands as judgment on our belief and our disbelief. We face, however, another kind of poverty. It is the poverty of trying to pin our hopes on whatever street we happen to live on. We march in many directions and serve many purposes. It creates the poverty of being unable to be one person because of the pressure of being so many persons.

The simplification of life is the first order of business in the practice of faith. Thoreau in *Walden II* pronounced the essence of his social message in two words: "Simplify, simplify." On a trip to Kentucky, I went with a friend to visit the remnants of an old Shaker village—Shakertown. During the eighteenth century, a small band of folks broke away from the Quakers in England and formed themselves into small communities called Shakers. This Kentucky village stands as a monument to the best and the worst of our religious instincts.

The Shakers did not persist or survive because they relied too much on their own human prescriptions of what God ought to do. The world was a mess. Surely, God was on his way to intervene and to set history right. They were resolute and celibate, unentangled with worldly concerns, focused only upon the imminent return of

Christ. They swept their meeting house floor after each evening service, and they would hang their benches and chairs on wall pegs so
that their house would be in order if Christ should return during the
night. While their instincts were devout, they stopped listening for a
word that would not fit their expectations. They confused their
desires and expectations with God's expectations.

The Shakers, however, also give us a glimpse of the essence of
devotion. They lived simple lives, spartan and single-minded in
every respect. One of their hymns was set to symphony music by
Aaron Copland in *Appalachian Spring,* a ballet in which Martha
Graham premiered in 1949 with the Louisville Symphony Orches-
tra. Its words constitute an ode to simplicity:

Simple Gifts
'Tis a gift to be simple
'Tis a gift to be free
'Tis a gift to come down
Where we ought to be
And when we find ourselves
in the place just right.
It will be the valley
of love and delight.
When true simplicity is gained,
to bow and to bend
We will not be ashamed
To turn, to turn
will, be our delight,
'Till by turning, turning,
We come round right.

As the vestiges of our lives become increasingly complex and we
feel caught in a whirlwind of voices, the urgent challenge is to hammer out some idea of ourselves that we can live with. The cry for
simplicity as the foundation of ethical behavior is grounded in our
longing for a single center to which our lives can repair.

The achievement of a measure of simplicity, of course, can
never mean the absence of complexity. The absence of complexity
would be sheer pretense. We cannot simply live on Seminary Place,
assuming that Bourbon Street is not there. These complexities
abound. We are confronted by brutal turmoil in Bosnia,

assassinations in Jerusalem, and widespread starvation and disease in Africa. We live in a world where our best efforts to cope with racism and sexism fall frightfully short. We walk uneasily on streets that have been terrorized by irrational killings. Our generation faces an aging population, decreasing confidence in government, fear of environmental disasters, a national deficit careening out of control, and the politics of self-destruction. Complexities abound. They are with us, and they are not likely to be gone with the morning.

Your hope, my hope, the hope of all peoples—faithful and unfaithful alike—is to find a place to stand. In the hail storm of competing expectations, we need a center of calm. We desperately need an operating clue around which we can manage the complex web of our responsibilities. The ethics of confession require a center of confession from which we can address the demands that cascade upon us. In the final analysis, this center of confession will be about choosing to be somebody. Making a confession will mean devoting ourselves to certain priorities.

The problem of focus and centering is especially acute for people who earnestly want to do what is right. With frantic fidelity, we try to respond to every call to serve and become distressingly unable to be every good thing to all good people. We are bent over by the burden of integrity—panting and out of breath. Finding a place to stand will not likely be settled by moving permanently to either Bourbon Street or on Seminary Place. Simplicity, the center of confession, transcends every street on which we will live. We will not find meaning in the street. The center is not a piece of geography. Centering is a matter of will and grace. It means retreating within to hear the quiet voice of God even while a clamor of voices is telling us what to believe.

Life's center is rarely stationary. Simplicity won't even mean getting planted in a point of view. Life is full of movement—shifting perspectives, seeing the world through different lenses. Our faith changes, our confessions change, our behavior changes as we learn and grasp the light of life more fully. So, the achievement of simplicity is more a process than a single event. No single event shapes all of life. We must follow Jesus each new day. As we face every horizon, we must declare anew the confession that Jesus is the Christ. It will mean something different today than it meant yesterday. Searching for simplicity is never done once and for all.

Simplicity is both a gift and a discipline. Simplicity is a gift of learning to listen. Prayer is one example of listening. In praying, it is not important what we say. Wait. Prayer's gift is what God says to us and through us. Listening means learning to be at home with our places in the world—learning to be at home on Seminary Place or Bourbon Street. Simplicity is a discipline because it requires devotion and practice. We cannot be everything to everybody. We cannot master every achievement. Simplicity means disciplining our energies to climb some specific mountain rather than daydreaming about climbing every mountain. Simplicity provides a mooring for saying "yes" or "no" to the demands that roll in upon us. Simplicity does not mean that we replace busyness with idleness. It means instead that we become less directed by purely external forces. We learn to listen and live by the light within.

Confessing and Behaving

Every confession has moral implications. What we say we believe turns out to be no belief at all unless we garner the courage to behave as though it were so. In actual experience, believing and doing are either integrated, or they belong to the tombs of stale and meaningless rhetoric. Confessional ethics mean that our living commitments bear real implications for our decisions and actions. They are not mere words. Belief and context meld together to form the cauldron of behavior.

Context always affects what ought to be done. The notion that we can dismiss the context or the situation from our efforts to determine what is the right thing to do reflects a naive refusal to take our own special place in history seriously. Our own peculiar situations are the only places where we can practice our faith. We have to engage the struggle to determine what our vision of God requires in the real life of action and decision where we live. Seminary Place and Bourbon Street are different places, but they are real places, and we live on both streets. The life of faith behaves differently in each setting because we face different challenges.

Our situations are often clouded. We have to act when we are not sure what is the right thing to do. Even worse, we very often do not have the luxury of waiting longer to decide. We cannot weigh the evidence any longer. The time to act has come. We are thrown into the cauldron of decision even when we wish we could wait so that we could understand more completely and could see more clearly. Our situations include clashes and tensions where easy answers and crystal clear decisions are often not an option.

Even so, the situation is not all that matters. Confessional ethics bring to every decision the power of confession. Christians face the complex dilemmas of human experience with both the power of reason and confession. Reason brings knowledge and good sense. Confession brings the reality of faith. Knowledge and grace come together to help us to decide what is right. Confession keeps our judgments in touch with the ultimate values and commitments that center our lives. Reason engages the gift of thought on life's most pressing dilemmas.

Confessional ethics look for what is right by searching out the intersection between the insight of thought and the wisdom of grace. Reason alone will not be enough. Reason alone could cause us to be content with balancing the ledger—an eye for an eye. Only confession will teach us of mercy. The caring of confession should not be confused with sentimental "do-goodism." The ethics of confession do not mean that evil and sin do not have dreadful consequences. The ethics of confession mean that the consequences of evil, no matter how dreadful, are never the final word. Judgment serves redemption. Love values the worth of the judged. The ethics of confession don't give us much room to discard people.

Confessional ethics also keep us from reducing ethical judgment to a prescriptive set of moral imperatives. We all yearn for a clear set of answers to every moral dilemma. Fundamentalist Christianity is often attractive because it seems to satisfy that craving. Fundamentalists risk all their faith on getting their doctrines right. Experience, intuition, and immediacy are suspect. Fundamentalism has an established load of religious truth. To embrace Christianity means to embrace a specific collection of religious affirmations. Every world religion today struggles with the appeal of fundamentalism. The parallels among Christian, Muslim, Jewish, and even Hindu and Buddhist fundamentalism are dramatic.

The word "fundamentalist," which was originally applied to a tendency with the American Protestant tradition, is now applied throughout the world to religious groups that replace priesthood before God with a package of received and settled answers to life's most difficult problems. The Jewish Defense League is a volatile, if not violent, example of Jewish fundamentalism. The overthrow of a dictatorship in Iran was managed by Islamic fundamentalists bent on establishing a theocracy. They wanted God in charge, and only Islamic fundamentalist leaders knew what God's being in charge looked like. Fundamentalist Christians who exclude churches from associations because people do not embrace the right set of Christian beliefs reflect yet another form of the treachery of fundamentalism.

Blaise Pascal was right when he observed that no evil is quite so courageously and joyfully done as when it is done in the name of God. We should beware of theocracies. They inevitably put in place not God's will but somebody's will who thinks for sure they possess the one and only truth from God.

Fundamentalism and modernism are kindred spirits. The modernism of the twentieth century believed that reason and science could find answers to every problem. Science could conquer disease, and government could establish justice and assure the public good. Fundamentalism believes that we have our arms around God's truth and the doctrinal "fundamentals" have been handed down. We are urged to submit our will to the will of the pastor as the anointed one of God. Both modernism and fundamentalism have a high view of people's ability to know the truth. Salvation means knowing the truth and following that truth word for word. The appeal is very strong. We can set people free of the struggle to know the will of God. We only have to accept God's truth contained in the fundamentals of our faith.

A faith that has been equated with a particular set of doctrinal propositions will issue into a morality that has been set forth in a specific set of moral prescriptions. In contrast, confession as a continuing dynamic of faith keeps both doctrines and ethics open to new light from God. Belief and behavior are alive. We can neither believe nor decide in advance. Yesterday's confession must be reaffirmed for today. Our confessing cannot outstrip our experience with God. Yesterday's behavior must be confronted again in today's confession. For example, earnest and faithful Christians in our day of faith once believed that "separate but equal" schools were the right thing. Our actions are sometimes wrong because our confessions do not see the truth. We have to repent. Stop, and start over again. Our actions were wrong because our confessions were blind.

No statements of belief will make us Christians. No decisions will make us moral. We confess our belief and our disbelief. We confess our joy and our despair. We confess our vision and our blindness. We confess our strength and our weakness. We confess that we are children of light and children of darkness. Our discipline of trying to do what is right is uneven. Our decisions carry both vision and blindness, belief and disbelief. Good and evil continue to compete for our devotion.

Moral principles serve as tutors for our deciding. Moral principles are stakes we drive down for what our confessing requires. The problem with most of us is not that we have too few moral principles. We generally have too many. Moral principles becomes shortcuts for moral choice. These principles should never be elevated to the status of prescribed truth. What we choose to do must continually be informed by what we believe and how we experience God in our lives. If doing is cut off from believing, doing right is cut off from being good. The good life does not emanate from making the right choices. The right choices emanate from right belief.

Our responsibility is always current. Every act of deciding what ought to be done should be made in the light of a living confession. Confession without morality has nowhere to go. Morality without confession has no reason to go anywhere. Our living confessions keep our moral principles from growing abstract and dispassionate. Listening to moral implications of our confessions keeps our beliefs from wallowing in a sea of self-indulgence. Believing breeds behaving.

The Practice of Love

The church's calling is to love because God is love. Believing anything means acting as if it is true. Believing that the ultimate reality underlying all creation is love has staggering consequences for what we do. We practice our faith most purely when we muster the courage to love. Our actions, even the loving ones, are rarely pure and unmixed. We are both possessive and giving. We love what we want. On the other hand, we should be bold enough to say that if God is love, no genuine act of love, no matter how compromised by ambition or desire, is without the blessing of God's presence. Our love both gives and takes. We affirm others, expecting to be affirmed. Yet, even in its diminished and abridged condition, if God is love, wherever love is present, God is present.

Love is faith's imperative. Wherever faith holds reign, love will be present. We have corrupted the idea of love with endless romantic and sentimental distortions. In the other direction, we have tried to make love into an abstract principle of morality. The reduction to either emotion or reason is a mistake. Love is not a feeling. Love does not mean resolving to like everybody. Likewise, love is not an external, impersonal principle by which to measure our lives. Love is a way of relating and acting in the world.

We relate to other persons in countless ways. We set ourselves over against others. We see other people as barriers to getting what we want. We climb over other people, making them instruments of our own achievement. Our faith teaches us a better way. Jesus said, "Love one another as I have loved you." He also said, "Whatever you do to the least of my brothers, you do to me." Love meets people because of their own value. They are God's gifts to the world. Love embraces other persons without conditions. Love acts for the well-being of others.

The question of ethics in the practice of faith is "what does love require of me?" The requirements cannot always be defined in advance or predicted precisely. We can talk generally about love's expectations. For example, we can say that love requires that we act justly. It requires that we feed the poor and clothe the naked. These general requirements, however, leave the heart of love behind. It is easier to feed the hungry than to feed an actual person who is hungry. It is easier to love everyone than to love someone. Love listens and cares and forgives in hundreds of specific and caring ways.

Finally, the practice of love as the heart and soul of our ethics of confession bases what we "ought" to do upon what God has done and who God is. We love only because God loves. Our loving finds all its energy from being loved. The ground of all our moral decisions is found in what God is like, how God relates, and what God has done in our history. Believing God's love means meeting people the way God meets us. God is love. In Jesus, God's love is lived down to earth. The ethical practice of our faith means bringing God's love down to earth in our time. What the church does will speak more loudly than what the church says.

Chapter 21
Plain Talk about Last Things

W e have said a lot more about "last things" than we know. By last things I mean to refer to subjects such as death and dying, heaven and hell, judgment and resurrection. They all seem remote. They are subjects that must be spoken more about in myth and poetry than with learning and logic. In dealing with such reckonings, we should be careful about claiming too much knowledge and prescribing too much certainty. People typically debate most vigorously about issues with the fewest clear answers. The deeper the mystery, the more scintillating the debate. When it comes to seeing how the world comes out, silence will be among our best teachers, and hope will be our last word.

The hazards in conversations about ultimate destiny crop up when we begin to stake our faith on some religious theory about such matters as heaven and hell. We should say to each other up front that nobody's theory matters very much. The foundation of being together as the church has little to do with delicate doctrines about the day of judgment. Final answers are rare. We have insight. We confess our faith and listen to another's confession.

Issues of ultimate destiny strike us with staggering force when we collide with our own mortality. As a young seminary student, I recall wrestling with the Christian view of "life after death." During my studies, the theologian and writer, Nels Ferre and I developed an enduring friendship. On one of the coldest April days I have ever known, I was visiting several days in Ferre's home in Boston, Massachusetts. Living in New Orleans, I was unaccustomed to snow in the winter, not to speak of the spring. Professor Ferre and I talked into the night about matters of ultimate destiny and the impact of believing in ultimate universal redemption upon the motivations of the moral life. We corresponded and met together on many different occasions. Yet to this day, the most lingering impression of our conversations, our days together and our years of correspondence, has

not been his ideas but his devotion. In the end, his devout piety
turned out to be a more important window on God's light than his
ideas.

Only a few months later after this particular visit in Boston, all
my easy conversations about last things were laid waste by the
untimely and tragic death of a friend. An automobile accident . . .
Suddenly, without warning, he was gone. No time to prepare for the
news. No time to say one more word. No time to enjoy one more
hearty laugh. No time for one more tilt of tomfoolery. Death had
ripped my friend away. The only thing left to do was to weep. In the
crevices of grief, talk doesn't help much. Our religious ideas don't
bring relief to the aching. Doctrines won't deliver us from despair.
The boundary situations of life where we meet death up close—perhaps even our own—are the only important context for confessing
our faith about last things. If our confessions do not ring true to
life's experience, they will dry up and blow away. Faith cannot live
by reason alone.

In the next few pages, I want to try to unravel three issues that
have complicated our life of faith and cast shadows on the witness
of the church. Then, in a final chapter, I will speak of the Christian
understanding of time and eternity and the meaning of hope. Before
we see our way clear to confess our hope, we need to face up to and
try to clear away some of the thickets of doctrine that have grown
up over our path, making our journeys of faith more difficult.

Heaven and Hell

Few of our discussions of faith are more burdened with complex,
esoteric language than the interpretation of heaven and hell. The
brambles are thick. When our understanding is limited, we seem to
make up for it with lots of words. Too many words are often the
best clue of too little understanding. We might test it as a general
principle: The longer we take to say something, the less we know
about the subject.

In the case of heaven and hell, our language is strengthened by
colorful and dramatic images. We cannot understand the language
of the Bible unless we distinguish between taking a description
seriously and taking it literally. When Jesus says "I am the vine," it
is to be taken seriously but not literally. If we insist on taking every
account of heaven and hell literally, we will grind to a standstill in

endless, and often mindless, hair-splitting debates. The Scriptures are rich with metaphor and drama, with figurative language and symbolism. Literal interpretations are short-sighted, and, more often than not, they lead us to serious errors.

The New Testament does not give an almanac of the end of time. Just as we should not look to Genesis for a scientific rendering of creation, we should not look to Revelation for a scientific account of the end of the world. The final victory depicted in the book of the Revelation and the careful descriptions of the new Jerusalem are powerful images of the righteousness of God and the ultimate victory of God's Kingdom. The good word is that evil will not prevail. In the end, the way of righteousness will endure.

To get caught up in the description of Satan and the physical dimensions of the Holy City causes us to get sidetracked in the wilderness of symbolism. The meaning of the words must be drawn from the power and grandeur of the images. Chasing after a literal rendering of these passages and transcribing them into the complicated theories of the millennium is a mistake. It is one more instance of our desire to be all-knowing. Faith does not call upon us to dispel the mystery. Let the mystery be. When we convert poetry into science, we wind up with nonsense. Metaphor is the language of mystery.

Speaking plainly, heaven and hell are not places in space. Heaven and hell describe our relationships with God. Heaven means achieving full communion with God. Heaven is more than God being with us. Heaven is our being with God. In contrast, hell refers to the absence of God. It is the absence of God's light in our lives. The "black hole" in astronomers' language is a wonderful metaphor of life without God. Hell means that the gravity of our own self-centered ways has become so strong that we shut out God's light altogether. The result is utter darkness—a moral "black hole."

Heaven should not be viewed as the ultimate compensation for our life of faith. The language is so familiar. "Accept Jesus and go to heaven." Our language leads us astray. Heaven is not a place to go as a reward for right religious or moral choices. Heaven is not akin to winning the lottery. The spatial descriptions in the book of Revelation are dramatic, articulating grandeur and perfection. The images help us speak in more vivid ways of the meaning of heaven.

But the question of "where is heaven" is a wrong question for which there is no right answer. The best we can say is that heaven is "where" God is.

"Whereness" does not apply to God or to eternity or to heaven. We will not search the galaxies and, at their edge, find heaven. Heaven is not a place in outer space. Space will never contain the realities of God and heaven. God is everywhere, and God is no-where. We cannot define God in terms of location. We are spatial beings. God is not. By heaven, we speak of the presence of God and our coming to live again in the likeness of God. Heaven might have been in Eden, but humankind chose to make the earth into their own kind of place. Heaven is the fruition of our long journey back to God's presence.

In a related way, hell should not be viewed as an arbitrary punishment of our sin. Hell depicts the ultimate outcome of life that is lived without God. Hell is the natural and inevitable outcome of our efforts to live by our own lights. We build our lives around temporal and passing values. In this sense, sin carries its own losses. The image of God meting our rewards and penalties of heaven and hell leaves us with a view of God that is very different from the vision of God embodied in the work and life of Jesus. Jesus did not come to his disciples as an arbitrary judge, handing out rewards and penalties on the basis of their behavior. Our doctrines of heaven and hell often reflect more of the human inclination to get even than God's presence as grace and mercy. Our ideas of heaven and hell should be secured from our childish views of God. Arbitrary judgment is childish. Simple, uncumbered grace is childlike.

Beyond the language of heaven and hell that has caused great confusion with the Christian faith, three major streams of Christian belief about ultimate destiny have been held by Christians down through the ages of Christianity. They are: (1) the conception of an everlasting dual destiny of heaven and hell, (2) the conception of conditional immortality, and (3) the conception of ultimate universal redemption. Let me discuss each of them briefly.

Dual Destiny. The most widely held view within Protestant circles of faith is the conception that heaven and hell are everlasting. In other words, heaven lasts forever—a thousand years is but a day.

Hell lasts forever. Hell is an everlasting punishment for our mortal sins. I find that most people accept or even assume this view as being the orthodox view of the church, being largely unaware that this view has been questioned and rejected by many devout Christian interpreters of the faith.

When we place this view alongside the teaching of the Scriptures or the revelation of God in Jesus, some problems exist. The idea of the eternal nature of hell places into eternity that which is contrary to the meaning of eternity—namely, the existence of our ultimate, enduring realm of evil. The doctrine of an everlasting evil lays waste the ultimate character of God in favor of an eternal dualism of good and evil. Chaos is never overcome. Evil persists for eternity. I believe the biblical view, including the view of God captured in images of the book of the Revelation, is that evil is subordinate ultimately to God's good presence. Though evil is real and threatens us profoundly, evil is not an ultimate challenge to God's grace.

Ultimate dualism places evil on the same footing with good. It holds that the judgment for which hell is the telling description is an abstract vindication of moral law. Hell is God's retribution. A dual destiny theory asserts that our choices before death are irrevocable and irreparable. Punishment as retribution occurs as a moral necessity. These ideas are clear and simple. They warn us urgently about our sin, but they stand forever against the ultimate reality of the God of grace.

Conditional Immortality. According to the view of conditional immortality, "the wages of sin is death." Hell, then, means ultimate death. It represents the complete loss of self. This theory unfolds in the following manner: People were created with the gift of immortality. The "tree of life" was planted in their midst. Humankind abandoned God's gift of immortality in the Fall. Through participation in the presence of Christ in Jesus, people recover their immortality. They put on immortality. To live outside God's presence means to remain under the bondage of corruption and, in due time, to become as though we had never been created. The ultimate outcome for the unrepentant sinner is utter and complete self-destruction. Evil destroys itself.

Conditional immortality obviously avoids some of the difficulties embedded in the theory of a dual destiny. There is no ultimate realm of evil. The lights go out. Evil becomes the victim of its own curse. It also underscores the seriousness of moral choice. Sin and evil bear ultimate and enduring consequences. Therein also lies its chief problem. If all creation is good because it comes from God, the ultimate destruction of God's good creation leaves evil victorious over the goodness of God. Evil destroys the creation of God.

Universal Redemption. The very utterance of the idea of universal redemption causes apoplexy among some Christians. If God doesn't get even, some of us want no part of God's ultimate outcome. We want to be in the front row to watch God hand out the "just desserts." It is true that the idea of ultimate universal redemption proposes that all persons will ultimately be redeemed. Like the concept of dual destiny, this view also finds strong support in Holy Scripture. C. H. Dodd, a major interpreter of the New Testament, contended that universalism is the only approach to interpreting ultimate destiny that is consistent with the New Testament and the teachings of Jesus.

Universalism has a very high view of God. God's grace and God's love are the ultimate realities revealed in Jesus. Universal redemption means that while God will never coerce, God will never abandon. God's caring pursuit of all persons will endure, and God's forgiveness knows no boundaries. Time is not a boundary. Death is not a boundary. Hell is not a boundary. Whenever a person chooses to accept God's forgiveness, the power of forgiveness becomes effective in his life. God's patient grace will finally win all persons to the new creation. God will never close the door. People ordinarily operate a different way. We close doors and prescribe retribution. Universalism contends that God never gives up on creation. God's creativity remains a force throughout eternity.

Ultimate universal redemption avoids the prescription that evil is eternal. Sin distorts and twists our lives, and the consequences of sin leave us afraid, isolated, and lonely. God's ultimate triumph is not based on some naive dismissal of evil or the consequences of sin. Judgment is a genuine part of God's world. Universalism, however, believes that judgment, including hell itself, serves the purpose of redemption. God's word is not retribution. Neither tragedy nor the consequences of sin will ever be God's final word. Universalism affirms that God's grace will outlast any person's rejection of God. Moral choice remains free, but God's love is eternal. God's love will prevail.

One of the objections raised to universalism is that it undermines the moral life by withdrawing the ultimate risk. Universalism does deny an ultimate peril. It says that evil will not be the final word. Universalism holds together the paradox of the severity and reality of judgment alongside the power and ultimacy of God's forgiveness. An early church father, Origen, put the matter this way: "Christ remains on the cross as long as one sinner remains in hell." This concept of ultimate destiny affirms that God's love is eternal and will endure beyond any measure of human rejection. God will always permit us to walk alone, even with the judgment and hell that decision brings. But God will never abandon us to our evil. God faithfully and persistently loves and forgives beyond the turmoil of our grief.

Judgment and Resurrection

Judgment day sparks emotions of fear and trembling. What do we do with the notion of the coming day of judgment? We should begin by being clear that judgment and redemption are not two different realities. Judgment and redemption are different responses to God's presence. God's presence rejects our self-centered and unloving ways. Jesus' life was a judgment upon idolatrous and self-serving religious systems. The proclamation of mercy is a judgment upon the absence of mercy. Wherever God is present, the holiness of God's presence brings judgment upon our unholiness. The Christian view of judgment is never of an isolated event, however. Judgment does not stand alone.

In both the Old and New Testaments, judgment comes for the sake of redemption. The final word of history will not be judgment, even though judgment is the final outcome of human sin. Sin and evil bring their own devastation, and the descriptions of the "day of judgment" point toward the seriousness of sin and the disastrous consequences of living without God. The "day of judgment" is not some certain date in the future on which history will close and each person will be brought before God for evaluation. The "day of judgment" conveys that our choices carry within them consequences that are certain and inevitable. Human sin carries within it an inevitable day of judgment, a dreadful day that we cannot escape.

Even in that dreadful day, God remains by our side. The consequences of sin are real and awful, but we do not face them alone. God goes with us to Babylon. God walks with us in our trials and stands with us in our weakness. The terrible judgment of holiness is matched by the embracing grasp of God's mercy. Judgment, in the Christian view, remains in the service of redemption.

Judgment divides and censures. The ultimate seriousness of the consequences of seeking to live unto ourselves is communicated as our being punished for "endless time." The time of judgment may be endless, but it is not eternal. "Endless duration" is a metaphor. It means that judgment is a telling moment in God's presence. Neither judgment nor redemption can ultimately be defined by chronological time.

The language of the Bible has two words for time. Our language has only one word for time. The biblical words are *kairos and chronos*. *Kairos* is the "time" of decision. It is the "time" of judgment and the "time" of redemption. It is time as defined by events and moments. *Chronos* refers to time as the succession of intervals that we measure by the clock. Judgment and redemption are not chronological events. They cannot be defined as some date on the calendar of history. They are the events that ultimately shape the meaning of history.

"To every matter," the Preacher of Ecclesiastes affirmed, "there is a time (*kairos*)." The *kairos* of judgment serves the ultimate purpose of God's redemption. Secular history chronicles human decisions and actions. *Chronos* means chronicle. It describes events as they took place by the clock. The "day of judgment" and the "day of redemption" are God's moments of *kairos* when the passing of chronological time is transformed in the "day of the Lord." Judgment and redemption belong to the *kairos* of God and not to the *chronos* of humankind. They are not calendar events; they are relational events.

The day of resurrection conveys the abiding Christian confession that death is never life's last word. The crucifixion of Jesus is overcome by the resurrection. The resurrection of Jesus demonstrates in history that God's life prevails against all odds, including the dread and misery of being assassinated by an unruly crowd. The resurrection is the evidence that the new life that is created by the presence of grace breaks through all of the barriers of time. The end of the clock is not the end of God's time.

In Christian doctrine, we put much emphasis upon the "resurrection of the body." This concept stands somewhat in contrast to the idea of the immortality of the soul. When we describe someone as "body and soul," it is a figurative way of referring to the whole person. We should not conclude from that figure of speech that a person has a soul located somewhere in the body. A person is a soul. Salvation relates to the whole person, and the notion of the resurrection of the body underscores that a person is not essentially a disembodied spirit. People are saved, not their souls.

Neither should the term body be construed as material. The key idea is wholeness. The form of the resurrection is not at all clear in any literal sense. We are left with the power of imagination to translate ultimate forms into spatial images. What we mean is that the resurrected person is no longer bound by the categories of time and space. We naturally find it very difficult to conceive of personal existence except in spatial and temporal ways. That's where we live. The life of the resurrection is life in the spirit, where the limitations of existence no longer bear down upon us. The challenge is to free ourselves of materialistic, time-centered thinking. God's being has no such burdens of limiting what is real and enduring.

The resurrection also reiterates the eternal significance of a person's unique presence in the world. A person "as a body" is a special and unique being unlike any other thing in the world. The doctrine of the resurrection preserves that uniqueness. No person ever replaces another person in the history of the universe. Creation is individual. There is only one of you. Resurrection means that we are not ultimately absorbed into some vague undifferentiated state. We are more than the dust. The concept of the resurrection assures that our specific presence in the world will not be lost in eternity. All of history and all of eternity are made different by our being here. The resurrection confirms the ultimate importance of our place in God's creation.

Chapter 22
In the End, God

People sometimes feel badgered by their religion—badgered to give, badgered to attend, badgered to believe right. The Christian faith is not the badgering kind. The Christian faith affirms, never dismisses. It embraces, but never pushes away. Nowhere have Christians acted more divisively than in their view of what is to come. Feuds erupt. Churches split. Weary of all our hostile words, some Christians quietly dismiss the entire subject as being irrelevant and unimportant. In part, they are right. No doctrines are final. Our faith is not about having the right answers to all of life's most mysterious questions. Christianity is about grace. One visit to the nursing home, listening to lonely people, is worth a twelve-volume set of writings on eschatology. Caring lies closer to the center of our faith than devising right answers to complex questions about last things.

While understanding that our words should remain tentative, a good place to start is here: Seeing the end clearly begins with seeing the beginning clearly. The affirmations of Genesis are as important to understanding the ultimate outcome of the world as the affirmations of the book of the Revelation. The end lies in the beginning. If we are to make sense of the end of time, we have to make sense of time's beginning. The Christian faith does not begin with time. The Christian faith begins with God. If our confessions of faith begin with "In the beginning God," we should be prepared for them to finish with "In the end, God."

Whenever the issues of beginnings and endings are discussed, we inevitably resort to the power of myth and poetry. The reason is this. We have no place to stand where we can observe the beginning and end. As I noted in our discussion of the truth of Genesis in chapter nine, metaphor and myth are very important elements of language that help us lay hold of the meaning of life's larger issues. The language of metaphor poses no threat to faith. Jesus was especially keen on myth. They were called parables. The stories called parables are not true in any historical or factual way. They reveal truth. Myth does not tell what is fact. Myth can tell us what is true. Myth enables us to describe the essence of ultimate reality and becomes our tool for probing the deep mysteries about us. Myth is not subject to the limitations of inductive reasoning and logical analysis.

In the stories of the book of the Revelation, as in the parables of Jesus, we are not given precise formulas for the circumstances that will surround the end of time. We are confronted rather with ultimate issues of our existence. The narratives give us insight for coping with the unpredictable and sometimes painful episodes of everyday experience. To dismiss the wisdom and insight of parable and myth takes away a profound means for understanding and relating to God's revelation. Myth gives us wisdom more than certainty. Through myth, we are seeking to "see the meaning of the end of the world." We have no place to stand to track the history of the world to its end.

Confusions about time trigger much of our confusion about the "end." In the context of faith, words like "end" and "final" do not refer primarily to time. They refer more to purpose. The end of history refers more to the goal in history than a date on the calendar. It seems that once every twenty-seven months, someone sets a date on the calendar for the end of the world. Wrong idea. Christianity is not about setting a date for the end of time. No one knows the date. Christianity speaks to the end of time as God completing the purpose of creation.

Eternity and Time

Our modern world is exceedingly time-conscious. We live by the clock, getting up and going to bed, going to work and "quitting time." Our language is dominated by where and when. We become absorbed by the passing of time, especially as we grow older. We monitor our behavior with clocks—clocks that ring the school bell, clocks where we punch in and punch out, clocks that chime in case we are not watching, clocks that alarm when our sleep is too sound, clocks that blow whistles in the city at noontime. We are time-centered people, measuring our lives by the number of days we have lived. He lived to be 82. She lived to be 77. He died when he was only 54. We measure our lives by time.

The genius of the Christian faith is that it gives us a look at our lives from the viewpoint of eternity. This faith we claim does not offer us an escape from time. The Christian faith offers us a new framework for understanding and thinking about our lives. Even while we are watching the clock, the Christian faith says to us, "Do not define your life by time." From the standpoint of eternity, we are more than time.

Time also ironically confuses us about eternity. Eternity should not be thought of as an accumulation of time. In fact, eternity has no reference to time. The message of eternity is that life is far more than the sum of our days. If we measure our lives by time, they are rooted in nothing and headed toward nothing. There was a time when we were not here, and we are moving toward a time when we will be here no longer. Time is nothing more than the duration between the "not yet" and the "no longer." If we define our lives by when we exist and how long we lasted in time, we have indeed built our dwelling on shifting sand.

If the future toward which we live is a future in time, we are utterly without hope. To the rich young man, God said, "This night, your soul will be required of you." If we live toward more time so that we are driven to acquire more things to make us feel good, nothing but tragedy awaits us. Our time will run out. Our clock will stop. When the ticking of the clock has finished for us, whether the clock reads forty years or eighty years will not matter very much. What will matter will be how we have framed those years.

We are more than the sum of our time. This reorientation contains the heart of the Christian gospel. In time, we live toward death. Life, in time, means nothing more than the interlude between birth and death. Basing the meaning of our lives on that duration means defining our lives by a whisper, a fleeting ray of light. No measure of time will ever be adequate to contain the mysteries of our presence here and the meaning of our relationships. We need to be shaken from our excessive reliance upon time. Time turns out to be a pitifully empty definition for the meaning of our lives.

This matter of following Jesus transforms how we look at our lives, including our time. Our progress toward death is refocused by the presence of eternity. Eternity is nothing less than a new way of looking at life. The vision of eternity teaches us that days are important only because of what we do with them and how we are present within them. Eternity focuses us upon a reality that the passing of time cannot take away. Through Jesus, eternity enters time, enabling us to see ourselves and the world beyond the boundaries of time. Jesus says to us, "Define yourselves not by time or its necessities."

Jesus urged his listeners to define themselves by the Kingdom of God. In other words, let God's reality be the measure of your life. This calling represents a different, radically different, self-understanding. The measure of our lives is no longer how long we have lived, but how deeply have we loved. Jesus was rather direct. Measure your life, Jesus says to us, by how much you love God and your neighbor—not by how long you have lived. The difference between living a long time and living a short time can get our picture on the Willard Scott weather show. It is a difference that is no difference. Loving God so intently that it recenters our priorities and changes our choices is a difference that differs. Jesus sets before us in history an entirely new way of seeing ourselves and conducting our histories.

The sight from eternity also changes the way we look at death. Death is pretty radical as a temporal matter. Death rips us away from one another. The loss of someone jolts us. It causes us grief and pain. The visits of death leave us bloodied and beaten. In the very face of death's agony, our faith affirms that life is larger than time's limits. Right now, a little more time seems precious. We long for a little more time to do the things we had always wanted to do. We cry for a little more time to have that conversation we always wanted to have. We reach for a little more time to make that trip we had always wanted to take. When the death of someone dear to us is near, a little more time is usually what we want.

Death is the end of time. We need some reality to help us understand that death is not the end of life. We miss the point of our faith if we think even for a moment that believing means getting more time. Death ends time. Outside time, terms such as "longer" and "shorter" become empty. Death is an event in time. The view from eternity is that time is an event in life, and life is eternal.

When we begin to see life the way Jesus saw life, the horizons between birth and death are not the ultimate boundaries. Birth and death are events in life. The Christian faith sets us free from thinking about death as the final enemy or the ultimate barrier. We begin, through the eyes of believing, to see that the real tragedy of our lives is not dying but that which dies within us while we live. We are people of the spirit. Building bigger barns is fun and exciting and good, honest labor. Building barns alone will not set us free.

Death is not the end of life. Death is the end of time. Time has a beginning and an end. The message that drives our faith is that we should not define our lives in terms of the beginning and ending of time. A chronology of days can make an interesting lesson of history, but a chronology will tell only about the days between birth and death. We seek to add days in the hope that the mere addition of days will add life. It will never happen. The extension of days will not bring life. It can only delay death.

Of time and eternity, we should learn that the difference between them is not quantitative. Eternity does not mean a long time. The meaning of eternity is that you and I are made for God. In Jesus, eternity entered time. In his life we could see what being made for God means in flesh and blood. In some ways, people did not much like what they saw. They preferred the main attractions of time. Time-focused people sought to end his life, by ending his time. We learned for all eternity that life could not be killed. Love will not ultimately die. Time and existence will crumble. God's love will endure.

The Last Word, Hope

Whatever else may divide us, hurt and even despair have a way of bringing us together. Pain invades the life of every person. We face moments when everything important to us seems to be lost. The aching overshadows the joy. The tears silence the laughter. In a moment of deep, unrelenting anguish, we simply want to give up. We want to be free of the hurt. It gnaws within us.

People don't much need a doctrine of hope. What people need is hope itself. When crippling anxiety and depression overtake us, we need hope that lifts our spirits. The Christian faith is not a faith that runs away from dealing with the harsh conflicts that consume us. Our ordinary experiences breed a multitude of deep human conflicts and hurt feelings. The Christian faith does not propose a naive joy that admonishes us to ignore the pain. The lessons of our faith may very well send us to a doctor. When our faith fosters a "grin and bear it" attitude or implies that seeing a physician or visiting a counselor is a sign of a weak faith, we should discard such dribble. It is nonsense. People desperately need help with their living. Every physician's help and every professional counselor's word can become words of God's hope. Christian hope does not live in the land of blind pretense. Our lives become tattered and frayed. We all need help with our living. The church encourages, fosters, and undergirds healing hands and voices because they are God's messengers of hope.

The hope of faith ranges even farther. The hope of faith enables us to see that tragedy and suffering are not our final condition. In the midst of the actual human travail, hope seems like a distant dream. The aching will not seem to go away. The hope that belief breeds within us is that suffering should never be the event through which we understand the meaning of our lives. Hope sometimes means leading someone down a difficult and painful road of getting well. Hope sometimes means letting go.

Only a few years ago, my friend, Pat, died from the ravages of breast cancer. Only a few hours before she died, I sat beside her and we talked of death. She had struggled so intensely, doing everything known to be done, undergoing every therapy, faithfully following all the regimens. The breast cancer won. Until the end, she was lucid, even asking if I would write down a final codicil to her will that pertained to some friends. Clear-headed and thoughtful, she and I talked about the meaning of her struggle and the uneasy prospects of letting go. She said to me, "I am going to embrace death in the hope that death is a friend." Only a day later, Pat died. Hope is not always a way out. It may also be a way into death.

Hope is born when grace breaks through the barriers of fear. We are the kind of creatures on the earth that are marked by our ability to intend. We are intentional beings. We live toward what we intend to be and what we intend to do. We act toward goals. We are driven by purposes, desires, and intentions. Much of what we do in the present is guided by what we intend to become and what we intend to accomplish. Career intentions affect what we study. What we intend to achieve affects how we do our work. Hope lives in the arena of our intentions. What we hope and what we intend are not one and the same, however.

Our intentions scatter all over the landscape of our lives. We mold intentions and discard them like broken clay at the kiln out back, but hope lives alongside our intentions. Hope rises above our intentions and tutors them, helping us to look beyond the fading trends. Hope enables us to live beyond the present, isolated moment and gives us energy to measure our intentions by a higher order of reality. Hope is the enduring presence of grace in our lives. Even when we are consumed by the pain of failure, or the disappointment of hurt, or the passions of present achievement, hope calls us to a higher vision of ourselves. Hope is the quiet call of God that we were created as one specific embodiment of grace. No person can love as you can love. No person can bear grace as you can bear grace.

In the historical presence of Jesus, we see a new prospect for assessing our presence here. Jesus holds before us the possibility of being a new creation. Being a new creation is a new light for interpreting our being here. We learn from Jesus, by what he says and what he does, that hope does not rest in survival. It was clear that Jesus wanted to survive. Jesus was not eager to give up and bear the pains of crucifixion. Rejection is never an easy experience. But the simple truth is this: Our hope does not ultimately lie in surviving. We will not. If we live only to survive, we lose. Death is the only outcome to our life in time that we can count on. The problems and victories of our lives will not stand on the loss or gain of time. We may gain a little or lose a little. Gain is generally better. Even so, the loss of time sometimes becomes an ally. Hope does not rest in the provisions of the gains and losses in time. If so, we have no hope.

Christian hope is the presence of eternity within our time-based experience, making the realities of God's grace a present force in our decisions and actions. So, we should not think of hope as a fanciful distraction. Hope does not turn our heads from the hard realities of life. On occasion, the work of hope is to focus us on the imminence of death. Hope resides amidst the anguish. The hope of faith does not pretend that our trouble is not real. Hope offers no glib assertion that "everything is going to be alright." Often, very often, everything is not alright. Hope, however, does change the impact of the trouble upon us. Hope changes the way we face that which is not alright. Hope gives us courage to struggle. Hope gives us the strength to live and grace to endure defeat.

Unlike naive optimism, hope faces the tragedy of all that is not right and fosters within us the courage and energy to work toward making things right. Hope rights the wrongs. Hope does not say, "Don't worry about it; God will take care of everything." Hope becomes the agent of God in making the world right. Hope searches for ways to overcome terrorism. Hope becomes a part of undoing the violence of abuse and abandonment that threatens us. Hope embraces the lonely. Hope carries coats to the elderly in winter. Hope takes the homeless home. Hope feeds the hungry and clothes the naked. Hope forgives the hurt. In very concrete, specific ways, hope is eternity breaking into the time of our lives. God's presence changes the character of our time on earth.

The Christian understanding of last things is not, then, chiefly about judgment day or heaven and hell. The Christian's last word is about hope. To be Christian means being present in time with the power of hope. Hope teaches us that God holds both the origins and the destiny of creation. History moves from God to God. We are God's children, and though we may walk outside Eden far into the land of wandering, God never abandons us. In Jesus Christ, we see God's hope in person. God creates us. God forgives us. God believes in us. As we become children of God's hope, we become free to forgive as God forgives and free to love as God loves. Hope is the power and presence of God within us. God is with us. God is in us. God is for us. Beyond hope, we can only be silent.